CHINA TEACHER

For my wife Wanda

my daughters DeNae and Lisa

and my son Lon

CHINA TEACHER

AN INTIMATE JOURNAL

J. R. LeMaster

New Voices Series v. 3

Florida Academic Press
Gainesville and London

Published in the United States of America by Florida Academic Press, Gainesville, FL, August 2005
Cover prepared by Gordon Woolf

Library of Congress Cataloging-in-Publication Data

LeMaster, J. R., 1934-
    China teacher : an intimate journal / J. R. LeMaster.
        p. cm. -- (New voices series ; v. 3)
    ISBN 1-890357-14-6
    1. LeMaster, J. R., 1934---Travel--China. 2. Teachers--Travel--China. 3. Education--China. 4. China--Description and travel. I. Title. II. Series: New voices series (Gainesville, Fla.) ; v.3.

    LA2317.L565A3 2005
    370'.951--dc22

2005011826

Contents

Preface   1

Introduction   3

August   7

September   11

October   61

November   99

December   129

January   157

February   189

March   211

April   239

May   267

June   295

July   325

Preface

I HAD NO INTENTION of going to China until I met Ralph K. Wang at a conference in New Orleans and invited him to speak at Baylor University. Once he had spoken, I accompanied him on a flight to Houston, and while we were flying over Texas he convinced me that I could make a contribution to education in China. In the weeks and months following Wang's visit, many details had to be worked out concerning my taking a leave of absence from Baylor University. Other details had to be worked out with the Chinese Ministry of Education, the Bureau of Foreign Experts, and Beijing Second Foreign Language Institute (now Beijing International Studies University). Progress was slow, but on August 28, 1980, my wife Wanda and I left for Beijing.

I do not claim that my journal is definitive in any way. From the outset, I attempted to record my impressions, observations, and experiences. I did not go to China as an authority on Chinese literature, Chinese history, Chinese religion, or Chinese politics. My field is American literature, and I claim no expertise outside my literary domain. I went to China to experience a world quite different from the one I had known, and my journal is a record of that experience.

Since returning from China, I have anguished over possible repercussions from disclosing the names of my Chinese friends. I have anguished over disclosing details of intimate relationships. But after much anguishing I have concluded that I have no story outside those relationships and those events. I hope people who choose to read my journal will see it for what it is, that is, a record of a journey.

I gratefully acknowledge my debt to former President Herbert H. Reynolds (now President Emeritus Herbert H. Reynolds) and Baylor University for granting me a leave of absence, and for released time and financial assistance in preparing my journal for publication. I am grateful to Ralph K. Wang for urging me to travel to China to teach, and for the friendship he has shown since we first met. I am grateful to President Tang Kai and my students and colleagues at Second Foreign Language University. They made my life richer than it had ever been before. I am grateful to members of the Bureau of Foreign Experts in Beijing for their care and concern while I was in China. I am grateful to Dongliang Xu for assistance in editing my manuscript, and to Ningkun Wu for reading it and writing an introduction to it. I am grateful to Jennifer Kozar-Carew and Ann Karaffa for special assistance in preparing my manuscript for publication. I am especially grateful to my wife Wanda, who not only agreed to go to China with me, but who has always lent me strength and courage in difficult times.

JRL

Introduction

by **Wu Ningkun, LHD**

EVER SINCE COMMUNIST CHINA opened its doors to the West in the early 1980s, an endless stream of American politicians, journalists, and academics have been visiting the People's Republic. Quite a few of them have turned their China experiences into memoirs. These travelers have often made macro observations on Chinese political and social life based on their stints in political and cultural centers such as Beijing and Shanghai. Professor LeMaster's Intimate Journal is a distinctly new China book.

Jim LeMaster was no "China hand," no politician. Poet and professor, he went to China to experience a world quite different from the one he had known. His Journal is a record of that journey and that experience, in which he attempted "to record his impressions, observations, and experiences."

As he avows in all modesty: "It does not purport to be a record of historical or political facts about China. The so-called facts about China are elusive, even for the Chinese people. My impressions are subjective, but they are no less real." Nevertheless, with the eye of a newcomer and the sensibility of a poet, his impressions are fresh, his observations acute, and his experiences first-hand. In the end, what we have is more, far more, than a record of a journey.

On the surface, the Journal is a detailed day-to-day account of the rigid routine followed by an American professor teaching in the capital of Communist China during the 1980-1981 academic year. It was an apparently monotonous life of commuting between the foreigners' hotel compound and his college and what happened in between, but the rich details speak volumes. More importantly, it is precisely this real-life framework that provides a solid setting for the unfolding of the panorama of life in the college, the city, and the nation under Communist rule, through specific incidents from everyday life in which he was directly or indirectly involved. And all this gains an additional dimension when placed in a larger context through frequent citations of momentous happenings on the world stage. With the immediacy of an eye-witness account, the history of China in transition is brought to life before our eyes, accompanied by a succinct running commentary.

As a dedicated China teacher, Professor LeMaster's first concern was with the 120 students he was to teach. His students were "attentive and eager," "curious and responsive," "bright and perceptive." They were also diligent and conscientious. However, he nevertheless had to face the fact that the life of each student was closely monitored, that each had to account to the school for everything he or she did as well as everywhere he or she went, and that students were obligated to inform on each other, as was the case in all work units. Privacy being out of the question, they were at the mercy of "fellow students and cadres carrying out their usual task of snooping and informing." It did not take the professor long to realize that they were slaves of the state, and he was "angry at a system that operates by fear and sorry for the victims of that system."

As the educational system "was designed to produce workers rather than thinkers," his students were trained to be tourist guides for the government. He deplored the lack of a comprehensive education among Chinese students and teachers alike. But he soon realized that "too much education could pose a threat to the party. Educated people cherish freedom, and demands for freedom could threaten party officials and rob them of their power. The future of the People's Republic of China hinges on the issue of education more than on any other. An educated citizenry is essential if China is ever to throw off the present political system and make progress toward becoming a modern state."

Professor LeMaster's concern extended beyond his students. His love for the Chinese people is felt throughout the Journal, whether he was in Beijing or on a vacation tour arranged by the government. Near the Friendship Hotel where he stayed ten months as a privileged foreign expert,

> I had seen row after row of mud huts, and I had tried to tell myself that no one could possibly live in such conditions, knowing that much of the population of China will continue to live in such

conditions for a long time to come. On our trip to Taiyuan, I had looked out the train window to see an area in which people were living in caves carved into the side of a mountain, and I reasoned the caves were comfortable compared to much of the housing I had seen. In Taiyuan the hovels looked desolate and cold.

One of the most touching little stories of the people in the Journal is about a little old woman who brought his hot water every morning. She "looked very bedraggled and beaten, but she managed a smile as she does every morning. She delights in filling the thermos bottles and making a cup of tea for me. The expression on her face as much as says, 'I like you. I envy you. My life is about over, but you must tell our young people the truth. Do not be afraid. If you do not tell them the truth, no one will.' I love the old woman. I feel a bond of friendship and love which is unusually strong." The old woman reappears again and again, like a haunting poetic motif, like an awesome portrait of Mother China.

Professor LeMaster did tell his young people the truth, as much as he could under the all-seeing eye of Big Brother. The students found his philosophical approach to American literature thought-provoking. In a lecture, presumably on modern American poetry, he focused instead on the intellectual milieu of modern America.

It gave me an opportunity to say a few things about dignity, respect, and the value of the individual human being. It had given me an opportunity to comment upon the nature of man and the relationship of the individual to the state. Some of the party members present likely found what I had to say a bit subversive, but the students loved it. The future of China belongs to its young people; only they can make China a better place in which to live.

After five months of his China experience, he confessed in a letter to a friend at Berkeley:

I frequently agonize over China—over the Chinese people. I agonize because I do not see bright prospects for the future. The government still consists of people with minds from China's feudal past. They are people with warlord mentalities; they still see the world as a fiefdom. At least they still see China as a fiefdom. Until Chinese government officials acquire a new mind-set, a more modern mindset, China has little possibility of entering into the modern world.

Furthermore, I am beginning to doubt that the Chinese way of seeing the world can be changed gradually or peacefully.

In June 1981, shortly before he was to leave China, he gave a combination lecture and poetry reading at a guest appearance at Jilin University in the city of Changchun in Northeast China. The students responded enthusiastically, but the Communist functionaries were offended, especially by his own poem entitled "Christmas: 1980." It was inspired by a young man who had burned himself on Christmas Eve in a park in Beijing.

> "A modern Moses," I told my wife.
> "Truly a Chinese Moses
> about to cross over."
> ....
> "There will be a leader," I said.
> "He will come out of the desert
> and march through the streets of the city.
> The people will strew his path with lotus blossoms
> while singing, Hosanna to our leader!
> Hosanna to our Chinese king!"

Unceremoniously put on a flight back to Beijing, the offending poet felt he "might have done a great service to those who suffer oppression in Changchun. I did not begin a revolution, but I fed a growing spirit of dissent. My trip to Changchun reinforced things I already felt and knew about communism." As he saw it, "the party is an albatross—a Chinese albatross."

It was not in vain that he "had lived in a land of poverty, fear, and suffering" for ten months. His poem "Christmas: 1980" attests eloquently to his love of the Chinese people as well as his faith in their future. Professor LeMaster can rest reassured that he has indeed made "a contribution that would count for something, not just for the time, but for generations to come," as he had initially hoped. The Intimate Journal, though spanning only ten months, is a true-to-life portrayal of "the real China" that remains substantially true of China today, and therefore more sterling than the gilded inventions of the Marco Polos or the Edgar Snows.

Dr. Wu Ningkun is Professor Emeritus of English at the Institute of International Relations in Beijing, and author of *A Single Tear, A Family's Persecution, Love and Endurance* (Atlantic Monthly Press, 1993)

August

Thursday, August 28

My wife Wanda and I had been excited about going to China for several weeks. We had secured the necessary papers. We had packed and shipped eight large boxes of books, clothing, cosmetics, and numerous items that we thought might not be available in China. For a month we had attended farewell parties, and when the day finally arrived for our departure, the sleepless nights of the previous two or three weeks seemed of little consequence. We were going to China, and that was all that mattered.

We left our home in Waco, Texas, at 6:30 a.m., August 28, 1980. Dr. Robert G. Collmer, a friend and colleague at Baylor University, drove us to Dallas/Fort Worth International Airport. We were also accompanied by Lon, our son, and by Mark LeMaster, our nephew. An hour late, our plane left Dallas/Fort Worth International Airport at 11:15 a.m., and we arrived in Seattle, Washington, at 3:30 p.m. We were concerned that we might miss our flight from Seattle to Tokyo, but as it turned out our concern was unnecessary. The flight to Tokyo was also late by an hour. We left Seattle at 5:00 p.m. and arrived at Narita International Airport on Friday, having crossed the International Date Line. With a twenty-seven-hour layover confronting us, we checked in at Narita International Hotel.

Saturday, August 30

Having slept for about ten hours, we enjoyed a fine breakfast. We took a walk in Narita before lunch. After lunch we rested, in anticipation of our flight to Beijing. At about 2:00 p.m. we boarded a bus and went to the airport. At 5:30 p.m. our CAAC (Civil Aviation Administration of China) flight began, and we were on the last leg of our journey. We talked about what we thought China might hold for us in the months to come, and while we were talking we landed in Beijing at about 10:00 p.m. When we arrived we were greeted by Lu Zhibao, Zhu Zheng, and Cheng Yu, who were all teachers from Second Foreign Language Institute in Beijing. They had brought a bus from the institute to transport us and our luggage to the Friendship Hotel, which proved to be about an hour's ride from the airport. Once we had arrived at the Friendship Hotel, we were taken to our quarters, consisting of two rooms and a bath. Fortunately, all three of the Chinese teachers spoke English. We talked for a while, and I inquired concerning when I might begin teaching at Second Foreign Language Institute. Lu Zhibao handed me 600 *yuan* (about U.S. $400) and informed me that someone at the institute would be in touch with me.[1] "Take a few days off," he said, "and rest." When the teachers from the institute left, we examined our quarters. We were shocked at what we would be living in for the next ten months. On the other hand, we were also tired. We went to bed believing that everything would look better the next morning.

Sunday, August 31

We awakened in Beijing, People's Republic of China, to discover that the Friendship Hotel was a compound for foreigners.[2] Surrounded by a huge wall, and with armed guards at the gates, the compound known as the Friendship Hotel contains nine major buildings. It contains a large swimming pool, tennis courts, dining halls, stores, and various other conveniences. We missed breakfast in order to explore the compound. We wanted to find our way around as soon as possible. Later in the morning, while on our way to lunch, we made our first friends, Ed and Gail Grejda. In China on a Fulbright award, Ed teaches at Beijing University; Gail, who is also a teacher, hopes to find employment through the American embassy. The Grejdas are from Clarion, Pennsylvania, and when we met them they were a bit lonely, a bit homesick, even though they had been in China only two days. Wanda and I spent the afternoon unpacking. It was Sunday, and we missed going to church, but we hoped that going to church would come later. When we had completed unpacking, we went to dinner. After dinner we went to bed; we were exhausted.

---

[1] The official name for the currency of the People's Republic of China is *renminbi* (RMB), which is denominated into the *yuan*. In China it is informally counted out as *kuai* (unit). Notes in common use are printed in denominations of 1, 2, 5, and 10 *yuan*. The *yuan* is divided into *fen* (cents). Paper notes are issued for 50, 20, and 10 *fen*; coins are in denominations of 1, 2, and 5 *fen*. When we arrived in Beijing in August of 1980, one U.S. dollar would buy one *yuan* and forty-nine *fen*; when we left in July of 1981, one U.S. dollar would buy one *yuan* and seventy-eight *fen*.

[2] When the term *friendship* is used in a title, it usually means "for foreigners." The Friendship Bus, which runs daily between the Friendship Hotel and the Friendship Store, is also for foreigners.

September

Monday, September 1

The weather has cooled off considerably since our arrival in China. The Chinese are complaining that "The Day of the Tiger," a spell of hot weather after autumn begins, has passed them by. Fall has come, and we have been told that fall is the best time to be in Beijing. We have begun to realize that we made many mistakes in selecting what to bring with us from our home in Texas. Known as foreign experts, the foreign teachers here dress very casually for everything. In that respect, they are remarkably like the Chinese, who have to dress casually to avoid criticism. In the winter, I am told, many foreign teachers wear Chinese clothes to keep warm.

Monday proved to be a good day. Ralph K. Wang came from Changchun to visit us. I had invited Wang to lecture in American Studies at Baylor University in the fall of 1979. At that time he was in the United States looking for teachers to come to China. It was while he was visiting Baylor University that he convinced me that I should teach in China. He had traveled for about eighteen hours on a train to Beijing to make sure that our quarters were comfortable and that arrangements with Beijing Second Foreign Language Institute were satisfactory.

It was good to see my Chinese friend again. We visited for an hour or so, talking about the Stricklands. Arney and Bobbie Strickland are from Lamar University in Beaumont, Texas. They are teaching at Jilin University in Changchun. We also talked about Baylor University. We talked about the possibility of an exchange program between Baylor and Jilin University. We also talked about Wang's brother, who lives not far from the Friendship Hotel and works for the Beijing Institute of Technology. After our visit, the three of us took a car to downtown Beijing, passing by the Great Hall of the People, the Chairman Mao Memorial, and other important sites such as the Forbidden City. We visited department stores, food stores, and gift shops so that Wanda and I could learn their locations. At about 4:00 p.m. we returned to the compound. When Wang had gone, Wanda and I went to the dining hall for dinner. We met many new people, some who had come to Beijing to teach, some who were in transit to other parts of China to teach, and some who seemed merely to be passing through.

Tuesday, September 2

We borrowed bicycles from Ed and Gail Grejda. We had heard that the Beijing Zoo was about a twenty-minute ride from the Friendship Hotel, and we wanted to go there. We left the compound shortly after breakfast to find that the streets were already filled with bicycles, horse-drawn carts, wagons, trucks, cars, buses, and nearly every conceivable means of transport. Early, I decided that one could stand outside the entrance to the Friendship Hotel and observe the history of land transportation. When we arrived at the zoo, we found that it was also crowded. Once we were inside we saw large, tree-lined boulevards. We also saw long canals, which were stocked with fish. Occasionally we observed a young couple holding hands, but they did not embrace. Before coming to China we had read that public displays of affection are forbidden. On the other hand, we found that women hold hands or embrace each other in public, as do men. Particularly, we noticed school girls with their arms around each other. In short, we learned that public displays of affection between the sexes is forbidden. Such displays by members of the same sex are common.

We wanted to return to the Friendship Hotel in time to have lunch in the dining hall, but we were lost. Furthermore, we could find no one who spoke English. Our only hope was to resort to gesturing, and that is what we did. I began making a gesture that the Chinese seemingly interpreted as a ship passing through a channel, or through a lock. They likely thought I was crazy. Wanda made a gesture in which she clapped her hands together and then spread them. Her gesture worked, but the Chinese only pointed across the zoo to indicate that the gate was on the other side. We moved in the direction of the gate and continued gesturing until we arrived at the main exit. Finally, we found our bicycles and made our way back to the compound. We had been lost, but we had also discovered that we could communicate without words.

A foreigner soon notices in Beijing that soldiers appear to be everywhere. Always they mix with the crowd and make themselves inconspicuous. They display no great sense of military superiority; nor do they appear to receive any kind of preferential treatment. Members of the People's Liberation Army are very much present—whether we are at the zoo, in downtown Beijing, or at our compound. At times I am impressed that as much as twenty percent of the population must belong to the army.

Before coming to China I had thought that many Chinese women belonged to the army, but I have found nothing so far to substantiate such an idea.

After lunch we slept for three hours. We were tired and we were suffering from jet lag. Also, we were resting for an evening out. When the alarm went off, we dressed quickly. We were taken to the Peacegate Restaurant for a banquet. Second Foreign Language Institute was sponsoring an evening of sumptuous dining for foreign experts teaching at the institute. We met many of the school officials—first party chairman, second party chairman, president, vice president, and so on. They were all friendly and courteous. The president of the institute gave a speech in which he welcomed us and stressed the value of our friendship to the Chinese. After the president spoke, we began eating and I talked with Lu Zhibao. We talked about American education and American politics. According to Lu, the Chinese are apprehensive about the possibility of Ronald Reagan's being elected president.

Wednesday, September 3

Wanda and I visited a market located across the street from the compound. We purchased soap and washcloths. I also found some matches, but what I thought to be pipe tobacco turned out to be tea. We were surprised by the market; it contained more things than we anticipated. Consisting of several shops, it stocked clothes, food of various kinds, bicycles, jewelry, candy, and many other items. When Ed Grejda had told us about the market, he had referred to it as the "local K-Mart." The name seemed appropriate.

Upon returning from the market we received a telephone call from Lu Zhibao. He informed us that he would stop by the next morning. I hoped to find out whether the boxes we shipped two months earlier had arrived. The boxes contain my literature books, and I must begin teaching on Monday. I also hoped we would be able to talk with someone about a job for Wanda. Otherwise she will be very bored once I start to work and she is left alone.

After talking with Lu, we went down the hall to inquire about the telephone. I had not been able to hear well. We were told that the telephone was fine, that the trouble was likely in a connection somewhere. We also talked with the floor manager about our electric typewriter and the converters we had brought from the United States. I had tried to use the typewriter with a 50-watt converter only to have the converter heat up badly. The floor manager suggested that I try a 1500-watt converter. I remonstrated that it would ruin the wiring in the typewriter. But once the floor manager had left, I tried the 1500-watt converter and found that it worked. I had found a way to convert 220 volts to 110, but I remained afraid that it would damage my typewriter.

Thursday, September 4

Ralph Wang came to visit at 8:00 a.m. We talked about Beijing and about Wang's visit to the United States only a few weeks before. When Lu Zhibao arrived, he was an hour late. It had taken him two hours to ride across town from the institute by bus. Buses are crowded. Long lines wait at bus stops almost everywhere. Such are the conditions in spite of the fact that many Chinese people walk or ride a bicycle. Wanda and I have not attempted to ride a bus. We have coupons from the institute allowing us to use a car, although I have been told that the car is to be used only for riding to work and to the hospital. We would be told conflicting stories about the coupons during the next several hours.

Lu wanted to discuss business, but I invited Ralph Wang to stay. We discussed the possibility of a job for Wanda at the institute, and Lu agreed that he would check into the matter. Such a job would have a number of advantages. It would supply extra income, and we could go to work together. The greatest advantage would be that she would feel useful. Since the cleaning is all done by the Chinese hotel staff, and since we eat all of our meals in a dining hall, the usual housewife chores do not exist. She will definitely need something to do.

Lu had a number of questions. For example, he wanted to know how much of my monthly salary I wanted in Chinese *yuan* and how much in U.S. dollars. He wanted to know whether or not I preferred to have part of my income mailed to our bank in Waco, Texas. We discussed money in some detail, and I found that the Chinese pay in cash. I was told that my salary would be determined after two months of teaching, and that

I should expect more than I was offered before coming to China. I presented Lu with a list of requests to take to the officials at the institute. I wanted a green residence card, a white identification card, a health card, and an official letter permitting Wanda and me to use hotels, buses, and trains at the same cost that Chinese citizens pay. I also requested coupons for purchasing cotton cloth as well as reimbursement for expenses we had incurred in preparing for our trip to China. Lu assured me that he would take my requests back to the institute, and Ralph Wang tried to impress upon Lu that foreign guests must be treated well.

Once Lu and Wang had left, Wanda and I went to the American embassy. I realized that it was not appropriate to drop in on the American ambassador, Leonard Woodcock, unannounced, but we did that anyway. We met the ambassador's secretary, who informed us that the ambassador was preparing to leave for a defense meeting in Washington, and that she would make an appointment for us to talk with him upon his return to Beijing. I wanted to talk with Ambassador Woodcock merely to let him know that we were in Beijing. Besides, I had once belonged to the United Auto Workers, and the ambassador had retired from the presidency of that organization shortly before being appointed to his post in Beijing. Early in the summer my brother Marvin, who is president of a UAW local in Ohio, had talked with Ambassador Woodcock at a labor union conference in California. At that time the ambassador had requested that I drop by to visit with him when I arrived in Beijing. Because of that, as far as I was concerned I had already been invited.

When we left the ambassador's residence, we went to the American consulate, in the Bruce House, where we met and talked at length with John Thomson, counselor for cultural affairs. We talked about the state of education in China. We also met and talked with Theodore M. Liu, first secretary of culture. He gave me two boxes of teaching materials, including some bilingual texts. From the consulate we went to the Friendship Store, where we wandered and observed for another two hours or more. When we returned to the compound, we visited the market across the street. We looked for a pair of sneakers for Wanda. We found a pair for four *yuan* and eighty *fen*, or about U.S. $3.00. Later in the evening Ralph Wang visited us again. We went to dinner at a Russian-built restaurant near the zoo. The building was massive. With its huge marble columns it was very imposing. As it turned out, Wang was scheduled to return to

Changchun the next day and wanted to share a farewell dinner with us. He also wanted an opportunity to offer us the services of his son-in-law, Mao Zhiren, who is a student at Beijing University.

As he had done many times before, Wang apologized for the primitive conditions in which people live in China. He also apologized for the primitive conditions under which teachers work. Wang is obviously disenchanted with his fellow Chinese because of what he terms their reluctance to change. He has lived in America—recently as well as in the forties when he attended the University of Southern California—and he likes America. He also hopes that his effort to bring qualified teachers to China will improve both the quality of education and the standard of living for many of his countrymen. Once again we talked about the United States and China. We talked about Wang's recent visit to the United States. We talked about Wang's family and about our being in Beijing. He would like us to visit Changchun in the spring, but much will depend upon the institute where I teach. The institute will likely take us on a tour of China in the winter, and they may be reluctant to let me travel to Changchun in the spring.

Friday, September 5

Wanda and I arose at 6:00 a.m. and walked for an hour. At that time of the morning one can see the Chinese performing many kinds of exercise. They take physical exercise seriously. One can also see that yards have been converted to gardens in which beans, squash, and many other vegetables are grown. We have observed that Beijing has little grass, and that where it exists it is clipped with hand shears. So far we have observed only one lawn mower in use, and it was at the zoo. Although we had read that Beijing is barren of trees, we have observed many tall, stately trees along the streets. The compound where we live contains many trees as well as beautiful flower gardens. Such is also true of the parks in Beijing. When we visited the zoo and the Summer Palace, I saw trees that I estimated to be more than a hundred years old. It is simply not true that Beijing is treeless.

Lu Zhibao called to tell me that I should be at the institute by 2:00 p.m. because the president, Tang Kai, would give a speech to all the foreign experts working for the school. I hurried through lunch in order to catch a car early because I knew that the trip would take about an hour. The Friendship Hotel is on the west side of the city; the institute is on the east side. When I arrived at the car stand, however, I was told that no cars were available. The dispatcher could not speak English, but when a car drove up about ten minutes later, I pointed at it and made very clear that I expected that car to take me to the Second Foreign Language Institute. The dispatcher understood, for he quickly dispatched the car and I was on my way.

Although Wanda and I had been in Beijing six days, I still had not seen the institute. The Chinese were concerned that we have sufficient rest after our long trip. Nor did I know how to get to the institute. Fortunately, I was joined at the last minute by Michael Assenmiker, who had come from Brussels to teach in Beijing. Michael spoke Chinese well enough to converse with the driver. Less worried because of being in the company of Michael, I gave myself over to observing the sights during our trip. I was particularly impressed by the suburbs near the institute. Everywhere I saw great masses of people. The roads were crowded with bicycles, cars, trucks, two-wheeled carts, and other conveyances. The carts were pulled by mules, but the hitch was strange. The tongue to a cart appeared to be fastened to the back of one mule while several others walked in front moving the load forward by a series of ropes. Heavy loads were being moved on the carts, including large slabs of concrete for building purposes.

When we arrived at the institute, we were early. Lu Zhibao was to meet me at the entrance of the institute at 2:00, and that left me about ten minutes in which to wander. I went into a classroom building. I wandered through the halls and looked into empty rooms. The rooms were empty because the Chinese rest for an hour or so after lunch. No one returns to work until 2:00 in the afternoon. In the heat of summer, work may be suspended until 4:00. I have also heard that on hot summer nights the people in Beijing carry their beds into the streets. I was thinking about the conditions under which I would be teaching when I met Lu. We went immediately to hear the president speak. The room had a bare concrete floor. Walls were painted a drab gray, and on one of them was a portrait of Mao Zedong alongside a portrait of President Tang Kai. The windows were covered by a dingy white material. They looked as though someone had hemmed a sheet or two and fastened them up with wire.

We were served much tea, as though it were a cure for all that is wrong in China—for all that is missing from the lives of the Chinese people. We were also offered Chinese cigarettes. During the meeting I became impressed that Chinese officials have watched too many American films in which the characters are always smoking and drinking. But the truth is that such gestures constitute a genuine effort to be hospitable. The Chinese people make every possible effort to be friendly. Nowhere have I observed any anti-American sentiment.

The president's speech was short. He divided what he had to say into two parts. In the first part he gave us a brief history of the school. He began by saying that the school opened shortly before the Cultural Revolution began in 1966. As were most other schools in China, the institute was closed during the Cultural Revolution. Throughout China intellectuals were suspect. Consequently, they were sent to work on communes in the countryside. In 1972 the institute was allowed to conduct what was called a "school with doors open." Such an arrangement simply allowed the teachers to teach those around them while they were working in the fields or in the factories. It was not until 1976 that the Gang of Four was ousted, at which time the institute resumed classes. When I heard President Tang Kai talk about these things, I realized why China is so far behind other countries in education. In the United States we customarily think of the Cultural Revolution as having lasted about five years. It actually lasted ten to twelve years and in that time devastated intellectual and cultural institutions. The intellectuals were displaced, and most things pertaining to Chinese intellectual and cultural traditions were defaced or destroyed.

President Tang Kai explained that English, Japanese, Spanish, Dutch, Russian, German, and a number of other languages are taught at the institute. The institute trains interpreters for the tourist trade, which is expected to grow rapidly now that China has opened its doors to the West. China also needs translators and interpreters for diplomatic service. The Chinese see themselves as in a great period of transition. They must compensate for the education lost during the years of the Cultural Revolution, and the officials at Second Foreign Language Institute welcome all the help they can get in putting their house of education in order. President Tang Kai stressed that idea over and over again. "Nothing is fixed," he explained. "The school is amorphous. We are groping for a direction." The heating, he explained, is very inadequate. Students and teachers must wear their winter clothes in the classroom. Electricity is rationed. The power is shut off when the week's supply has been consumed. Not enough money is available to employ people to keep the school clean. The halls and rooms are often dirty.

From what I could gather as President Tang Kai continued, only one thing is constant in Chinese schools, and that is the insatiable appetite the Chinese student has for knowledge. The Chinese student will not miss a class, I have been told, unless he is too ill to get out of bed. He will not make a disturbance. He will always do more than he is asked to do. He will always be courteous and respectful toward his teacher. He knows that his future depends heavily on his receiving an education. He also knows that thousands of others are waiting to take his place. China has several major universities, and the largest, which is Beijing University, has an enrollment of about eight thousand students. Chinese students know they are fortunate to be in school.

When I had arrived and looked at the conditions under which I would be teaching, I was depressed. But when the president had completed his speech, I felt better. I felt that I was facing the greatest opportunity of my life, an opportunity to help people who obviously needed help more than any other people I had ever known. I was determined I would make a contribution that would count for something, not just for the time but for generations to come. I left the institute feeling good, feeling optimistic about what was to come. I went away feeling happy that among the rough and rickety desks, the dark and drab hallways and classrooms, I would face a challenge unlike any that I had ever known.

After dinner Wanda and I went to see a Chinese movie. Large banners duly inscribed with Communist slogans hang on either side of the screen, and I recalled that one of the elevator operators in our building had introduced himself as Comrade Ma Tunga. As I sat watching the movie I wondered about the many paradoxes surrounding me. I thought of Miss She Yong, a beautiful girl of eighteen who also operates an elevator in our building. I have been trying to help her with her pronunciation of English. Perhaps Lu Zhibao is right when he says that the young people have changed, that the future belongs to them, and that they are rapidly departing from the old ways and the old ideologies. I hope he is right.

Saturday, September 6

On Saturday morning we met Lu Zhibao at the entrance to the Palace Museum, known in the old days as the Forbidden City. It served as a permanent residence for the emperors of the Ming and Qing dynasties. Built between 1406 and 1420, in the reign of Yongle, a Ming emperor, the Imperial Palace has a history of 560 years. When Pu Yi, the last of the Qing emperors, was overthrown in 1911, a total of twenty-three emperors had lived in the Imperial Palace while exercising supreme feudal (autocratic) power over the country.

Unlimited wealth seems to have gone into building the Imperial Palace. The Chinese estimate that 100,000 artisans and 1,000,000 laborers worked in press gangs during the reign of Yongle alone. The Imperial Palace covers 720,000 square meters. It is surrounded by a wall 10 meters high and 3,400 meters in length. It is surrounded by a moat 52 meters wide. Containing four gates, the Imperial Palace consists of outer and inner courts. The outer court contains three great halls—the Hall of Supreme Harmony, the Hall of Complete Harmony, and the Hall of Preserving Harmony. The inner court contains three main palaces—the Palace of Heavenly Purity, the Palace of Union, and the Palace of Earthly Tranquility—as well as six east and six west palaces. The Palace Museum contains 900,000 pieces of art from all periods in Chinese history as well as relics from the courts of the emperors of the Ming and Qing dynasties. Some of the halls and palaces are kept as they were originally furnished, and because all explanations are in Chinese one needs an interpreter.

In the afternoon Lu Zhibao took us to the Summer Palace, not far from the compound where we live. The Summer Palace, according to Lu, was built by the Empress Dowager Cixi in 1880. When the emperor died, the heir to the throne was only seven years old. Consequently, Empress Dowager Cixi ruled for him. She did many controversial things, including having the Summer Palace built. At the Summer Palace one sees lavishly furnished chambers and many other impressive things, but the most fascinating object at the Summer Palace is a marble boat. According to Lu, the money used to build the Summer Palace was originally appropriated to build a fleet of ships to protect China from foreign invaders. Empress Dowager Cixi did not think China needed the ships and used the money instead to build a lavish palace with a covered walkway approximately two miles long. The walkway winds along Lake Kunming, and above it towers Longevity Hill. Across the lake from the walkway one can see the Temple of the Sea Dragon and Seventeen-Span Bridge. At the end of the walkway, however, one comes upon China's famous marble boat. Built by Empress Dowager Cixi to mock those who criticized her for using the money intended for a fleet to build the Summer Palace, the marble boat is full size.

The most interesting part of the day was the conversation we had with Lu Zhibao. We talked about various subjects. For example, we talked about ancestor worship. Lu told us that his father, who had died about five years earlier, had practiced ancestor worship. Lu's father's generation was the last to practice ancestor worship.

The younger generation does not believe in it, according to Lu. Lu Zhibao also told us that he could not be with us on Sunday because he had to take his father-in-law to the hospital for an examination. He explained that his father-in-law is paralyzed and must be pushed four miles to the hospital on a cart. Once a drama critic of considerable reputation in Beijing, Lu's father-in-law suffered a stroke which left him paralyzed. When I inquired of Lu concerning what caused the stroke, his answer was, "He ate too many chickens." Lu went on to explain that his father-in-law had been too fat and had suffered from high blood pressure.

We talked about young people, for half the population in China is twenty-five or under. The ideas of the young people, said Lu, are different from those of their parents. Young people want things now; they are tired of waiting. Before leaving the United States, Wanda and I had read that the legal marrying age for Chinese men is twenty-six or twenty-seven. But that has been changed. Men are permitted to marry at twenty-two and women are permitted to marry at eighteen. China's young people protested and eventually got their way. Setting the legal age for marrying high was an effort on the part of the government to keep the population in check. Housing is very inadequate, and young couples do not live with their parents as they once did.

We also talked about capital punishment. According to Lu, Chinese young people are opposed to the death penalty. But the death penalty is still common, and most major crimes are committed by young people. The accused appears before a judge, and if he is found guilty he is sentenced. If he is given the death penalty, he is placed before a firing squad.

"China has too many people," Lu told us. "There is no room for criminals." Although the death penalty is common, China's prisons are full, according to Lu. Thinking about those who are executed, and about the great masses of people in the streets of Beijing, I wondered about disposing of the bodies of the dead. When I inquired, I learned that they are not buried in cemeteries. Rather they are cremated. Sometimes they are hauled to the crematorium on a cart. The ordinary Chinese worker has no access to a car or a truck. Such things are too costly.

Lu Zhibao loves to cook, and he assured us that he will invite us to his house for dinner before we leave Beijing. As he put it, it will give us "an opportunity to see a typical Chinese home." We have seen many of those "typical Chinese homes" from the outside, and they have a forbidding look about them. Many of them look like long rows of mud huts, and in the mornings the Chinese emerging from them resemble bees coming from a hive. Lu contends that he lives in a typical home. He does the cooking; his wife does the washing. He says they also constitute a typical Chinese family in that they have one child. They cannot afford much, he told us, because the school, which supplies their flat and furniture, is poor. The flat is supplied with electricity, running water, and central heating. Lu's salary, as well as that of his wife, goes mostly for food and clothes. Those are the major things a Chinese family has to buy. When he goes to a doctor or a hospital, he pays only ten *fen*—about five cents in U.S. currency. His monthly salary is seventy *yuan*—about forty-eight dollars. Lu's wife also works, and between the two of them their monthly salary is the equivalent of eighty-seven dollars.

We talked about basic differences between the Chinese and American people. Lu observed that Chinese people conceal their emotions. He likes the fact that Americans express their emotions, that they are more likely to laugh, weep, or do whatever seems appropriate for the occasion. Lu Zhibao regards Americans and American life very highly.

Sunday, September 7

Wanda and I walked to Purple Bamboo Park. When we arrived at what we thought was the park, we found that it was not. We stopped a beautiful Chinese girl and inquired as to whether she was a student. Speaking English fluently, she told us that we were on the grounds of the People's

School, which we took to mean the People's University. We returned to the main road and made our way to Purple Bamboo Park, which is only a forty-five-minute walk from the Friendship Hotel. We paid ten *fen* (about six cents) and entered the gate to find a beautiful lake and many fishermen. It was Sunday afternoon, and many people were there. The Chinese enjoy family outings, especially outings in a park. We also saw young lovers taking their Sunday afternoon stroll, much as they once did in America before automobiles became plentiful. We took a number of photographs while at the park, most of which were of fishermen and babies.

When we returned to the Friendship Hotel, I tried to get the news on the radio. As it turned out, I found a program in English on Radio Moscow. The program consisted of short speeches by two Soviet authorities concerning the normalization of relations between China and the United States. The speakers were obviously opposed to such normalization. They claimed America's involvement in China to be nothing more than an effort to spread imperialism throughout the East. They dismissed the present Chinese-American effort to cooperate as a danger to the free world. On the other hand, Chinese leaders have been denouncing Soviet hegemony as the most immediate danger to world peace. Chinese leaders expect the Soviets to take the Middle-East oil fields by force in the near future, thereby touching off a major war. The radio broadcast was an effort to inform the Chinese that the Soviets disapprove of any alliance with the United States. That it was in English was probably designed to let the Americans know that too.

Monday, September 8

It was Monday, my first day to teach at Second Foreign Language Institute. At 7:00 a.m. I left the compound in a car containing three other foreign teachers. Traffic was heavy, and we had a young driver who liked to take chances. When we arrived at the institute about an hour later, I was met by Lu Zhibao. Lu took me to my first class, and when we entered the room he said to the class, "Good morning, comrades." It was then that I was first impressed by the significance of the party to every phase of Chinese life. Every work unit has its cadres or functionaries. The cadre represents the party to the workers, or students, and he or she is responsible for political indoctrination. At Second Foreign Language

Institute, everyone except the foreigners attends an afternoon of political instruction each week. The session consists of a discussion of party policies, of documents issued by the government, and of particular problems of both local and national concern.

After he introduced me, Lu Zhibao left the classroom. I began lecturing on the nature of language. I wanted to test the reaction of my students to my voice. I wanted to find out how well they knew the English language. I wanted to find out what to expect when I lectured in the future. As it turned out, my students were attentive and eager. Occasionally I walked down the aisle in order to be near them, to allow them to become familiar with my being in their presence. When I had completed my lecture, I began asking questions. They responded cautiously, as though they were afraid. I asked who the class monitor might be and found that she was a very charming young woman by the name of Liu. I asked her to prepare a class roster and bring it to my office.

After class I went to my office where two American teachers were complaining to three Chinese teachers about heavy teaching loads. I stayed in the office for about an hour. Realizing that I would accomplish nothing in the midst of such bickering, I took a car and returned to the Friendship Hotel. After lunch I thought about my first classroom encounter with my Chinese students. Then I spent an enjoyable afternoon reading.

Tuesday, September 9

On the way to the institute we passed a truck with a wheel off. An axle had broken, and the truck had fallen to the ground. We also passed farmers driving their cattle on the road as well as many wagons and bicycles loaded with produce of one kind or another. One cart was loaded with the carcasses of goats, another with plucked chickens which had had their entrails removed, and another with onions. The Chinese are very fond of onions and garlic.

At 8:00 a.m. Lu Zhibao introduced me to another class of students. I teach all of Grade 77, which is called Grade 77 because the students in that grade entered the institute in 1977. At least I had been told that. I had also been told that the institute did not resume classes following the Cultural Revolution until 1978. Regardless of the explanation, I teach Grade 77, which consists of five sections or classes.

Again I heard Lu Zhibao say, "Good morning, comrades." Then he introduced me to the class. Once he had introduced me, he left, and I was on my own. I began by telling my students about myself. I told them about where I was born, about where I grew up, about my education and teaching experiences, and about some of my interests. They appeared to be excited. I gave them a list of writers we would be studying and was amazed when I found that they had heard of many of the authors. I was even more amazed when they told me they had read books by such writers as Mark Twain and Nathaniel Hawthorne. I lectured for fifty minutes, and I could tell that all was going well by the way their eyes sparkled at various times throughout the lecture. When the bell rang at the end of the class, they surrounded my desk. I had no recourse but to remain and talk with them. I found that they were desperate for books. They have been told the same story over and over: "The school is poor and has no money for books. The government does not have sufficient U.S. dollars to purchase books. Those books that are purchased must be in the sciences." My students will obviously do anything for books, but no solution to their problem is readily available.

While thinking about books, I made my way down the hall toward my office. Shortly before I reached the door, an attractive young woman stopped me. She smiled and said, "I am Tan Luying. Thank you for being our teacher. I will be your assistant. I will do anything you want done." I thanked her and told her that I would keep her offer in mind, and I will. She wants to learn, and I will do all I can to help her. Ah, but if every English teacher in America would send one book! What a difference that would make to thousands of Chinese students. China has many schools. Beijing has many schools. They need teachers, and they need books. The Cultural Revolution left them destitute. They need to read about America. They need to read American literature. They are ready. They are eager. The future of Chinese-American relations could be greatly influenced by making available the books that Americans discard. To the present generation of Chinese students, books are the greatest of all possessions. I sat at my desk and thought about ways in which I might secure books for my students.

Wednesday, September 10

It may be that Chinese youth are being corrupted by youth from the

West. My Chinese students play disco records and throw a frisbee at class break. China is also being invaded by Madison Avenue. In downtown Beijing mammoth billboards resemble those along the streets and highways of the United States. Billboards are used in advertising everything from refrigerators to automobiles, and they are obviously catching on in China. New products are advertised almost every day, and construction is going on almost everywhere a person looks. Furthermore, the buildings going up often have a giant crane on the construction site to lower materials into place. In some places, metal scaffolding has replaced bamboo scaffolding, which has been used for centuries. Much construction is taking place in Beijing.

At 10:00 a.m. we had a meeting called by disgruntled American women in the English department. They were trying to elicit sympathy over what they termed unbearable teaching schedules. After the meeting, I decided that I would visit the school library. When I visited the office of the head librarian, who spoke no English, I was told that the library was closed. When I insisted that I be allowed to see the library, one of the librarians produced a key. Once I was inside I was a bit sorry that I had insisted. I found the entire school library to be about thirty feet by sixty feet. The books were all on shelves, and the English section—from all English-speaking countries—comprised seven shelves which were about ten feet long and seven feet high. When I checked for American literature, I found three or four dozen books at most. I found dictionaries and encyclopedias to be plentiful, but I found little else that might be of value to a faculty member or to a student.

The day was productive in one respect. In the afternoon Wanda and I took the bus to the Friendship Store in downtown Beijing.[1] We walked from there to the American embassy where I made a plea for literature books for my students. Theodore Liu, the first secretary of culture, thought I was interested in books for all of my students. He was pleased when he found that I would settle for a copy for myself and one for each of my five classes. I reasoned that a copy for each class would be better than no books at all, and he gave me eight copies of a four-book set called *Highlights of American Literature*. I was not sure

---

[1] The bus left the Friendship Hotel at 1:00 p.m. and left the Friendship Store for the return trip at 5:00.

how I would make a set of books serve an entire class, but I felt I had a beginning toward making books available.

Thursday, September 11

On the way to the institute I sat in the front seat with the Chinese driver. Jeanne Lonnoy, from Brussels, sat in the back seat with a young French woman and a young Japanese woman. Jeanne and the French woman spoke French for the fifty minutes or so that we were en route. The Japanese woman laid her head back and pretended to be asleep. I was never introduced to either of the young women by Jeanne, whom I knew to speak German, French, English, Chinese, Russian, and some Japanese. At different times during the trip, I interrupted the conversation between Jeanne and the French woman. I even tried to follow their conversation in French, but my French had depreciated too much over the years. Unable to enter into the conversation, I felt lonely. I realized that for the first time in my life I was beginning to understand what it means to belong to a minority group. The feeling had been building for some time, particularly at school where almost everyone knows and speaks Chinese. I was beginning to feel left out—left out of the conversation and consequently out of the world one cannot enter without knowing the language. All day I had the distinct feeling that I belonged to a minority group and therefore could not enter into the life of the community. It reminded me of what had happened when my wife and I visited Purple Bamboo Park on Sunday.

I had felt fine when we began our walk, but at that time the Chinese people still all looked alike to me. I had not come to see them as distinctly different personalities. To me they were still the "Chinese people," but while walking around the lake at the park I began to see them as individual human beings. It happened in an instant as I shifted my gaze from the lake to the people in front of me. Since that time a great number of ideas have entered my mind. The possibility of waging war, for example, must demand that the enemy be viewed in such an impersonal way. It must demand that one view the mass and refer to them as the Chinese, the Japanese, the Germans, or the Viet Cong. On the other hand, when the mask of indifference is swept away and people become distinguishable human beings, one feels an empathy. In China one also feels great sympathy because of the level at which most people must live. To my amazement, when I went into the classroom on the Monday following my experience in the park I found my Chinese students to be persons with whom I could identify.

At one point in our trip to the institute, I turned to Jeanne and commented that our Japanese friend appeared to be tired. Jeanne explained that the young woman was in Beijing with her four-year-old son, that she had left her husband in Japan, and that she would be in Beijing for several months. I gathered that she was lonely, that she missed her home in Japan, and that she missed her close friends and relatives. I gathered that she was also feeling what it means to belong to a minority group—to be isolated and alone much of the time, and to be isolated with only a few people who speak the same language the remainder of the time. Thinking about the young Japanese woman in the back seat, I told myself that I could not belong to a minority group for the remainder of my life. The pain is too great.

When we finally arrived at the institute, the driver entered through the back gate. We drove down an alleyway between walled-in dormitories. The walls are a common sight in Beijing, as I am told they are throughout China. The Chinese people live behind walls, work behind walls, play behind walls, and even go to school behind walls. In spite of all that, the Chinese people seem open and cordial. It could be that they have physical walls in order to escape having to erect the psychological ones so characteristic of Americans. Chinese walls can be seen and therefore dealt with in a simple and concrete way. Psychological walls are much more difficult to manage. At any rate, I have become a wall watcher. I watch to find out what walls are made of, how high they are, how thick they are, and most of all I look for what is being walled in as well as what is being walled out. The latter is often difficult to determine, but walls seem to lend the Chinese people some semblance of privacy as well as peace of mind. Perhaps that is their greatest value.

When I arrived at my office, I lit my pipe, poured myself a cup of tea, and began to think about the class I would teach. When I entered the classroom at 8:00 a.m. I found that I had five visitors. One of the visitors was a man who appeared to be in his late forties or early fifties. Upon examining his very proper uniform, I decided that he must have come to represent the party. Two women whom I had never seen before were present, as well as two Chinese teachers whom I had met. At break time, after fifty minutes, I located Lu Zhibao and asked for an explanation concerning the invasion of my class by new people. He informed me that one of the ladies, an attractive one, was a party cadre who was visiting the class "to see how it was coming along." When I inquired about the official-looking man, Lu explained that he was attending the class under the sponsorship of his work unit. I pushed for details but got nowhere. I had been wrong about which one was the party cadre, and after discussing my visitors with Lu I concluded that he knew little about them.

When I returned to my office after class, I looked at the literature around which I would build my next lecture. Feeling the need to schedule more closely, I began looking for a school calendar. I found a spring calendar from the year before on my desk, but it was in Chinese. A young Chinese teacher brought me a current calendar and sat down to help me label the months in English. She explained when the Chinese holidays were and when we would dismiss classes for spring break. I told her that my lack of knowledge of the Chinese language posed many barriers to my planning well and functioning well. The young teacher supposed that the institute would likely supply me with a tutor but added that the arrangement would be awkward. The tutor would need to come to the Friendship Hotel, she explained, and both the institute and the hotel have severe restrictions concerning that. Furthermore, a tutor would have to travel for two hours each way on a crowded bus. That, I surmised, would be asking too much.

In the afternoon Wanda and I went for a walk. We talked, and I began to realize that she was also feeling what it means to belong to a minority group. She has not found a job yet, and she spends more time in our apartment than she should. She feels lonely and isolated. She has talked with representatives from two schools about teaching oral English. But she has never taught school in her life, and she does not relish the idea of teaching. She needs to find a job with an American firm; she needs more contact with speakers of English. To work in an American firm and establish acquaintances with Americans would make her life in China more enjoyable. She needs to be occupied. She needs to overcome the feeling that she belongs to a minority group.

Friday, September 12

On the way to the car stand I met Lisa Wichser, who also teaches at

Second Foreign Language Institute. I told her about my feeling as though I belonged to a minority group. She said she had felt that way since she was sixteen, and Lisa is probably twenty-seven. When we arrived at the car stand, we found that a nearly loaded car was waiting for one more passenger; as Lisa got into the car she said, "I think everyone should have to undergo that experience." While I waited for the next car, I wondered about her parting words. I also wondered why she had felt that way from the time she was sixteen.

As it turned out I rode to the institute with a Japanese man who spoke no English. He and I sat in the front seat with the Chinese driver. The back seat was occupied by a teacher from England, whose name is Jim, and a teacher from France, whose name is Isabella. I listened as Jim and Isabella talked about the news as it was reported in the morning paper. I learned that the People's General Assembly had been meeting in the Great Hall of the People for several days. Some concerns which the assembly had been addressing itself to included rates for parking bicycles and rates for admission to city parks. Another item in the news concerned accountability in medicine. According to the story as Isabella related it, a Chinese doctor was treating a patient who died. Because the relatives did not think the patient should have died, they set about beating the doctor. Another item in the news had to do with the income of peasants. According to the morning newspaper, the average annual income for a Chinese peasant working on a commune in 1979 was eighty-three *yuan*, about fifty-five dollars in U.S. currency. The story, of course, makes sense but it omits much of what the story should be. For example, a peasant earns points for his work. He also supplies his needs from the commune store. At the end of the year he and his fellow peasants may be paid a bonus provided the year is prosperous for the commune. If the harvest is good, he may do well. On the other hand, if the harvest is poor, he and his family may suffer.

After I had taught my morning class Lu Zhibao came by and suggested that we take a short walk and look at some of the campus. He also informed me that some of the boxes Wanda and I had shipped from Texas had arrived. I was glad to hear about the boxes because I had come to doubt that the boxes would ever arrive.

I was also glad for the walk because I had not seen the campus. As it turned out, Lu wanted to talk; the walk was only to allow Lu the opportunity to pose a question: "Frankly, Dr. LeMaster," he said to me, "why did you really come to China?" I was momentarily shocked to find that he suspected ulterior motives on my part, but I repeated the story that I had told him before concerning Ralph Wang's visit to Baylor University and how he had convinced me that I could make a worthy contribution to education in China as a foreign expert. When I had completed the story once again, he seemed very pleased, very willing to accept that I was telling the truth. In the retelling, nevertheless, I found myself wondering whether I was telling the truth. Why had I come to China? I was at a loss for an answer that would satisfy me. I supposed I had had psychological reasons. I reasoned that my coming to China had had something to do with success. I supposed that I had had to get away and view any gains I might have made from a distance. Whatever the reason, I was glad that I had come to China.

When I returned to my office, I marked the first book in a set of four entitled *Highlights of American Literature* and sent it to the press. The press will print 150 copies and will have them ready in two weeks. My students will each have a text to read. On the way home in the afternoon I was told that the entire four volumes of *Highlights of American Literature* were being pirated in Shanghai (printed illegally). When I heard about the pirating in Shanghai, I remembered a story I had read in the newspaper before coming to China about efforts by Chinese technicians to copy a Boeing-made aircraft. I remembered that someone in China had told me that the effort had failed; it seems that the Chinese could not duplicate the airplane's exact center of gravity. My students will have books, however, and perhaps that is more important than the present state of Chinese technology.

In the afternoon Wanda and I went to Jingshan Park. We got off the bus across the street from the Great Hall of the People and walked for about forty-five minutes through streets filled with shops and family dwellings. While we walked we stopped and purchased chocolate ice cream bars at a price of five *fen* (about three cents) each. The cost of entering the park was also five *fen*. We climbed to the top of Coal Hill where we could look far out over the city of Beijing. What I found most impressive was that we could see two cities in one. We could see an old Beijing with its low and drab looking buildings, but we could also see a new Beijing with its impressive high-rise buildings. What one actually sees from the top of Coal Hill is a giant city in a rapid state of transition. When one stares out over the city in almost any direction, one realizes that the Chinese are serious about modernizing. He or she realizes that the high-rise buildings mark a new beginning for China, just as he or she realizes, when he or she sees a young couple "necking" on the side of the mountain, that this too marks a new beginning. It was a pleasant afternoon. The view from the top of the hill, and the lovers, made it a day to remember.

Saturday, September 13

I suffered terribly throughout Friday night from an inflamed throat as well as from congestion in my chest and head. The dust in Jingshan Park was taking its revenge. On Saturday morning I went to the clinic to see the doctor, but seeing a doctor in China is almost as difficult as seeing one in America. Wanda and I had still not been issued our medical cards, and without a medical card one must first answer numerous questions as well as pay for the medical service. After the questions, I was allowed to see a woman doctor who appeared to be about forty years old. She knew a few English expressions and managed to ask where I hurt, whether I had diarrhea, and whether I had a heart problem. She had fairly well exhausted her English vocabulary by that time and decided to check my throat. She immediately prescribed three kinds of medicine—a lozenge to soothe my throat, an antibiotic, and a granular substance to mix in hot water, a substance which tastes terrible and which the foreigners at the compound refer to as Camel Dung Tea. When the bill came, I was surprised. The office call cost two *yuan* and the medicine cost one *yuan* eighty four *fen*. My total bill was $2.56, and I would be reimbursed for that by the institute.

Mao Zhiren came to visit us. We served tea and inquired about his studies. Mao explained that his graduate work in international economics is time-consuming but not very difficult. When we asked concerning what he would do when he completed his graduate work (called postgraduate work in China), he explained that he would stay and teach at Beijing University. Mao wants very much to study in America, and I have been trying to help him gain admission to the graduate school at Baylor University. He will need financial aid, for Chinese families have no access to large sums of money. We also asked him whether he might like to return to Changchun to be with his family once he graduates. He said that he would not. He has been in Beijing for two or three years, but his wife and two daughters live in Changchun where his wife teaches at Jilin University. Such an arrangement strikes both Wanda and me as strange, but it is not strange to Chinese families. They have learned through years of hard and desperate living to adjust to whatever is needed to survive. To survive with honor seems to be the goal of those with whom I talk, but among the youth exists a growing desire for material possessions and comfort.

We postponed our trip to Beijing University. In the meantime Mao agreed to look for appropriate books from which he will tutor us in the Chinese language. His offer is not entirely for our benefit. While he tutors us in Chinese, he will practice his English. He often does not understand what we are saying, although he pretends that he does in order to avoid embarrassment. I had discovered that Lu Zhibao did the same thing. Before he left I told Mao that we often hear what sounds like cannon shots early in the morning, and he told us that the military conducts target practice not far from where we live. When he left, Wanda and I agreed that Mao is a fine young man.

Sunday, September 14

I wanted very much to accompany Wanda on a trip to Miyun Reservoir, but I was still suffering from a cold. As it turned out, Wanda went alone. As for me, I typed letters. I worked on my journal. I did much thinking. I thought about how different our lives are in China. I thought about our friends and colleagues back in Texas. At noon I went to lunch and sat alone. I was still thinking. I tried to review my past in such a way that it would make sense. Will we fit in when we return to Baylor University? We have been in China only two weeks, but life in China is different. When I had completed my lunch, I went back to the apartment to work on lesson plans for the next week of classes. How could I lecture on American literature without talking about religion? How could I keep from sounding overly zealous, and even solicitous? I set about preparing a lecture on Puritanism and the Enlightenment in America. How much would my students already know? Would they have a sufficient stock of Western ideas to understand what I was saying? I scurried about for a beginning place, and finally decided I could best begin by explaining to my students some basic philosophical concerns such as metaphysics, epistemology, and axiology. I would define those terms and illustrate them, hoping that I could prepare my students for what I had to say about Puritanism and the Enlightenment.

Wanda came home from Miyun Reservoir at 5:30 p.m. She explained that three buses of foreigners had gone on the trip, but that few of them had spoken English. She explained that she had eaten a number of kinds of fresh fish for lunch, that she had enjoyed a pleasurable boat ride, that she had toured the dam and the reservoir, that she had enjoyed viewing the countryside, including a number of communes, but that she had done it all feeling very much alone. As for me, when I had completed preparation for my lectures I slept. I knew that I would need more than the medicine given me at the clinic if I was to be ready for classes on Monday morning.

Monday, September 15

Once I had my lecture underway, I found that I had to refer to medieval ecclesiastical structure, to the Greek philosophers Plato and Aristotle, to the Latin Humanists, and to a number of other sources to make meaningful distinctions between the Puritan concept of a world order and that of the Enlightenment. I stopped lecturing frequently and asked for questions, but few came. As abstraction led to abstraction, I could tell that some of my students were lost. I could also tell that others were following what I had to say with great satisfaction. The smiles on their faces told me that they were pleased with their own knowledge, with their ability to comprehend, and with my having confirmed for them things that they had already thought through for themselves. I think I succeeded in establishing for them the context out of which American literature grew, and for some of my students that context will make a great difference in their study of American literature both now and in the future.

After my morning class I went to a meeting called by the head of the English department. He addressed the foreign teachers, but he said little that we had not heard before. His major concern was that we were all adjusting to being teachers in a Chinese school. He solicited questions, and I took advantage of that to complain about my not having received the necessary papers to function well in Chinese society, including identification papers. The liaison to the Bureau of Foreign Experts was summoned and charged with expediting the issuing of the papers. I also inquired about being reimbursed for postage on boxes Wanda and I had shipped from Texas. I was assured that my request would be handled quickly and that I would be reimbursed.

Tuesday, September 16

Again I lectured on Puritanism and the Enlightenment. From my experience of the day before, I decided that I had better use three models based on European feudal society in order to explain intricate relationships involving God and celestial structure, the church and ecclesiastical structure, and the society and civil structure. Because the models proved successful, I found that I could profitably elaborate on particular differences between the seventeenth-century Puritan theocracy and the late eighteenth and early nineteenth-century Enlightenment in America. Occasionally I stopped to answer questions, and when I had completed my lecture I could tell that my students were pleased.

On the way home from the institute I read the world news from *News from Foreign Agencies and Press* (September 12, 1980).[1] I was particularly interested in what I might find about Prime Minister Robert Muldoon's visit to Beijing. When Muldoon arrived, flags were flown for miles along the boulevard leading to the Great Hall of the People. From New Zealand,

---

[1] *News from Foreign Agencies and Press* and *Xinhua News Agency News Bulletin* are news bulletins circulated in and among work units. The former contains international news and is referred to as "The Blue Sheet" because it is printed in blue ink. The latter contains news about China and is referred to as "The Red Sheet" because it is printed in red ink. Articles appearing in *News from Foreign Agencies and Press* and *Xinhua News Agency News Bulletin* originate in various places. The following consists of a list containing the dates of the articles that I used from each news bulletin as well as the sources of the news stories.

News from Foreign Agencies and Press: September 12, 1980, from AP, Beijing; September 10 and November 29, 1980, from UPI, Beijing; November 28 and December 4, 1980, from UPI, Beijing; December 3 and December 4, 1980, from Reuter, Beijing; December 3 and February 16, 1981, from UPI, Washington; February 16 and March 24, 1981, from AFP, Beijing; March 24, April 15 and April 16, 1981, from UPI, Beijing.

Xinhua News Agency News Bulletin: March 7, 1981, from Xinhua, Beijing; March 6 and April 20, 1981, from Xinhua, Beijing; April 19 and April 21, 1981, from Xinhua, Beijing; April 21 and June 3, 1981, from *Guangming Daily*, Beijing; May 31 and June 11, 1981, from Xinhua, Beijing.

Muldoon was the first head of state to meet with Zhao Ziyang, who was elected premier on Wednesday, September 10, by China's National People's Congress. Zhao is an economist, and at a recent banquet held in the Great Hall of the People he gave Chinese leaders a preview of what he intends to do about China's lagging economy. Premier Zhao intends to turn China into a modern industrial state by the end of the decade of the nineties. Such an intention is curious because the growth of cities will prove essential to turning China into an industrial state. Presently, only 20 percent of the population lives in cities. To quote Zhao: "We should vigorously expand the decision-making power of enterprises and the power of their workers and staff to participate in management, restructure the economic system step by step, combine regulation through planning with regulation by the market and run our economy by relying on economic organs as well as on economic leverage and legislation" (p. 1).

Zhao is a protégé of Vice Chairman Deng Xiaoping, and Deng is the driving force behind Chinese plans for modernization. In his speech Zhao promised to "promote socialist democracy, strengthen the socialist legal system, improve the leadership of our government at all levels and enhance stability, unity, and liveliness in the country as a whole" (p. 2). Zhao's major effort concerning the economy appears to be that of relieving the state of its powers of decision-making concerning the economy. As he explained to a delegation from Japan, a delegation which included Yoshira Inayama, head of a Japanese Steel Corporation, the world's largest steel company, "The experience of China and other countries shows that over-concentration of power is detrimental to democracy" (p. 2). In short, Zhao said that the leaders of economic enterprises should have responsibility for and power over those enterprises without interference from the state. What appears to be implied is the return of more power to the people, and that this appears to be the case seems evident in Zhao's fondness for the word *democracy*. In the press one reads and hears *democracy*, *socialism*, and *socialist democracy* in attempts to describe the future of the People's Republic of China. One does not encounter the word *communism*. Although this likely reflects current ideological differences between China and the Soviet Union, it appears to amount to more than that. Chinese leaders are consciously adopting the language that best reflects their aspirations concerning the future of China. If such is the case, the present rift between Moscow and Beijing will grow over the next few years. It is sad that Americans are not well informed concerning what is happening in China, politically or in any other way. Perhaps Americans can count on cultural exchange programs and business to bridge the gap for a short while, but sooner or later we must recognize the fact that we are staring into the face of an awakening giant, one that will play a large role in shaping world civilization in the twenty-first century.

Wednesday, September 17

When the weekend came, Wanda and I traveled with other foreign teachers to a resort about 250 kilometers from Beijing where we saw a Buddhist temple and about eight monasteries. Because I was excited about the coming trip, I asked one of the Chinese teachers concerning the state of religion in China. Her response was that Buddha was important during the Tang Dynasty, and that he is still somewhat important in southern China. When I asked about the importance of Confucius and his ethical system, her response was that the importance of Confucius had been destroyed in the Cultural Revolution. I dropped the subject at that point; she appeared to be uncomfortable while answering my questions. Sometime in the future, however, I will ask for her opinion concerning the future of religion in general in China.

My conversation with the Chinese teacher, combined with the fact that I have been trying to explain to my classes the influence of religion in shaping American culture, brought back memories of an experience that I had had in 1976. At that time my family and I still lived in Defiance, Ohio, where we had lived for twenty years. It was during the afternoon in the fall of the year that I received a phone call I had not expected. I was working in the garden when my wife called me to the phone. When I picked up the receiver and identified myself, the other party said, "Jim, Dad is dead. We would like you to come to New York. Mother very much wants you to come." Not knowing what to say to this request, being made by the oldest of three sons of a former teacher of mine, I finally said that I would discuss the matter with my wife and return the call the next morning.

I was shocked. I was stunned. My old teacher had died, and he was in his early fifties. He had just returned from teaching for two years in Laos. Before that he had taught for two years in Thailand. And before that he had taught for twelve years or more at Defiance College, in Ohio. He was a young teacher at Defiance College when I arrived in 1955 as a freshman, and he was an inspirational teacher. I came to like him very much because I was not a strong student, and more than anyone else he instilled confidence in me. He had a way of making a student believe in himself or herself. He was always positive and never seemed to doubt that his students could do almost anything. On the other hand, he was Jewish. He was not paranoid about being Jewish, but many times he found himself cut short of fulfilling his aspirations because he was a Jew. Being cut short hurt him terribly, but he tried to compensate by encouraging his students to accomplish great things. That was his one accomplishment. Through his students he could transcend his Jewishness and accomplish many things vicariously. Yes, I liked him very much. I liked him even more when after several years from the time I was his student he came home from teaching abroad and brought me a poem I had written in his class as a sophomore. It was a rather bad poem, but he had saved it. He wanted me to have it as a token of our friendship.

I decided that I would go to New York, that I would pay my last respects to a man who had been instrumental in shaping my life. I owed him that much, and I owed it to his family as well. My wife helped me pack my clothes, and the next morning I called New York. Once again I talked to Lloyd, the oldest son. He asked me to take the earliest plane possible because the funeral was scheduled for 2:00 p.m. I was horrified at the idea, for I had never so much as seen a Jewish funeral.

I flew to New York and helped conduct the funeral, and I am glad I did. Perhaps it is because I am teaching in China that I have been thinking about my old professor. Perhaps it is his dedication to helping others that I cherish. Whatever it is, I feel a debt of gratitude, and I feel that my being here is one small way in which I can pay tribute to him. He would have wanted it this way. He would have approved. I often think of him when I am teaching my Chinese students, for I know that he would gladly have done what I am doing.

In the afternoon Wanda and I went to Beihai Park. The scenery was breathtaking. The parks in Beijing are clean and well decorated. We climbed a hill to visit a pagoda, and from the top of the hill we looked out over Beijing. The city is heavily polluted, and I could see why several people had told me that Beijing is more polluted than New York City. I wonder what it will be like when the winds of March blow dust and sand into Beijing from the Gobi desert. We have been told that March and April are hard on everyone because of the dust. I held a clean handkerchief over my mouth and nose as much as I could while we made our way down the hill and through the streets toward the Beijing Hotel. Wanda decided to take pictures of the people in the streets as well as in the shops. In one instance she stood in a doorway and focused for a picture of a woman working on a piece of pottery. When the woman realized what was about to happen, she screamed and ran. I was not surprised, for I had been told that the older Chinese people are camera shy. Some are not familiar with cameras, but there are two other reasons. Some are superstitious, and some are still afraid that any picture might be used by the authorities.

Thursday, September 18

On the evening of the seventeenth we had had dinner in our flat. Wanda had succeeded in finding a job, with the United States Department of Agriculture, and we felt we had to celebrate. She will work for about two months. The job has to do with setting up and operating a large exhibition in Beijing of United States farm equipment. The United States Department of Commerce is also involved. The object of the exhibition is obviously designed to open up the China market to industrial equipment, machinery, and a great number of things that United States manufacturers would like to sell to the Chinese. Hopefully, the manufacturers and the United States government will realize that they cannot sell to the Chinese unless they buy from the Chinese. The fact that the Chinese have no U.S. dollars is a large deterrent to their purchasing American goods. Until the problem is solved by way of barter, or by some plan of currency exchange, China will not be a viable market for anything produced in the United States. As for our dinner, our celebration, we had cheese, bread, and beer. It was a good celebration, even though Wanda does not begin working until the first of October.

It was Thursday, and on the way to the institute I listened to Don Krumm, from Washington, D.C., hold forth on statistics about Beijing. He told those of us in the car, for example, that Beijing moves 50 percent of its eight million people by bus or electric trolley, 45 percent by bicycle, and 5 percent by car. I thought the statistics were interesting by way of comparison to those of any major city in the United States. While listening to Don, I watched the traffic, the endless stream of bicycles, and I saw, for example, a woman being taken to the hospital on a platform mounted on the back of a bicycle. Covered with a quilt, she was bouncing every which way. I wondered how she could possibly survive the trip to the hospital. I saw bicycles loaded with onions, cabbage, and melons on their way to market. I saw many large, two-wheeled carts loaded with chickens and farm produce of various kinds. I noticed that in some cases the drivers of the carts were asleep. The animals pulling the carts apparently knew where they were going and how to get there.

Friday, September 19

On the way to the institute, Don Krumm, Christine Wang, Jeanne Lonnoy, and I talked about Michael Assenmiker. Young and inexperienced, Michael is teaching French with an older Chinese man. The Chinese teacher has assigned Michael sixteen hours of teaching each week along with other duties. Also, he is trying to intimidate Michael into assisting with a book which the older teacher is researching and writing. Michael has protested, but his protests have accomplished nothing. When he goes to the school officials and succeeds in having his work load reduced, the Chinese teacher merely assigns him a new round of responsibilities. Such is Michael's dilemma as Jeanne explained it. Jeanne is in her early sixties and is very motherly. I am sure she is a great consolation to Michael.

When I arrived at my office, I had a cup of hot water. I have come to appreciate the fact that the Chinese seem always to be sipping a cup of hot water. It had not occurred to me that such an act might have practical reasons until I had a bad cold. One of the Chinese teachers advised me to drink plenty of hot water. Steaming hot water keeps the head opened up. It also keeps the dust and pollution washed away. I sip a cup of hot water every chance I have because it keeps my sinus passages open and soothes my throat. I am told that in winter drinking hot water will be even more important. Because coal is plentiful, the people in Beijing heat with coal. The result is that Beijing is heavily polluted with coal dust in winter.

According to my Chinese colleagues, very few people die of heart attack in Beijing, but cancer of the throat, larynx, and lungs is common. Such information alone is reason enough to drink hot water.

My students continue to be curious and responsive. They have begun asking questions, but they prefer to ask them in the privacy of my office. For several days they think about an idea I have given them and then they come with questions. Always they seem excited about learning. Always they seem excited that I am lecturing to them about American ideas, about American thought, and about American literature. They listen closely, and when I entertain questions they ask very perceptive ones. When I came to the institute to teach, I was told not to expect my Chinese students to ask questions. Some of my students are still afraid. They remember the Cultural Revolution when asking questions often led to criticism. But I can see hope in their eyes, and I can see it in their behavior. Some are asking questions inside themselves until they can acquire the courage to ask them aloud as others are doing. I encourage them to talk with each other about the ideas they are encountering. I encourage them to evaluate everything I say, to test it first of all for common sense, and then to test it for whether it should or could make a difference in their lives. They like the approach, and they appreciate that I will be open and honest with them.

Tan Luying is twenty-two years old, although she looks as though she might be sixteen. In talking with her I have also learned that she is remarkably intelligent. She came to my office to tell me that she has been reading about the Temple of Heaven in order to function well as a guide when she visits the Temple of Heaven with Wanda and me on Sunday. I told Tan to mark a map indicating the places we should see together throughout the winter. She was thrilled with that idea, and I am sure she will bring a map well marked for my approval. As it turned out, however, Tan wanted to talk about other things. She stayed with the topic of sightseeing only until the office cleared. Then she posed the topics of morality and religion. Young people in China, Tan said, are less moral than old people. She attributed the difference in morality to the fact that religion was outlawed during the Cultural Revolution. Chinese young people, she added, those coming after the Cultural Revolution, are selfish. She asked me about my own convictions, about whether, as she put it, I was religious. I told her that I considered myself a Christian, that my wife and I are members of the Presbyterian Church. At that point she remarked, "I think religion is important to the human spirit; I think it is good." I was surprised because Tan grew up in a time in which religion was strictly forbidden. She confided in me that her mother was still a follower of Confucius, and that her mother had instilled the teachings of Confucius in her children. Our conversation was interrupted by several teachers who entered the office, but I sensed that Tan Luying went away without having completed what it was she wanted to say about religion.

Saturday, September 20

We set out on a trip to Chengde at 6:30 a.m. I had mentioned the trip to some of the Chinese teachers the day before and had noted resentment on their part as we talked about the trip. I could understand their resentment. Foreign teachers are paid ten to twenty times what Chinese teachers are paid to teach the same classes. Foreign teachers are taken on tours of China by the Bureau of Foreign Experts, but Chinese teachers cannot afford the trips. Even though Chinese teachers are miserably underpaid, teaching is not exclusively a woman's job. Everywhere one looks in Chinese society he sees men and women working alongside each other. He sees women sweeping the streets before early morning traffic. He sees them driving buses as well as operating heavy equipment. He sees women carrying bricks and buckets of sand at construction sites as well as laying bricks and setting steel girders high up on the tops of buildings. He sees women in the fields early in the morning as well as late in the afternoon. They work alongside men in tilling the soil, in planting crops, and in cultivating. Wherever one sees men working in China, he also sees women working with them. Chinese women have been liberated, but the responsibility they bear for supporting the family makes many of them wish they had not been.

Chengde is about 250 kilometers northeast of Beijing. Surrounded by mountains, it is a beautiful summer resort as well as the world capital of Buddhism. Built during the reigns of the emperors Kangxi and Qianlong (1662-1795) of the Qing Dynasty, the compound known as the Li Palace was completed in 1703. Surrounding the compound are temples known as the eight outer monasteries, the architectural characteristics of which were borrowed from the Han, Tibetan, and Mongolian nations. During the sixteenth and seventeenth centuries, the Russians invaded Chinese territory repeatedly, and this worried the Chinese nationalities in the north causing them to split away from China. As a result emperors Kang Xi and Qian Long spent five to six months in Chengde every year conducting military maneuvers, protecting the border, attending to state affairs, and entertaining the chiefs of the northern nationalities. Head of the government as well as state religion, the lama of Tibet was frequently a guest of the emperor. He also had much influence in determining the architecture of the palace and the outer monasteries. One of the temples was modeled after the residence of Banchang, in Rigeza, Tibet, the head of lamaism throughout China.

One sees great marvels in Chengde. For example, one sees a statue of Buddha measuring 22.28 meters in height and 15 meters around the waist. Made of wood, the statue weighs 110 tons. This giant statue has fifty-two hands, so it can serve everyone, and forty-five eyes, so it can see throughout the universe. Ten thousand Buddhas of gilded clay serve as the disciples of the great Buddha. These miniature statues are supposed to indicate that the followers of Buddha are many. When one has spent a day in Chengde, he or she realizes how important the Buddhist religion once was to the Chinese people. Now the temples serve only as tourist attractions, and that has been the case only since 1980, when Chengde was first opened to foreigners.

Sunday, September 21

On the way to Chengde, I had watched the countryside from the train window. I was overwhelmed by the beauty of the mountains in northern China. I was impressed by the utilization of land, by the terracing that went so high up the mountains it boggled the imagination, by the irrigation of crops and conservation measures resulting in efficient use of every drop of water available. Passing through northern China was like passing through another time in history. I watched plows being pulled by oxen and people carrying their burdens in baskets and earthen jars suspended by ropes from a pole across the shoulder. Grain, I observed, was being cut by hand with a knife or sickle. I watched peasants flail grain with an instrument that has been around for thousands of years. I watched them as they beat the kernels of grain from stalks on an earthen floor and then tossed the grain into the air so that the wind would blow the chaff away. In the background, always, were the modest dwelling places of the Chinese people, dwelling places which had been constructed by piling stones on top of each other to make walls and then filling the cracks with mud. The floors were earthen, and sometimes only a curtain covered the entrance. Some of the houses had doors, but even in Chengde some houses did not. Temperatures north of Beijing drop to below zero on the Fahrenheit scale, and Chengde has a considerable amount of snow in the winter. As I looked at houses where a family of seven or eight lives in one small room, I wondered about the great sense of dignity and fear Chinese people seem to possess everywhere I went. For centuries the Chinese people have survived. I hope the future of China will have political stability so that these people will have an opportunity to better their living conditions. After centuries of suffering, they deserve a chance to share the luxuries and comforts belonging to affluent societies. The trip to Chengde made me want to be caught up in the rhythms of Chinese life.

Monday, September 22

On Monday morning my class went well. I conducted a review in order to supply my students with a natural context from which to ask questions. I also gave them an outline of events, names, and dates as preparation for lectures to come. After class, I hardly reached my office door when I was approached by one of the Chinese teachers. She asked if I would be willing to help her for a few minutes. She seemed a bit shy about asking, so I quickly assured her that I would do anything I possibly could. She had been preparing a unit to teach her students on films and filmmaking in America. She confided in me that she was having difficulty because she had never seen an American feature film. She asked me about certain terms used in her book, *English Today*. She asked questions about production companies and about free-lance filmmaking. When we completed our discussion, I was surprised to hear her apologize for being dumb and taking my time. I hastened to assure her that she was not dumb, that she could not be expected to know about American films and filmmaking, and that she was really very perceptive concerning what she had read. She was pleased and thanked me as she went on her way.

The name of the teacher who came for help is Shao Jingfeng. As is the case with most people in China, she has not traveled. I decided that I would give her the brochures Wanda and I had brought back from Chengde. That way she could see many of the sights in Chengde. After she had gone, I made a point of asking one of the foreign teachers concerning Shao, and what I learned was pathetic. Shao's husband lives in Africa, where he teaches French. Her four-year-old son lives in Shanghai with her parents. The arrangement is not satisfactory, but as is the case with many Chinese families, government assignment has kept Shao's family apart. Although she misses her family, she dedicates herself to teaching and helping her students. She hopes for a time when she can be with her husband and son, but that does not appear to be a possibility in the foreseeable future. Shao's case is a common one in the People's Republic of China. For the remainder of the day I could not help but think of Shao.

Tuesday, September 23

The day of the Festival of the Moon is a grand occasion in China. Celebrated throughout the country, it marks the end of the growing season. As seems to be the case in all ancient civilizations, two festivals mark the growing year—one in the spring and one in the fall. The ancient Greeks celebrated the Greater Dionysia and the Lesser Dionysia, and these probably influenced what we in Christendom celebrate as Christmas and Easter. All such festivals appear to be bound up in myths and rituals pertaining to death and rebirth. At any rate, for the Festival of the Moon the parks in Beijing were decorated with colorful lanterns; flowers were displayed throughout the city; lights were strung on public buildings; and the Chinese people enjoyed many festivities. Many stories exist concerning moon cakes, which are traditionally eaten on the occasion of the Festival of the Moon. According to one of those stories, during the Yuan Dynasty, before the Ming Dynasty, the Mongolians had taken over China and the peasants planned an uprising to free themselves from Mongolian rule. The uprising was to take place throughout all of China simultaneously, but a problem existed concerning how to circulate news about the time of the uprising among the peasants without alerting the Mongolians. According to the story, news of the uprising was sealed in moon cakes and the moon cakes were distributed among the peasants. The uprising took place on schedule and the Mongolians were defeated. The date of the uprising is now celebrated as the day of the Festival of the Moon.

Moon cakes are round, resembling the shape of the moon, and for centuries the peasants throughout China have gathered with their families and friends on this day, a day of the full moon, to celebrate the overthrow of the Mongolians, but more importantly to celebrate the end of the growing season. It is their way of giving thanks for a bountiful harvest, and in that sense resembles Thanksgiving Day in America. When the Chinese gather at night under a full moon, they cut each round cake into small pieces and distribute the pieces among those present, symbolizing unity in the family as well as in the community. Then they sing songs and tell tales about the past, but most of all they enjoy one another's company as they give thanks for a bountiful harvest.

Lu Zhibao brought moon cakes to my office. "Go to the park with your wife and friends," he said, "and eat the moon cakes under the full moon. That will bring you prosperity and happiness during the coming winter." I thought about his generosity in bringing the moon cakes. I thought about his being humiliated as a young teacher during the Cultural Revolution, about his being sent into the countryside to perform hard labor, and then I marveled at what I interpreted to be his optimism concerning the future. Lu Zhibao is not bitter. He tries to leave the past in the past. He loves his countrymen, and he wants a better life for all of them. He is one of the most unforgettable human beings I have ever met.

I had an opportunity to talk with Tan Luying again. She told me about her father, who died ten or twelve years ago of high blood pressure. She told me that her father went to Europe when he was young, that he studied medicine in Brussels and became a doctor, and that he returned to China to help his people. When he returned to China, he had changed. He had been converted to Catholicism. He met a young woman and married her, and the woman became Tan's mother. He also converted his young wife to Catholicism, according to Tan, and during the Cultural Revolution Tan's parents remained devout Catholics. Afraid of reprisal, they worshiped in their home. They brought up three children—Tan and two brothers—to believe in God. When Tan told me these things I understood why she had said that she thought religion very important to the human spirit, but I did not understand the comment she had made concerning her mother and Confucianism. Her mother had been brought up as a follower of Confucius and had been converted to Catholicism by the man who had gone to Europe to become a doctor. As far as I could tell, Tan was saying that her mother never discerned any great conflict between Confucian ethics and the Catholic religion. As she talked Tan seemed to be telling me more about herself than I had previously grasped. She is remarkably religious.

Tan talked until we were interrupted by a Chinese teacher who wanted me to help her prepare a lesson. The teacher's name was Qi Wenqin. She also wanted to talk about my schedule for the spring term, since she is responsible for all of Grade 77, which I teach. We settled on a schedule which calls for me to meet all of Grade 77 once a week and for conducting seminars with a different group of my students each day of the week. She apologized for assigning me what she thought to be too much work, but I assured her that I could manage. She was gratified and asked for my advice concerning the entire schedule for the spring semester. I made suggestions, and she seemed pleased. When she left, she asked me if I would be kind enough to help her with her English. I told her that I did not want to embarrass her by correcting her. She replied that she would be honored instead of embarrassed. I promised her that in the future I would be as much help as I could. Then I left to take a car to the Friendship Hotel where I would have lunch.

Wednesday, September 24

On the way to work I talked with Don Krumm. We agreed that we would visit the Bureau of Foreign Experts and request permission to tour a commune, a hospital, a power plant, and a factory. We both want to see such installations, and we agreed that it might be more convincing if we went to see the appropriate officials together. While talking we also discovered that we would both be going to Qufu and Taishan over National Day. At Qufu we will visit the birthplace of Confucius, and at Taishan (Mt. Tai) we will climb seven thousand steps to the top of the sacred mountain, where we will spend the night. Don seemed as eager to see Taishan as I was. Many stories exist about Taishan, and I have been told that it is very beautiful.

After my class Lu Zhibao came to my office. I told him that Wanda and

I had shared the moon cakes he had given us and that we liked them very much. In turn Lu told me about how he spent the Cultural Revolution; at least he told me about the Cultural Revolution as he wanted me to see and understand it. He explained that violence led to the closing of all schools. When this happened, he was sent into the countryside to work with the peasants. Because he had an education, he explained, he was given a job as secretary of a commune. He stayed in the countryside and worked as secretary of the commune for eight years. During that time he came to know the peasants in the commune very well, and he still refers to them as his friends. He holds great admiration for the peasants with whom he worked, because they saw him through the Cultural Revolution without any harm coming to him, and for that he is grateful. "The peasants in the countryside are slow to change," he said. "They hold on to the old ways." Lu sees in them the essence of the real China, the China that has existed for centuries without having been very much affected by change.

In the afternoon Wanda and I went shopping in Wangfujing Street. We were looking for a padded jacket that I might wear in the classroom. We looked in the shops but found nothing suitable. However, I purchased a collection of prose pieces by Yang Shuo, a Chinese fiction writer who died in 1968. Wanda purchased a metal container for storing cakes and pastries. Since I must leave for the institute before the dining hall opens, we have a pastry and a cup of coffee each morning for breakfast.

What I experienced in Wangfujing Street made me dislike the Chinese people en masse as much as I like them as individuals. They seem to have no sense of courtesy in crowds. Men and women make their way through large crowds by pushing and shoving. They have made an art of maneuvering in crowds. In one shop Wanda and I watched a crowd gather for books to go on sale. They pushed, shoved, waved their money, and I thought a fight would surely break out. I was reminded that for the Chinese people many things are in short supply, and that a chance to purchase warm clothing for winter, for example, might be the last chance before the next winter. The Chinese have learned to survive, and at times they must scrap to do that.

I came home worn out from making my way through the masses of humanity in Wangfujing Street. Every day in Wangfujing Street is the same. There is no time when the shops are not crowded. I was also told by Wanda that many of the young people wandering in the streets as well as in the shops are out of work. Until my shopping trip I was convinced that every Chinese person fits into the system somewhere, that everyone has a job. Wanda explained that she had recently read an article in a magazine deploring the fact that unemployment among the young is growing, that there are simply not enough jobs to go around. When Chinese young people graduate from middle school, they take an examination to determine who will enter a university. In Beijing about five percent of those graduating from middle school actually enter a university. All others are given jobs based on their scores in school until the jobs run out. Those who are not assigned jobs are advised to go to the countryside and work until jobs open up in Beijing, but many of them do not go. The young people in the countryside do not like to work with them because they are not capable of working as hard as the country youth. They are frequently criticized and called "lazy" by the country youth. They have a hard time adjusting, and for that reason many prefer to stay in Beijing and roam the streets. As would be expected, unemployment among China's young people is affecting the crime rate. Crime is increasing and social planners are trying to find solutions, but as of yet they have found none.

When my wife told me about the young people and unemployment, I wondered what would happen if a free labor market ever came about. Many Chinese people do not like being forced to work at one job all of their lives. Nor do they like having little or no say in selecting the job. Recently I have heard stories that sound disgraceful. For example, I have been told that Beijing University has as many teachers as it does students. Many of them do not teach, but they will remain on the payroll until they die. One nearby school has a president who is in his nineties. He has not been to the school or a school function for many years, but he remains the president and will likely do so until he dies. Such a system calls for having vice presidents, who appear to be more numerous in Chinese universities than they are in American universities. Instead of being retired, Chinese teachers and administrators are moved to the top positions, creating a top-heavy bureaucracy. Much of this may change in the foreseeable future, as indicated by what is happening in the Chinese government. In government the old guard is being retired; younger men are filling their positions. The old men are in their seventies and eighties; the younger officials are in their fifties and sixties. This retiring of the old guard constitutes a great achievement for China. It may prove to be the means whereby the system is altered to allow for modernization.

Thursday, September 25

The morning was brisk. While teaching my class, at about 9:00 a.m., I gazed out an open window to see a nice, hard rain coming down. I was conducting a review with my students, but I also talked to them about taking risks, about the necessity of being wrong until one can be right. I used my efforts to learn the Chinese language as an example, and they found that humorous. I reminded them that I have been mispronouncing their names, but I also assured them that I will continue trying until I have the correct pronunciations. My explanation seemed to convince them. They asked more questions and talked more freely than they ever had before. I was pleased.

Before I dismissed class I explained that I had brought a few books to lend them. Immediately after class two groups of my students came to borrow books. Once they had left my office, Tan Luying came to teach me the Chinese language. We looked at pictures of my wife, our three children, and me. We also looked at pictures of my father, my mother, and my brothers. Then we looked at pictures of my wife along with her father, mother, sister, and brothers. Tan enjoyed the pictures immensely. She asked if she might take some of them home to show her mother.

After viewing the pictures, we set about taping the sounds of the Chinese language so that Wanda and I might study at home. Tan read the sounds into the recorder, but she did not approve of what she had done. She asked to read the sounds again, and we recorded a second time. When she completed reading the sounds for the second time, it was almost noon.

Friday, September 26

I lectured to my students concerning the necessity of talking—of expressing opinions and resolving differences. I explained that their country, as well as mine, had fought too many wars, and that wars start when people stop talking, that is, when they stop trying to understand each other. I encouraged them to talk in class. I encouraged them not to be afraid of making mistakes. Again I used the example of my mispronouncing their names. Making mistakes, I explained, is often necessary to becoming accurate. Being wrong, I reasoned, is a risk we take in order to be right. It is the price we pay for learning, the price for progressing from ignorance to knowledge. My students asked questions, and they talked freely.

For the last few weeks I have talked extensively about Puritanism in the American colonies, but the subject always leads me to observations about religion in America. I try to minimize the subject, but I cannot suppress it. One cannot talk very long about American literature without talking about religion. It has been such an integral part of American culture from the very beginning that there is no escaping it. I also talked about the two-party system and the coming presidential election in America. We are examining some of the background, some of the culture, while we wait for the press to complete the printing of our literature books.

After class I met Lu Zhibao at my office. He had come with my pay for the month. He stayed for about an hour and we talked. Since Wanda and I have agreed to attend a Protestant church while we are in Beijing, I asked Lu whether he might attend church with us. Lu has never attended a church service in his life, and he would like to attend with us, but I doubt that he ever will. Although the government has declared that the Chinese people have the right to believe, or not to believe, in matters of religion, most are still afraid of what might happen if they were seen in church.

When Tan Luying came I asked whether she might go to church with Wanda and me on the coming Sunday. She was obviously shaken by my question, but she could not explain because Chinese teachers were present. She had come to help me with my Chinese lesson, and I could tell as we worked that she was deeply bothered by my question. When I asked, she replied, "I think I am not welcome; the church is for foreigners. It is not for the Chinese." When I remarked that the Chinese do attend, she was obviously more bothered. Once the Chinese teachers had left the office, almost an hour later, she decided that she would try to explain. "I cannot go," she said. "I hope you will understand. The government has said that we are free to go to church and worship, but that comes from the officials at the top. The officials lower down do not agree. If I go to church, the party will know it. Someone will be there to observe me, and I will be reported. It is not that I do not want to go; it is simply that I am not free to go. Please try to understand." I assured her that I understood and that she should not worry. I told her that she should come to the main gate of the Friendship Hotel on Sunday, that we would talk while we toured the Temple of Heaven. When she left, she told me that she was looking forward to a good time, and that I should convey her regards to Wanda.

For a long time I sat and pondered what Tan had said about going to church. For the first time in my life the matter of being free to worship became one of life's significant issues. I had taken it for granted. Furthermore, I had not seen through the party structure enough to realize that what is law does not necessarily lead to practice. When Tan left I was infuriated, and I have been infuriated ever since. I have taken for granted the basic freedoms that are missing from much of the world, and largely because I have known no one until now who was personally denied those freedoms. To know makes a difference, and I now know many fine people who are denied freedom of worship.

At dinner we joined Jeanne Lonnoy. I told her about my conversation with Tan Luying. She was not surprised. "You must keep in mind," she said, "that they are slaves of the state. You must keep in mind that they do not have freedom, and whether they like it or not makes no difference." I asked Jeanne whether she thought Tan might be unduly alarmed. She responded by saying that Tan had likely been very accurate in her observations, that someone would have observed and reported her to her work unit (the institute), and that the reporting would likely have been done by an official in the church. "They are not like us," Jeanne said. "They cannot do what they want." Jeanne did not stop. She assured me that my classes were being monitored, that everyone who visits our apartment is observed and reported, and that my interpreter, Lu Zhibao, is obligated to be an informer for the Communist Party. It is because of such conditions, she added, that one should not become friendly with one's interpreter or anyone else in the institute. The worst thing one can do, she continued, is to confide in a Chinese person. "At all costs," she concluded, "a Chinese citizen must be loyal to the party. He or she must inform party officials of any suspicious or unacceptable behavior, and that includes informing on each other." Because Jeanne is in her third year at the institute, I must weigh what she has said carefully.

I left dinner angry. I had caused Tan Luying to be afraid. I now understand why she was visibly shaken by my asking her about church in the presence of her teachers. Further, Jeanne had substantiated that what Tan told me pertaining to lower and higher officials is true. The government passes laws, and the party circumvents them. The result is that the people are not greatly affected by the laws. Their lives go on as though the laws had never been enacted. As I see it, Zhao Ziyang has a tremendous problem on his hands. He wants to separate the government and the party so that the party has no power over the government, but I fail to see how that can be done without outlawing the party altogether. Any attempt to break the power of the party will surely result in a bloody purge, but Zhao Ziyang will have to break the power of the party if he is ever to bring about the social democracy that he envisions for the Chinese people. As it is, the party is an albatross—a Chinese albatross.

Saturday, September 27

After breakfast Wanda and I took our book on Chinese language and retired to a beautiful garden in the compound. We studied Chinese for about an hour and a half. After studying Chinese we began searching for my hat. We searched in the dining hall and in the barber shop. I inquired of the barber concerning my hat, and because he understood no English he attempted to have me sit for another hair cut. Finally, I stopped trying to communicate and left the barber shop. We went to the dining hall next. It was time for dinner, and I thought I might have left my hat in the dining hall. While eating steak and fried potatoes, I inquired among the women who wait tables concerning my hat, but none of them spoke English. One of the women left and returned with a man who spoke English and I explained to him about my hat. He explained that it had not been turned in, but that I should check with him in a few days. I knew that it would be returned to me if a Chinese person found it. It would never be appropriated by a Chinese person. Of that I was confident. I have come to respect the integrity of the Chinese people. I have come to recognize that they will not steal regardless of how much they might want or need something. It is a virtue which I cherish, a virtue which might be more profitably practiced in the West. As it turned out, I need not have been alarmed. I had left my hat in my office at the institute.

When we had completed our meal, we went to the market across the road from the Friendship Hotel. I needed an earphone for our tape recorder. When I study the sounds of the Chinese language in my office, my office mates complain that they cannot work because of the interference. Since we had purchased the cassette recorder in Texas, and since it was manufactured by General Electric, I doubted that I could find an earphone for it in all of China. On the other hand, I wanted to loaf for a while anyway, and I decided that I would search for an earphone. We visited one shop and failed. But I remembered that I had seen radios in the bicycle shop. Fortunately, when we entered the bicycle shop I saw that a Chinese man was examining a small radio, and that he had an earphone plugged into the radio on one end and into an ear on the other. I walked up to the counter and gestured to the clerk that I wanted to see one of the earphones while all the time pointing to the one the man was examining. The clerk understood and immediately brought one of the earphones from behind the counter. I plugged it into my cassette recorder, and much to my surprise it worked. I had been wrong in thinking that I could not find a Chinese-made earphone to fit my General Electric recorder. I relished the idea that I would have the luxury of listening to my Chinese lessons in privacy.

Sunday, September 28

Wanda and I had received a phone call from Mao Zhiren informing us that his father-in-law, Ralph Wang, was in town and that he wanted to visit us at 9:30 on Sunday morning. It was Sunday morning, and we had planned to go to church. But after my conversation with Tan Luying I was not as eager to go to church as I had been. I was pleased that Ralph Wang was coming to visit. I knew that we would have a good talk. As it turned out, he was coming from Changchun to meet the president of Lamar University, who had brought several university administrators and their wives with him. They were accompanied by a representative from Gulf Oil Corporation. Gulf, like a number of American oil companies, is trying to negotiate an agreement to drill for oil in China. American companies are presently surveying China's oil reserves, and will likely succeed in signing contracts with the Chinese government for drilling.

Ralph Wang arrived shortly after we returned from breakfast. Mostly, he wanted to check on our welfare. He wanted to make sure that we were being treated well and that we did not need anything. We talked about his having visited us in our home in Texas, and he explained that he had once considered California the best place to live in the United States. "Now," he said, "if I were to live in America I would want to live in Texas."

We explained to Ralph Wang that Wanda had lost a large section of a tooth the evening before and asked for his advice. She was worried because she had no idea how she would communicate with a Chinese dentist. Wang set her at ease by telling her that his son-in-law, Mao, would accompany her to the dentist and serve as interpreter. Mao would come to our apartment in the evening to help us study Chinese, and we would discuss the matter with him at that time. In the meantime Wang stayed for almost two hours. We had a pleasant visit, and we were gratified that he was concerned for our welfare.

In the afternoon we met Tan Luying at the gate of the Friendship Hotel and went to the Temple of Heaven. Tan had been looking forward to our outing for several days. She had been looking forward to meeting Wanda. We rode a bus, and it was packed with passengers. We rode for an hour and a half before we finally arrived at the Temple of Heaven. Tan presented Wanda with a beautifully embroidered tablecloth containing a likeness of the Temple of Heaven. She walked us through beautiful flower gardens while all the time talking about the Temple of Heaven—when it was built, why it was built, and what numerous structures symbolized. She explained, for example, that a large circular mound or altar, located in the center of a large, walled-in enclosure, was constructed using entirely symbols of nine, and that the circular wall symbolized the umbrella of heaven. The round wall was inside a square wall, making an interesting geometric design, and the square wall, Tan explained, symbolized the shape of the earth to the Chinese at the time the Temple of Heaven was built in the fifteenth century. What I appreciated most about the Temple of Heaven was that it told me much concerning Chinese thought and Chinese values. It told me much concerning fifteenth-century Chinese beliefs.

The Temple of Heaven contains a number of arts and crafts shops. They are posted "For Foreigners Only," and the Chinese people are denied entrance to them. When Tan took us to the Temple of Heaven, I refused to frequent the shops, because I felt it would be an insult to her. I was still angry concerning the churches, and my anger grew as I looked at the signs forbidding the Chinese people to enter shops on the grounds of a national monument in the capital of their own country. Through one of the shop doors Wanda saw a piece of furniture which attracted her attention. She went in to examine the piece, but Tan and I remained outside. While in the shop Wanda found a piece of jade which she wished to purchase. She attempted to purchase the piece of jade with Chinese *yuan*, but the clerk would not sell it. The clerk insisted that she had to have foreign certificates of exchange. She presented the clerk with a card authorizing her and me to make purchases in the people's money, but the clerk persisted. Wanda and the clerk argued, but I could tell that they were accomplishing nothing. The clerk came outside and asked Tan to come inside and interpret. I refused to enter the shop. I listened from outside the door, and I realized that Tan's explanation did not impress the clerk. I rushed inside and grabbed our "white card" from the hands of the clerk while screaming *bu* (no) and angrily rushed out the door. The absurdity of it all was beyond my endurance.

Fortunately, the issue of segregation is in the news in Beijing. Many Chinese are angry over being excluded from shops designated for foreigners only. Such shops are so designated because tourists can pay higher prices than can Chinese citizens. The arrangement is humiliating to the Chinese; it is also embarrassing to many of the foreigners who live in Beijing.

After the incident in the shop, we boarded a bus and returned to the Friendship Hotel. We said our farewells to Tan and expressed our gratitude for her help and generosity. I left her with visions of the Hall of Prayer for Good Harvest and the Circular Mound Altar in my head. I thought of all the symbolism of the numbers three and nine built into the Temple of Heaven when it was erected during the Ming Dynasty, near the end of the fifteenth century. I thought of the numerous altars I had seen for burning incense and making offerings. Then I thought of Dante's *Paradiso* and *Purgatorio*. The Hall of Prayer for Good Harvest was built without beams or supports, built of marble with a beautiful dome on the top. For its time it must have been a remarkable feat in engineering. It still stands as a remarkable feat in engineering. I hope we will have an opportunity to visit the Temple of Earth, the Temple of the Moon, and the Temple of the Sun before we leave Beijing.

Monday, September 29

In my class I talked about British and French romanticism along with American romanticism. Impetus for American romanticism, it seems to me, came from both of those countries. After class students came to my office to borrow books. They particularly asked for books on American literature, history, economics, sociology, and psychology. Tan Luying also came to the office. Since she had spent the day with us on Sunday, and since she would not let us pay her in any way for her time and service, I presented her with a copy of *Making Sense of Grammar* (a book which was originally published by an old professor of mine who had studied at Columbia University under Otto Jesperson, but which I had recently revised and edited for publication by Columbia University Teachers College Press). I also presented her with a copy of *A Jesse Stuart Reader*. She was pleased. She informed me that she would help me learn to pronounce the names of my students once we returned from the National Day holidays.

In the evening Wanda and I accompanied other foreign experts to the Great Hall of the People for a National Day celebration. Sponsored by China's national minorities, the celebration consisted of singing and dancing as well as instrumental music. The pageantry surpassed anything we had ever seen. Those of us who were from the West were awed by the spectacle, and we were impressed by the lack of sex and violence characterizing similar performances in the West. We observed Chinese art at what I thought must be its best, and we returned to our compound pleased that we had come to China.

Tuesday, September 30

After class Lu Zhibao came to my office. He solicited my response to the celebration held in the Great Hall of the People the night before. He had also attended, but he had not been as favorably impressed as I had. On the other hand, he had attended many such occasions. He asked me to watch for appropriate American literature that he might translate and make available to the Chinese people. He explained, "We will have to avoid the highly sensational in such a venture. Too much sex and violence will bring a reaction from the older people as well as from school officials and the government." I presented him with a copy of Jesse Stuart's autobiographical *The Thread That Runs So True*. Even before coming to China, I had felt that Jesse Stuart would be loved by the Chinese people if they could read him. After having been in China for a month, I am convinced that his stories of the hills will be well received once they are translated. I asked Lu to read *The Thread That Runs So True* so that he could give me an honest opinion concerning its appeal to the Chinese people. He was pleased that I requested such an evaluation, but because of his fears I doubt that he will ever attempt a translation. I also gave him a copy of the first poem I had written since coming to China. Upon reading it he remarked, "It contains many of the qualities found in classical Chinese poetry."

Once I completed my conversation with Lu, I turned my attention to a student who had been waiting to see me. Her name was Liu Liming. She had missed my first lectures and had come to ask questions about them. I asked why she had just entered the institute instead of entering at the beginning of the semester. She explained that she had dropped out of school four years earlier to take a job translating for the government and that she had most recently been engaged in translating Marx and Lenin. She applied for permission to return to school, she continued, and had been granted permission to return for one semester to study the American language and American literature. But the permission did not come through until the semester was under way. She assured me that she would work hard, and that she would visit me frequently for help so that she could learn faster because of being allowed to return for only one semester. I told her I would help her all I could, and that she should feel free to visit me when she thought I might be of help. Liu Liming left my office with a smile on her face; she was obviously gratified. Once she left, I caught a car for the Friendship Hotel. I had to prepare for the trip to Qufu and Taishan. I would finally have an opportunity to see the birthplace of Confucius.

October

Wednesday, October 1

It was National Day, the thirty-first anniversary of the People's Republic of China. The day appeared to be as important to the Chinese as the Fourth of July is to Americans. The streets and parks were decorated. Throughout the city large buildings were outlined by lights much in the way Americans decorate their houses at Christmas. But in Beijing the buildings decorated are the largest available. The lights created a Christmas atmosphere as our bus took us across town to the station where we would board a train for Shandong Province.

Our train rolled through the night, but I did not sleep well. I lay awake and watched the passing countryside as well as I could while thinking about the month I had spent in China. I thought about the many things which had crowded their way into that month, and I thought of the people I had come to know and love. I was pleased to be in China; I was happy to be teaching 120 young people. I also thought about my life before coming to China. I realized that at some time in recent years my wife and I had arrived at upper-middle-class respectability, all of which seemed far in the past as our train carried us through the night. I realized that Thomas Wolfe was right in his observation that one cannot go home again. I know I will always long to return to China and visit my friends. One thing I have learned about the Chinese people is that they are capable of love. Unlike any people I have met before, they wear their hearts on their sleeves. They take risks that many Americans will not take. For the sake of friendship they will risk being disappointed and hurt. They seem not to have learned the art of self-defense as far as their emotions are concerned. This appears particularly true among Chinese young people. They approach others as totally trustworthy, and they make themselves completely vulnerable in doing so. It is as though they had never been lied to, had never been abused, and had never been cheated. One could describe the condition as ignorance and innocence, but to feel a bond of complete trust is refreshing.

When our train arrived at the station in Qufu, in Shandong Province, I was excited. Qufu is an old city. Confucius lived from 551 to 479 B.C., and five hundred years before his time Qufu was a thriving city seven times its present size. The Kong family mansion (Kong Qiu being the original name of Confucius) and the Temple to Confucius make up a sizeable portion of the present-day city, and the family cemetery is twice as large as the city itself. The mansion, the temple, and other buildings were constructed over a period of several centuries. Since Liberation, in 1949, they have been under the protection of the government, but many of them, and even the stones in the cemetery, were vandalized during the Cultural Revolution.

The Temple to Confucius occupies the central part of the city. Rulers from every dynasty after the Han came to the temple to pay homage to Confucius. Construction of the temple began in 478 B.C., the year after the death of Confucius. Expanded and rebuilt by many emperors over the centuries, the temple now contains 640 halls, chambers, and pavilions as well as 54 giant arches. The main structure, Dacheng Hall, is thirty-two meters high and thirty-four by fifty-four meters at the base. At one time Dacheng Hall housed a dozen intricately made statues of Confucius and his disciples, but they were damaged in the Cultural Revolution. The two corridors flanking Dacheng Hall contain seven hundred tablets with inscriptions—valuable material for the scholar who wishes to study Chinese culture.

East of the temple lies the Kong family mansion, in which the descendants of Confucius lived for centuries. As powerful landlords the descendants were rulers over a large area in ancient China, and the mansion contains many rare cultural ornaments and documents. For example, the mansion contains bronze vessels which are three thousand years old, and which were once used in ceremonies paying homage to Confucius. It also contains nearly ten thousand volumes of documents and files from the Ming and Qing dynasties, especially of value in studying those dynasties.

Not far from the north gate to the city is the cemetery containing the remains of Confucius. In ancient times many kinds of trees were planted in the cemetery by disciples of Confucius. The tradition of presenting China's wise man with trees has been kept, for today the cemetery contains twenty-two thousand pines and cypresses, some of which date back eight hundred years. The twenty-two thousand trees were all planted before Liberation in 1949; since that time another forty thousand have been added, making the cemetery the largest man-made garden in China. Containing more than seventy generations of Confucius' relatives, the cemetery now includes a large tract of land surrounded by a wall seven kilometers long. On National Day the Chinese people were out in great numbers to pay respect to the sage who had been condemned as a capitalist landowner during the Cultural Revolution.

I had come to explore Qufu, but my exploration led me more to the person who accompanied me as guide. Her family name is Sun, and we seemed to be friends from the moment we met. As we walked the streets of Qufu, she told me many things about herself. I wished Wanda could have been with us, but she had stayed behind to begin her new job. She would have enjoyed Sun Shaoyong immensely. As we walked she told me that she was from Chengde, that her father was a school principal, that her mother was a teacher, and that she was in her fourth year at Qufu Teachers College. She told me of her daily schedule, and I marveled. She rises at 5:00 a.m., she said, and jogs for half an hour. She then bathes and has breakfast before beginning classes. She studies until 11:00 p.m., and she studies seven days a week. I asked her whether she had a boyfriend, and she replied that she had never had one. "There is not time," she added. "I must get my education. There will be time later, perhaps, when I have completed my education." We walked and talked for more than two hours, and all the time I was overwhelmed by her intellect, her charm, her openness, and her willingness to confide in a complete stranger. I reminded her that she could not have walked in the streets of Qufu with me only a few months earlier. She was very aware of the changing conditions in China, and we were both glad to have met in Qufu and to have walked and talked together on an October afternoon. When evening came and she was preparing to return to her college, she asked me if I would bestow upon her an American name. I could tell that she was serious in wanting an American name, and I named her Sheila. When she got into a car to return to her school, she was crying. I suppose that she was crying because she was happy to have an American name. As for me, I still do not know what to make of our meeting, but I remain impressed that Sheila is one of the finest young people I have ever met.

Thursday, October 2

We arose at 5:30 a.m. After breakfast we boarded a bus bound for the sacred mountain Taishan. In as much as Qufu resembled a medieval town, the countryside between Qufu and the city of Taian echoed the feudal society of the Middle Ages. To explain the atmosphere no sufficient means exists. One has to have been there to observe the ancient practice of plowing with the ox, the grinding of corn with a stone, the thousands of peasants working in the fields, the practice of flailing grain on an earthen floor, and many other practices about which one reads in history books as belonging to European feudal society. I sat in my seat and marveled. At the same time I wondered how such a way of life could ever be pushed aside in the name of modernization. Life in the Chinese countryside has been the way it is for at least two thousand years, and I wonder if there can ever be any substantial change.

We arrived in the city of Taian well before time for lunch, and for the first time since coming to China I saw many human beings in harness. They were pulling long carts—more than twenty feet long—loaded with concrete reinforcing rod, scrap metal, huge stones, and many other things. I saw one cart which I estimated to contain more than a ton of steel rod. I watched the cart puller's muscles ripple as he pushed against the harness. The streets contained many such carts, with lighter loads being pulled by women and children. I had never before seen anything resembling the carts in Taian. Much of the freight was being moved by human beings instead of machines or animals.

A bus took those of us who wanted to ride halfway up the mountain. Some of our party decided to climb all seven thousand steps, but I saved my energy for the second half. I was glad I did, for the second half ascends steeply until one is well above the timber line. The Mount Tai Range extends through Jinan, Changqing, Licheng, and Taian counties in Shandong Province. The main peak rises to a height of fifteen hundred meters above sea level in Taian County. (It is known as the Eastern mountain, the mountain of the sun, and the mountain of the gods.) Every fall the old women of the area come to climb the mountain and offer their shoes to the gods in hopes of finding a resting place in heaven. Many stories exist concerning the old women who climb the mountain. Some cannot complete the climb and must crawl or be carried to the top. Some, whose feet were once bound, must hold to a railing for support while they climb.

One of the Chinese teachers accompanying us talked of his grandmother and of the fact that she suffered greatly as a young girl because her parents subjected her to binding. She lay on a bed and cried away much of her youth, he told us, because the pain was so intense that she could not enjoy life in the least. The binding had a purpose, for small feet were considered beautiful and were a sure way of attracting a husband of means. The history of women in China has not been an admirable one. Baby girls have generally been considered useless. In times of drought and famine they have often been put to death at birth, or left on their own to be destroyed by the elements. Allowed to live, they have at times been bartered or sold by their families for food or for animals to hitch to the plow. The story is a sad one, and life remains hard for Chinese women.

We spent the night at the top of Mount Tai. The next morning we arose early to see the sun come up. Legend has it that if one watches the sun rise while standing at the top of the mountain he will enjoy a long and prosperous life. At the top the wind is strong, and at night the weather is very cold. No way exists to keep warm, but I didn't care to sleep anyway. I was rooming with a Chinese man about my age named Ts'ang Yin-po. Ts'ang is an American-trained physicist who teaches at Beijing University. I was pleased to be rooming with him because I had many questions concerning China, and I thought he might be the right man to answer my questions. Professor Ts'ang proved amenable, and we talked well into the night.

Ts'ang began by telling me that he had a family in New York, an American wife and a son. He related to me that he had been in China teaching for four years and that all during that time he had been trying to have his visa renewed so that he might rejoin his wife and son. He attended Taiwan University before Liberation and then went to the United States as an interpreter for the United Nations. He traveled widely as an interpreter and finally gave that up to enter the University of Florida. He lived in Florida for thirteen years and then moved to New York. He had come to China to teach on other occasions, but this time his visa expired and he has been unsuccessful in his efforts to have it renewed. Last summer his wife and son came to Beijing to visit him, and at that time he and his wife called at the American embassy. He is optimistic that his visa will eventually be renewed, and that he will return to the United States to be with his wife and son.

Professor Ts'ang has studied China closely, as I quickly learned when he began answering my questions. He told me that Zhao Ziyang and

Deng Xiaoping are both liberal and pro-West. He also told me that a great gap exists between the level at which laws are passed and the level at which they are applied. The young people, he volunteered, want nothing to do with the Communist Party. To them, he explained, the party is outdated and useless, a millstone about the necks of a billion Chinese people. Ts'ang told me that his students laugh at the ineptness of party officials and refuse to join the party. To China's young people, added Ts'ang, the party is a joke on the one hand and a serious threat to progress on the other.

Because I have read a number of accounts pertaining to what the government has been doing to improve Chinese education, I asked Ts'ang for his evaluation of the state of education in China. He responded by saying that most Chinese teachers are poorly educated, too poorly educated to be teaching. Admitting that testing as a means of selecting college students is the right approach, he explained that a system of testing had been in operation for only two years and therefore had not had time to prove itself. Said Ts'ang, "The system of education will have to be changed. The system is one introduced by the Russians in the fifties, and even they have since then abandoned it as inadequate. The system is designed to prepare people for jobs rather than to educate them. Pedagogy is largely ignored in Chinese education, and because China was closed to the outside world for thirty years teachers need a comprehensive education. They need to study much more than the subject to be taught. Because of the isolation in which the Chinese people have lived, all Chinese students need a comprehensive education." As Ts'ang explained, nevertheless, too much education could pose a threat to the party. Educated people cherish freedom, and demands for freedom could threaten party officials and rob them of their power. The future of the People's Republic of China hinges on the issue of education more than on any other. An educated citizenry is essential if China is ever to throw off the present political system and make progress toward becoming a modern state. As for Professor Ts'ang, he warned me against being too optimistic. The party is the government, he explained, in spite of the premier's desire to separate the party from the government. Such a separation will not take place, he assured me, because it would mean the death of the Communist Party in China, and too many party officials enjoy their positions far too much to allow a premier or anyone else to change the system.

After we had stopped talking and Professor Ts'ang had gone to sleep, I lay awake and thought about all he had confided in me. The wind blew viciously across the top of the mountain as I thought of the millions of Chinese people enslaved by a system, but I also realized that for more than two thousand years they had known poverty and hardship. I went out to the edge of the mountain in the middle of the night and stood alone while looking down on the lights in the city of Taian. I thought of the student I had met in Qufu, and I realized that I would never see her again. I recalled that while we were walking in the streets of Qufu she had purchased peanuts for us to eat. I still had some of the peanuts in my pocket. I recalled her laugh. I recalled her smile. Then I took two of the peanuts from my pocket and hurled them over the side of the mountain. "We will be friends forever on the top of the mountain," I told myself.

On my way down the mountain the next morning, I began thinking of home, of being with my wife in Beijing, and I wondered whether the mountain works some sort of magic upon all of those who visit it. We had watched the sun rise, and I felt that my life would be happier and richer for having visited the home of the ancient Chinese gods.

Friday, October 3

I was glad to be on the train and headed for home. I was tired from having climbed the mountain, but I was more tired from watching food and supplies being carried to the top of the mountain on the backs of human beings, both men and women. Each man carried 120 pounds, with 60 pounds balanced on either end of a pole. Women carried less. By the time the carriers neared the top of the mountain they were in great pain, and I shuddered to think that they would likely have the same job until they can no longer make it up the mountain. That the individual is not likely to live long while performing a particular task makes little difference. That the job is the last thing he would like to do makes little difference. Jobs are assigned; they are not chosen. As for me, I lay on my bed and looked out the window as we rolled across the flatlands. We crossed the Yellow River, and for a little while the sound of the wheels on the track lulled me to sleep. It would be good to be home in Beijing. I remembered the medieval appearance of the countryside between Qufu and Taian; I also remembered Qufu as a medieval town. I had the feeling that we were returning to civilization, at least to the best example of civilization to be found in China. When we approached the train station in Beijing, I told myself that I had had enough traveling for a spell, that I would be content to teach my classes and do my writing.

Saturday, October 4

I had not believed that the mountain would exact revenge upon me, but it did. I was extremely sore. My stomach was irritated. When Wanda and I went to breakfast, I had to ride the elevator to the lower floor because I was too stiff and sore to manage the steps. In the afternoon I sat at my desk and wrote while Wanda visited the shops in Xidan Street. She returned about six o'clock, and we dressed for dinner at a restaurant called the Big Duck, one of a number of restaurants in Beijing specializing in Beijing Duck (Peking Duck). The dinner was sponsored by a German trucking firm, and the guests were the staff who had come to China to organize an exposition.

Sunday, October 5

I did not sleep, and when I awakened the next morning I faced the prospect of teaching. Indeed the mountain was taking its revenge. My stomach was sore; my legs were stiff and sore. But I knew that I had to go to the institute, for I had traded classes on Friday for classes on Sunday in order to take the trip. I felt better once I was in front of the class, but after an hour I felt considerably worse. I rested for ten minutes and returned to class for a second hour. After class I hoped to avoid everyone and catch a car for the compound, but that did not work. Chinese teachers came to my office with questions about literature, and students came to borrow books. In the meantime I was recruited to read proof on a news tape, and Tan Luying came to tutor me in Chinese. The office seemed a madhouse until noon, at which time I slipped away. I knew that the day had not ended, for Mao Zhiren would come in the evening to teach Wanda and me Chinese.

Monday, October 6

I decided that I would begin the new week of classes without lecturing because I did not think I could concentrate well enough to develop an idea coherently. The mountain was still exacting revenge. When I met my first class, I announced that we would do three things. First, as I explained, I would read them two of the poems I had written since coming to China. Second, we would look at a copy of the United States Constitution so that they might understand a little more about American government and law. Third, we would examine some of the literature they had been assigned to read. I had scheduled things that I could do while sitting, and the class went well. Once class was over I went to my office hoping for a time of relaxation, but I was to be disappointed. Diane Stark, another of the foreign teachers, came to the office complaining that she was ill.

The remainder of the morning was a comedy of errors. When Mrs. Stark came to the office, I was helping a Chinese teacher prepare a lesson for her students. The teacher immediately ran to secure permission for Mrs. Stark to go home. One of the school officials came to the office to grant permission personally, but after he left Mrs. Stark became engrossed in conversation with the Chinese teacher. At 11:30, about half an hour before the cars were to leave for the Friendship Hotel, she decided that it was time to go home. The Chinese teacher accompanied her to the car and instructed the driver that he was to take Mrs. Stark home immediately because she was ill. I said nothing, although I suspected that the illness was feigned. Mrs. Stark laughed, joked, and generally enjoyed herself between the time the official granted her permission to go home and the time she actually left. At any rate, I was glad to see her go. I would enjoy the quietness of her absence for a while.

Tuesday, October 7

The trips taken during the holidays were taking their toll throughout the compound. The foreigners who had not taken the trip to Qufu and Taian had gone to Inner Mongolia, and many of them were ill. On Tuesday few foreign teachers showed up at the car stand for the ride to Second Foreign Language Institute. In class I continued the routine I had established of not lecturing, and again my students responded well. After class I found that Mrs. Stark had decided not to come to work; I had the office to myself. Normally, Patrick Cassidy, who shares the office with Mrs. Stark and me, would also have been there, but Tuesday is his day off because he teaches on Saturdays. My students came for books, but I had lent them all. Then I was visited by one of the Chinese teachers. She wanted to know whether I might lecture for an additional two hours each week, to another class of 120 students. She had come from a meeting with the students, and they had proposed that I lecture to them. I realized that if the proposal were implemented I would be doing part of the work of every Chinese teacher in the English department. The Chinese teacher, Qi Wenqin, also proposed that I consider and report back to her on how to restructure the curriculum in the department so that it might prove less repetitious and less boring for the teachers.

Qi Wenqin's proposals took me by surprise. I did not come to China to do the work of the Chinese teachers, and I did not come to tell the officials how to run their school. On the other hand, I could tell that Qi Wenqin was serious when she assured me that she would take my suggestions to the officials for their evaluation. I explained to her why I considered the system inefficient, and why much of what we teachers do proves counterproductive. She agreed with me as I explained to her that the system is designed to produce workers rather than thinkers, and that because of the new emphasis on modernization students will have to be educated to handle more than a job. Students in China, I urged, will have to have a comprehensive education similar to that given to students in the industrialized West. She appreciated my remarks and asked again that I prepare a statement for school officials. I promised her that I would. In the meantime, I must think about her suggestion for changing class schedules. I must consider whether I can afford the time required to prepare and deliver another lecture each week.

Wednesday, October 8

Some days are uneventful, and Wednesday proved to be one of those days. It was one of those days of walking and thinking. It was one of those days that one would just as soon not have lived through but did, and found nothing on the way to make it either redeeming or satisfying. In the afternoon I went to the embassy to plead for more books for my students, but even that did not work well. Theodore Liu, who is in charge of the books, was not in his office when I arrived at 2:30. I next went to the Friendship Store and looked at winter coats only to discover that

I did not have enough money on me to purchase one. I was glad when 5:00 came and I could board the bus for home, although I had the feeling that such a restless day could lead to no less than a sleepless night. As it turned out, I was right. I lay in bed and thought the night through, solving no problems and getting no sleep.

Thursday, October 9

I had given the lecture I delivered to my students on three other occasions. Consequently, it required little in the way of preparation. My students were excited by the lecture, and after class they called at my office requesting copies of poems I had written about China. Others came to return or borrow books. Tan Luying came to tell me that she would stop by later for our usual Chinese lesson, and then the teachers came. Qi Wenqin came to find out what I had decided concerning her proposals. While we were in the middle of our discussion, Patrick Cassidy came in to complain that he was being mistreated. For some weeks he has been acting as representative to the institute for Harvard University in recruiting outstanding students for possible admission to Harvard. The gist of the matter was that Patrick had chosen a slate of students to take a competitive exam for entrance to Harvard, but the school officials did not agree with his selections. Teacher Qi had been involved in making the institute's selections, and Patrick was angry. He accused the school and Qi of making political choices rather than choices based on ability or the likelihood of a student's succeeding at Harvard. What began as a discussion between Patrick and Qi Wenqin turned into an argument. While they were arguing I was informed that a meeting was scheduled and would take place in our office in a matter of minutes. The meeting, of course, would stop the argument, so I was glad when it began. Tan Luying came to tutor me in Chinese and stood outside the door waiting for the meeting to end, but it lasted the remainder of the morning. At 11:40 I proposed that we adjourn and postpone all discussion until we could call another meeting. I looked forward to the quietness of my room in the Friendship Hotel.

Friday, October 10

I was completing a week of lecturing on American romanticism, and I must admit that my having to lecture to Chinese students has had a very good effect on me. I have been forced to evaluate what I say more closely than I have in the past, and I have been forced to make sense of what I have been saying about literature in a cultural context. In some ways I have gotten a closer look at American literature than ever before because I have had to explain it to people who know little about the culture from which the literature comes. I have gained new insights into American literature, but perhaps the real challenge will come next Wednesday when I lecture to all of Grade 77 on existentialism and Ernest Hemingway's "A Clean, Well-lighted Place." Explaining existentialism to people who are extremely pragmatic may prove difficult. At any rate, I will enjoy seeing how far the minds of my students, and the minds of Chinese teachers, will stretch.

Tan Luying came to help me with my Chinese lessons. She seemed pleased that I could articulate the sounds and follow her example in reading exercises from the book we are using. I was not as pleased as she because I knew that when she went away I would not be able to read the exercises correctly. She is very patient with me, and she always encourages me to believe that I am making great progress, even when I know better.

I had given Tan a brochure about Baylor University the day before, and she was excited about the brochure, saying that she would like Baylor to be her university. Tan's mother is over seventy, and she would like for Tan to go to America where life offers much more than it does in China. Her brothers would also like her to go. Her father saved money and deposited it in a foreign bank before he died, although I have no idea how much money he saved. According to Tan, the money remains in a foreign bank. She will have access to it, she says, when she has left China. If Tan succeeds in going to America, however, she will need someone to look after her. She is immature by Western standards. She prides herself on being a Chinese daughter to Wanda and me, and we enjoy the role of mother and father.

Saturday, October 11

Wanda had severe pains in her legs and feet during the night; she has not been ingesting enough calcium. At about two or so in the morning she had to get out of bed and attempt to walk off the cramps in her legs and feet. She walked from her bed to mine, about six feet, before she collapsed, completely fainted. I laid her across my bed. Then I slapped and shook her several times in an effort to bring her back to consciousness. Just when I was ready to run for help she opened her eyes and began to speak. She spoke slowly and indistinctly at first, but as she talked her voice grew stronger. We had had a scare, and I knew that something would have to be done.

We slept late, but we got up in time to leave the compound at nine for a tour of a cloisonné factory. Before the tour I knew little about cloisonné except that it is expensive. During the tour I found out why it is expensive. Cloisonné pieces are all handmade, and to produce a cloisonné vase, for example, hundreds, and sometimes thousands, of tiny pieces are glued to a copper base one at a time. Many of the pieces are so minute that they must be located in the appropriate place with a small pair of tweezers. Many people usually work on one piece of cloisonné, and total production time for a small piece usually exceeds a month. I had never dreamed that so much work could go into producing one vase. I was also a bit shocked by the working conditions we observed. With only four days off each year, some of the workers must go blind early in life because of the poor lighting and detailed work they perform. They appeared to be happy, but my guess is that they dared not appear otherwise.

In the afternoon we took the bus to the Friendship Store, where we purchased two scarves and a pair of shoes for Wanda. We also purchased a winter coat for me, one with a heavy cotton-padded lining. Beijing winters are cold, and the institute is never adequately heated. I have been told several times that I will have to wear heavy Chinese clothes in order to keep warm. Because it was a rainy and cold day, shopping for winter clothes seemed to be the sensible thing to do. In the evening, hungry from our shopping trip, we experienced our first Mongolian hot pot. Several of our friends had raved about how delicious Mongolian hot pot is, so I anticipated a great feast. But I was disappointed. The meal consisted mostly of dipping slices of raw mutton into hot water and then eating them raw. When one tired of eating mutton, he or she had the choice of doing the same thing with raw cabbage or another vegetable. Throughout the meal, I ate everything I do not care for in a manner that I do not care for, and that I did it made no sense. Fortunately, we had scheduled a bridge game to begin early in the evening, and because we had been late in beginning the meal we excused ourselves early. I don't think we will ever invest in Mongolian hot pot again. The bridge party, on the other hand, was enjoyable.

Sunday, October 12

Again I did not sleep well. I had been suffering from constipation. There appears to be no way to adjust to Chinese life, particularly to the greasy food. After breakfast I went to the clinic and came home with four kinds of medicine. Tan Luying would come to accompany us to the Summer Palace in the afternoon, but because it was rainy and cold going to the Summer Palace did not appear wise. Wanda and I decided that we would go shopping instead. I needed pipe tobacco, and I wanted to find calcium pills for Wanda. When Tan came we took a car to a shopping area about three miles from the Friendship Hotel, where we purchased heavy wool jackets to wear under our coats. We purchased a pair of Chinese cotton-padded shoes for me. We also purchased a pair of shoes for Wanda, a second pair. My shoes cost four *yuan* fifty, and hers cost three *yuan* ninety. We did not find the calcium pills, but we did find the pipe tobacco. We purchased some soap and a few other things before returning to the compound with Tan for lunch. It was a pleasant afternoon. Tan enjoyed visiting with us in our apartment. She enjoyed playing the role of daughter, and we enjoyed being parents in a strange and new country.

We escorted Tan through the main gate and watched as she boarded a bus for home. I then took Wanda to the health clinic to inquire concerning calcium pills. The doctor was cooperative and gave Wanda the pills. Following our visit to the clinic we waited in our room for Ralph Wang, who was en route from Guangzhou to Changchun. When he came, Wang wanted to talk about his son-in-law, Mao Zhiren, and about Mao's application for admission to the graduate school at Baylor University.

Monday, October 13

Beijing was very cold. I went to the institute as I had during the weeks before not realizing that I would suffer from the weather before the day ended. The cold was penetrating, and the halls at Second Foreign

Language Institute serve as wind tunnels. With cold feet, I delivered the first of a series of lectures on early political currents in America. I prefaced my lecture by explaining that the presidential election in America was only a few days away, and that I shared the concern of my students over relations between the United States and China. I explained that I was aware of their reaction to Ronald Reagan's proposal for a two-China policy. I also explained that a two-China policy had been in effect since China was recognized by the United States. I explained that nothing had really changed in the United States' relations with Taiwan, that is, that business between Taiwan and the United States had continued as usual. What I did not know as I talked with them was that President Carter had just announced that nothing had changed and that in doing so he had infuriated government officials in Beijing. I took it that his announcement had something to do with his campaign strategy. All reports received in China indicated that he was running poorly against Reagan and that he would have to do or say something spectacular to win the election. My students had difficulty believing that the Chinese had been deceived by United States policy. They asked me what I believed about the candidates as well as how I perceived the election. I told them that I favored Reagan, particularly because of President Carter's apparent helplessness in doing anything about a sagging United States economy. I also told them that I thought Reagan would win the election, that Americans were a bit fed up with President Carter's penchant for vacillating instead of making up his mind concerning the crucial issues facing the nation. I explained that I did not think Reagan's being president would have a negative effect on Chinese and United States relations.

Tuesday, October 14

On Tuesday Beijing was even colder than it had been on Monday. On Monday evening Wanda had come home with a present for me, a pair of long cotton underwear. I needed the underwear and I needed wool socks. I was eager to arrive at the institute because I was concerned about Tan Luying. I was concerned that she might be ill, for she had not been by to see me. I was even more concerned that she might have been criticized for spending too much time with foreigners. As it turned out, she had been ill, and when I next saw her it was in a place

I least expected. I was not sure the person I saw was Tan Luying, for she was standing along the road not far from the institute by a bus that had broken down. As we passed the bus, I thought I saw Tan, but I dismissed it as a case of mistaken identity. I wanted to stop the car and see if my first impression was right, but I decided that I would look foolish if the person I saw proved not to be Tan. After class, at about 10:00 a.m., Tan came to my office. She confirmed that it had been she standing beside the road. She told me that she had been ill, and I suspected that her illness had resulted from her standing in the rain outside the gate to the Friendship Hotel while waiting for us on Sunday. She reasoned that her illness came from staying up late the night before visiting us to prepare for our trip to the Summer Palace. In either case, we were to blame, and I felt bad about that.

Tan explained that her mother had been severely critical of her for having had dinner with us at the Friendship Hotel. I told her to tell her mother that we had insisted, that Tan had ridden in the cold for more than an hour on a bus, had stood in the rain for at least half an hour waiting for us, and had then gone shopping with us in her wet clothes. I knew what I was saying would make no difference; I knew that Tan would not tell her mother. But I wanted her to know she had done the right thing as far as Wanda and I were concerned. She was pleased to be reassured, but she was not critical of her mother. Her mother, she explained, is very good to her because, as she put it, her mother explains to her how to behave in situations Tan has not previously encountered. As far as Tan was concerned, her mother was right in correcting her.

When Tan went away, I was visited by Zhu Zheng. Zhu Zheng is a little man who serves the institute in a number of capacities. For example, he serves as liaison between the English department and school officials. He asked if I would write a letter for him, a model letter recommending a Chinese student for admission to an American university. Because he had never written such a letter, he came to me for help. I told him that I would be glad to write a letter that he could use as a model, a letter that he could use over and over by adjusting a few details. That was one of a number of projects I would have to complete in the afternoon. I would also have to prepare my lesson for the next morning.

Wednesday, October 15

The little old woman who brings my hot water every morning looked very bedraggled and beaten, but she managed a smile as she does every morning. She delights in filling my thermos bottles and making a cup of tea for me. The expression on her face as much as says, "I like you. I envy you. My life is about over, but you must tell our young people the truth. Do not be afraid. If you do not tell them the truth, no one will." I love the old woman. I feel a bond of friendship and love which is unusually strong. I love to see the smile on her face when she sees me each morning. I love to see the satisfaction she receives from making my tea. On this particular morning she seemed to know that something was about to happen, but she could not tell me about it. She does not know a word of English. Her smile was warm and gracious though, and I felt that she knew something that she very much wanted to tell me.

Lu Zhibao came to my office to talk. He told me that he and several other Chinese teachers would attend my lecture on Hemingway and existentialism. What he did not tell me was that some of the school officials and party functionaries would also attend. I spotted them as soon as I walked into the room, and I had the distinct feeling that I was on trial. I also had my mind made up that I would not be intimidated, that I would say nothing less than what I had come to say.

I began my lecture with some generalizations: "Religion has been a central fact in Western culture for almost three thousand years. The Hebrew's God proved central to thinking and living in the West until a short time ago. An intellectual revolution, paralleling an industrial revolution, posed the first real threat to beliefs almost three thousand years old." Having begun in this way I lectured for two hours on existentialism and the effort existentialists have made to account for man's life in an indifferent universe. Everyone seemed to be listening closely, and I frequently left the podium to walk among my audience. I wanted to be close to the people in the audience. I wanted to detect any objections or resentment.

When I finally completed my lecture, I asked for questions, but few came. Two young men were brave enough to ask questions, but they were careful about how they worded them; they were obviously and deliberately cautious. None of the teachers asked questions; they were afraid of being criticized. They were intimidated by the presence of school officials and party members. Once I dismissed my audience, students swarmed around me in great numbers. They were full of questions, but they refused to be overheard asking them. They could not afford to be overheard by anyone who would be critical. Lu Zhibao finally came to my rescue, and I walked out after informing my students that I would answer their questions the following week, that first we needed to examine Hemingway's story "A Clean, Well-Lighted Place" as a case of existentialism.

I went to my office with Lu Zhibao, and we talked. He was pleased with the lecture. He assured me that he could follow what I had said even though he had never heard of existentialism prior to my lecture. As for the remainder of the day, I knew it would be anticlimactic. I went back to the Friendship Hotel and had steak for lunch. Then I went home to work and to wait for a call concerning objections by school officials and party functionaries to my lecture. The call never came; by evening I was relieved.

Thursday, October 16

I returned to lecturing on political patterns in the early American republic. Because the presidential election was coming up, I wanted to take advantage of that to explain to my students how the two-party system works. I went back in time far enough to begin with European influences, influences by such people as Locke, Hobbes, and Rousseau. I talked about how these men supplied ideas that proved highly influential in shaping American political life. My students were remarkably interested. They are excited over the upcoming election, even though they have been told to be suspicious of Ronald Reagan and his proposed two-China policy. I talked with them about some of the reasons why President Carter might be turned out in November. I talked about "bread-and-butter issues" and about what inflation is doing to the American economy. I talked about the necessity of education in a democracy, and the responsibility each citizen has to make the system work. I stressed the fact that each citizen has the right to vote the way he or she wants, that one has complete freedom when he or she enters the voting booth. I talked about a number of problems facing Americans, and my students seemed to appreciate the fact that I would admit that such problems as crime and racial discrimination actually exist.

After class one young man inquired of me concerning how one joined either the Democratic or Republican parties, and he was surprised at my answer. He was surprised to hear that one neither joins nor carries a party membership card. He had difficulty in accepting my explanation that one can identify with a party and still vote the way he wants. While we were talking word came that the press had completed printing our books. I was happy because we could begin examining early American literature. After the background lectures I had given them, I expected my students to find the literature exciting.

Friday, October 17

I was eager to end the week. On Sunday we would go to the Great Wall of China. I repeated the lecture that I had given to my Thursday class. The Friday class also seemed to appreciate willingness to discuss what I consider to be President Carter's shortcomings. After class Tan Luying stopped by my office to help me with my Chinese lessons. She was disappointed that I could not translate from English to Chinese. She was also disappointed that I could not answer her questions in Chinese. Once again we resorted to my trying to read the sentences in Chinese after she had read them to me. She found my effort very amusing and laughed much of the time while we were studying. Fortunately she has a good sense of humor. I have not had time to practice, and she knows that I have not been progressing as rapidly as I should.

In the evening Wanda and I went with other Americans to a dance-drama called *Tales of the Silk Road*. The story in the dance-drama was set in the Tang Dynasty (A.D. 618-907). Zhang, a master cave painter, is separated from his daughter, but they are reunited with the help of a friend, a Persian merchant. The story begins with painter Zhang's saving Enus, a Persian merchant who is about to perish in a desert sandstorm on the Silk Road, but the painter's daughter, Yingniang, becomes lost. Years later, at a Dunhuang market, he finds her, then a slave-dancer in a the-atrical troupe. The painter is too poor to redeem her, but Enus, now head of a Persian caravan, gives some of his riches to secure her release. Father and daughter are united, but the local magistrate in charge of trade has designs on Yingniang. To prevent her from falling into the magistrate's hands, the painter entrusts her to Enus, who in turn takes her to Persia.

In this foreign land she considers Enus as a father. She also develops a deep friendship with the Persians and exchanges skills with them. Later Enus comes to China on a mission and returns Yingniang to her motherland. The corrupt magistrate, in the meantime, is duly revealed, apprehended, and punished. *Tales of the Silk Road* was written in 1977. It was obviously written for propaganda purposes in that the magistrate's fate corresponds to that of the Gang of Four, who are presently awaiting trial. The scenery in the presentation was spectacular, however, and the dance-drama had obviously been well rehearsed. We foreigners were told that costumes, props, and other necessary materials for the production cost more than for any previous stage production in the history of the country. I believed what we were told, for it was one of the most elaborate productions I had ever seen.

Saturday, October 18

After breakfast we went to the market across the road from the Friendship Hotel to do some shopping. We purchased cotton-padded shoes for Wanda, who had been complaining of cold feet. We also purchased several pairs of wool socks. The weather in Beijing is rapidly becoming colder, and we were afraid the socks might not be on the market when we really needed them. After lunch we boarded the Friendship Bus and went to the International Club. Wanda wanted to have her hair cut, and she had heard that the beauty parlor in the International Club was the best place for that. I went along because I thought she might want to go shopping after having her hair cut, and because I wanted to look for pipe tobacco. I sat in the lobby most of the time and waited for her. When I was not sitting, I was pacing. I tried to purchase a newspaper, but the woman at the newsstand would not accept Chinese *yuan*. I became furious and argued with the woman, but arguing did not get the results I wanted. As far as I could see, the system contained no logic. Perhaps it was another case of my not appreciating what I am supposed to accept, and understand, with considerable patience. Others seem to understand; at least they pretend they do. I can see why tourists might accept the system as it is. They are minimally exposed, and they can walk away from it. I cannot walk away, and I see no logic to being paid in a currency with which I cannot purchase a newspaper.

Sunday, October 19

The day arrived. We were going to the Great Wall of China. We would also visit Ming Tombs, and I was excited. As it turned out, I had built up too much anticipation. I began the trip with a sore throat, but I was determined not to let that bother me. The nearer we came to the wall, the heavier the traffic became. We finally left our bus and walked the last half mile or so in order to waste as little time as possible. We climbed the steps, and for the first time in my life I looked out over the Great Wall of China. It was a spectacular sight. Back in the fifth century B.C., during the Warring States Period, some dukedoms built defensive walls to consolidate their domains. After Qin Shi Huang, the first emperor of the Qin Dynasty (221-207 B.C.), achieved the unification of China, he linked up and extended the walls built by the northern dukedoms of Yen, Zhao, and Wei to form a continuous wall running from Liaotung in the East to Lintao in the Northeast. This was undertaken to hold off chieftains of the Han and other nomadic tribes living in that area north of the Great Wall from attacking the predominantly Han area to the south. Later dynasties continued to repair and extend the Great Wall for the same purpose. The Great Wall as it stands today dates from the Ming Dynasty (1368-1644), which, during its 276 years, was repaired on at least eighteen occasions to lengthen and reinforce with slabs of stone and huge bricks what was originally an earthen and rock wall. Presently the wall is in poor repair. Once we were on it, we walked only a short distance until we came upon a section that had all but fallen away. Furthermore, I could see that beyond the next rise the wall had completely fallen away. There was no point in going farther. The wall stands as a great relic from China's past, but in the future no wall will suffice. China must enter the twentieth century if it is to do business with the modern nations of the world.

As for the Ming Tombs, I was disappointed. There was little to see. On the other hand, the American embassy was sponsoring a picnic at the tombs, and we joined the foreigners for the picnic. At about four in the afternoon we boarded our bus for home. In my pocket I carried a piece of the disintegrating wall as a keepsake and a reminder of the time I visited the Great Wall of China.

Monday, October 20

My students told me that they had spent half a day trying to read forty pages of Cooper and Freneau. Some had given up in despair because they did not understand what they were reading. A general complaint was that they encountered too many words for which they had no meanings. Some of the diction in the pieces they read is dated, and I gathered that much of the difficulty could be accounted for in that fact alone. On the other hand, for those who had not tried I could not think of an acceptable excuse. They had had almost a week in which to read the forty pages. I made an assignment for the following Monday and told them that I would examine them over what they read. I don't know whether such an approach will work, but I am determined to find out what they are capable of reading and adjust my assignments accordingly. They have been cooperative in the past. They have taken extensive notes from my lectures, but they need to read the literature and learn as much as they can through reading. I am optimistic that they will grow accustomed to reading literature from a text.

After class Tan Luying stopped by and returned books she had borrowed. She also borrowed a book about Jack London. For several days I have had the impression that she has something to tell me, but always she is prevented from telling me whatever it is by the presence of other people in my office. She inquired whether Wanda and I had enjoyed our trip to the wall, and I told her that we had. She said that she had gone to Fragrant Hill Park with some of her classmates on Saturday and that they had enjoyed themselves. She seemed to be in unusually high spirits, as though something good had happened to her.

When Tan had left another of my students came to see me. She had been missing from class for several days and had come to tell me of her whereabouts. As she explained, she had served as a tour guide for a group of American tourists, and they had befriended her. She was excited because they had made her feel good about them as well as about herself. They had given her ten or a dozen of their names and addresses and promised that they would write to her. She was concerned because she cannot afford the postage to answer their letters. They offered her money, but she could not accept it. Accepting gifts from a foreigner, including money, is strictly forbidden. I told her to answer the letters when they came and that I would mail her letters to her American friends. I knew that she was afraid of being criticized for corresponding with foreigners, but I said nothing about that. From the smile on her face, I knew that she was pleased by the prospect of continuing her friendships with the Americans for whom she had served as tour guide.

At lunch I purchased a loaf of bread and then placed my order. I sat with Ed Grejda, Ken Rosen, and a woman whom I did not know. When I joined them, Ken was explaining that he knew a number of foreign experts who were leaving China during the next few days. As he explained, contracts are to be signed by the end of the month, and rather than agree to stay throughout the year many people are packing to go home. As far as the schools are concerned, that will mean a new round of jockeying for foreign teachers in a market where the number is critically short. I cannot accept the idea that people are leaving because of money; they knew the salaries would be meager before they came. They simply feel frustrated. They have not adjusted, and they do not savor the prospect of trying for another ten or eleven months to accomplish what they have failed to accomplish in the time they have been here. Some of them are frightened by the prospects of a bleak winter, but most are simply convinced that they cannot make the adjustment to the rhythms of life in China, so unlike anything they have experienced. In such cases, they are wise to go home. They would lead difficult lives if they were to stay, and they would not be of much value to the schools they serve. Such short-term visits are costly to the Chinese government, but both the government and the foreign teacher gamble on the undertaking. Considering the time lost and the cost of transportation home, the foreign teacher loses almost as much as the government does. In any event, new faces will appear around the Friendship Hotel to replace the old ones.

The people who live at the Friendship Hotel constitute a strange lot. Some of them are new divorcees. Some are Westerners who have taken Chinese mates and have come to be with their wives or husbands, in some cases because the Chinese spouse can secure neither a job nor citizenship in the country of the foreign mate. Some are drifters. One couple, for example, was in Italy for eight years before coming to China. They were in England a number of years before that. They are Americans, but they enjoy drifting and have no intentions of settling in one place. Some belong to the restless young, such as Lisa Wichser and Penn Ritter. They came to China for no apparent reason other than that they are young and restless. Once they have matured, have acquired a few years of experience, they may join the drifters. On the other hand, they may join one of the other groups. Perhaps those who are leaving are doing so because they are restless. Perhaps after two and a half months in China, they feel an urge to move on. Any way one cares to view the people who live at the Friendship Hotel, they are a strange and interesting lot.

Tuesday, October 21

Trying to adjust to a culture as different as China's results in many emotional crises. Insecurities manifest themselves in many ways, and for evidence of that one need only observe the foreigners around him or her. Some become ill and miss work frequently and for long periods of time. They come to feel that they cannot face the Chinese people and their way of living any longer. Some foreigners ride through the streets of Beijing on their bicycles, sometimes as far as fifty miles in an afternoon, because they think wearing themselves out will bring sleep, and therefore relief from their anxieties. Others become obstinate and disagreeable, particularly directing their hostilities toward the Chinese, whom they feel to be responsible for the emotional and mental disorientation they are experiencing. Some develop feelings of inadequacy and insecurity concerning their marriage and become jealous when their wives talk to other men, especially foreign men. The Chinese man seems to pose little threat to the American male. The American male is threatened, however, by other Americans, the French, the Italians, and the Germans. He seems to be less threatened by the Japanese, or by Asians in general. Among the foreigners in Beijing, insecurities are obvious to any observer.

As for my class, we examined selections from Cooper's *Leatherstocking Tales* as well as two poems by Freneau. My students enjoyed discussing the literature; they enjoyed my talking about the American Indian and the frontier. Lu Zhibao has told me on several occasions that my students often come to him and express their gratitude for my literature course. They frequently remind him, he says, that they are always learning something new. Such information, I am sure, finds its way back to the Chinese teachers and to school officials. In our most recent talk Lu also reminded me that contracts are to be signed in a few days and that I could expect considerably more than the Chinese have been paying me. He said that he would talk with the officials before they made a decision and offered me a contract. I expressed my gratitude for his support, although I felt guilty at the time knowing that my salary was already about twelve times the amount of his. He confided in me that he teaches in another school every Monday morning in order to make another four and a half *yuan* per week. Usually such practices are forbidden, so I hope he has permission from the officials. I also talked with Lu about my interest in assembling an anthology of contemporary Chinese literature for publication in the United States. He advised that for the best literature and translations I should examine *Chinese Literature*. He offered to locate several recent volumes of the journal and bring them to me so that I might work at home.

Wednesday, October 22

I had to lecture to all of Grade 77 and to the Chinese teachers. I continued where I left off the week before on the topic of existentialism and Hemingway's story "A Clean, Well-Lighted Place." I began by talking about Albert Einstein and his theory of relativity. I discussed how Einstein's work accelerated the knowledge explosion accompanying industrialization. I then gave the class a list of generalizations usually agreed upon by existential thinkers along with a list addressing the same issues taken from the thought of St. Thomas Aquinas, who lived in the thirteenth century. I proceeded to explore the two as very different ways of looking at man's world, and at man's place in the universe. Once I had demonstrated radical changes of thought taking place between the thirteenth and twentieth centuries, we then looked at Hemingway's story. My students were amazed at how such a brief story could say so much about life in the modern world. After class they gathered about me in a group of twenty-five to thirty. They were excited; they were inquisitive. I only hoped that I had started some of them thinking on their own, that I had inspired some of them to look beyond the canned explanations they have been given throughout their lives.

After class Lu Zhibao brought me three bound volumes of the journal *Chinese Literature*. "You'll need these," he said, "in doing the project you have planned." When I inquired concerning where he got the volumes, he told me that he had borrowed them from the faculty reading room. After we had talked for a while, he left and I began to examine some of the poems and stories in the volumes he had brought me.

I rode back to the Friendship Hotel in a car with Don Krumm. Don and I had previously agreed that we would stop at the Friendship Store on the way home and buy flowers for our wives. Don bought cut flowers for his wife, Louise, and I bought two plants for Wanda, a passion plant and a geranium. We made our way home with the flowers and plants and then went to lunch.

In the afternoon I took a long walk. I also visited the office of the Bureau of Foreign Experts. There I met a Chinese lady who had gone to the ballet with us the night before, and we talked. We talked about life in Beijing and about future events to be sponsored by the Bureau of Foreign Experts. She was extremely cordial, filling and refilling my teacup as we talked. On the way home from the Bureau of Foreign Experts I directed an American tourist to where he could purchase a copy of a newspaper printed in English. He and I talked, and I was pleased when he inquired about the football season at Baylor University. He went on his way, and I returned to my room to continue the work I had earlier walked out on in order to enjoy some fresh air and exercise. On the way back to my room I told myself, "It is good to be in China."

Thursday, October 23

We arrived at the institute later than usual, and I missed the old woman who smiles at me each morning as she pours water to make my tea. When I arrived, she had already delivered water to my office, but when she saw me in the hall she returned to my office and made tea for me as if to say, "We are friends. I like you." She smiled in her usual way, and I knew that she looked forward to that moment as much as I did. The old woman looks as though she has worked hard all of her life. I would like to know the story of her life, for I am sure it is one of hardship and deprivation. She fascinates me. I see both pain and kindness in her eyes. I see both resentment and love. Several days ago I tried to write a poem about her, but I tore it up because it seemed to go nowhere. Perhaps I will try again.

Wanda has suggested that I come up with a plan for having Tan

Luying spend more time with us. When she came to my office after class I thought I would present her with such a plan, but the dean of the English department was waiting for me. Tan went away, and the dean explained that the school would sponsor a trip to Fragrant Hill Park on Sunday. I often think about Tan. I think of her future in China, and then I think of a possible future for her in the United States. Her future in China will be bleak and oppressive. I am not sure what we might do to help her, but I will continue to explore ways of making her life a little more enjoyable than it has been.

Two of my girl students came to my office with tears in their eyes. They had served as tour guides for American tourists, but they were afraid to correspond with the Americans. Also, they had no money to pay for postage. I explained to them that air mail costs seventy *fen* (about forty cents) and that a letter takes ten days to two weeks to reach its destination in the United States. I told the girls to write. I told them that I would mail their letters and pay the postage, using my return address. I also instructed them to have their American friends relay all letters through me. In short, I agreed that when letters arrived I would carry them to the girls in my briefcase. I know that what I agreed to is illegal. It could be very dangerous for the girls. Furthermore, I have begun to wonder about the wisdom of my decision. Mail addressed to foreigners is commonly opened for inspection, after which it is taped closed and sent to the intended receiver.

What bothers me most of all about the two girls is that they are typical of Chinese girls their age. They are brought up to be completely honest. They trust completely except where fear of political reprisal outweighs the trust. They are likely right in trusting their American friends, but such trust often proves to be a disadvantage to Chinese girls now that Westerners have infiltrated China. For example, the other day Diane Stark, a teacher at Second Foreign Language Institute, told of attending a dance at the International Club where she listened to a story told by a teacher from the Sudan.

As the story goes, one of the best schools in Beijing has ten male students from the Sudan. The Sudanese students became familiar with Chinese girls, and after a time of gift giving, along with expressions of concern and friendship, the men convinced the girls that they should become lovers. The girls became mistresses to the Sudanese men, and they were reported to the school officials shortly after. In disgrace the girls were sent off to work in Inner Mongolia. The Sudanese men apparently could not understand why they could not have mistresses. Nothing happened to the men except that they lost their mistresses, but the girls will face a life of hard work and shame because of their poor judgment. Such naiveté as that exhibited by the girls is hard to imagine. On the other hand, the girls did not intend to become mistresses. They expected the young Sudanese men to be honorable and trustworthy. The girls merely wanted attention and friendship, but because of their immaturity they were easily deceived. That girls of college age do not know how to protect themselves from public disgrace seems impossible, but it is true. Furthermore, most such incidents involve foreigners. When both the girl and the young man are Chinese, both face the likelihood of public disgrace, and that serves as a deterrent to sexual immorality. When a Chinese young person is found to be having sexual relations outside of marriage, he can expect not only to be humiliated and disgraced, but also to be sent off to a God-forsaken outpost like Inner Mongolia. If for some reason he is allowed to stay with his work unit, he will be avoided by the people who were once his friends, he will be assigned the worst possible jobs, and he will be the last in the work unit to be extended privileges or to be promoted. He will be made to feel the disgrace of his immoral act every day of his existence, and that is a more deadly kind of punishment than being sent into the countryside.

Friday, October 24

Friday was a routine day except for the evening. After dinner Wanda and I went to a Chinese movie called *Falling in Love*. Only once before had I attended a Chinese movie, and on that occasion I walked out because I was fighting a cold and because the theater was stuffy. This time I stayed, and I am glad I did. Because I had heard that Chinese movies are sentimental and childish by Western standards, I wanted to see one for myself. Many foreign teachers were present, and many snickered and laughed at what I saw as a statement of ideals—the ideal of romantic love, the ideal of responsibility toward one's family and community, and the ideal of making life count in terms of service to one's fellowman. It occurred to me while I was watching the movie and listening to the foreigners scoff, that the Western world might profit from such ideals, that perhaps such ideals are not really outdated and that those of us who consider them to be so are selling life short. Nowhere in the film did I see any overt political messages; rather it seemed to say that one has an obligation to love and respect his or her family, neighbors, and countrymen. Nowhere did the film advocate hating those who are different. Nowhere did it advocate discriminating against those who see life differently or those who believe in things different from those any one of us believes in. On the other hand, the film had obviously been made to instruct the viewer in those virtues that produce happiness and a feeling of well-being.

Unlike Western films, *Falling in Love* contains no endorsements of illicit sex. It contains no nude scenes or pornographic displays of any kind, nor does it contain traumatic scenes of violence and hatred. The film advocates nothing to tear down and no institutions to smash. It merely presents the story of a Chinese family in which there are three sons, how those sons found love at home, and how they came to mature into responsible citizens. By Western standards *Falling in Love* is immature, but it is a kind of immaturity which has virtue, and I admire film makers as well as artists who see an opportunity, and grasp it, to make their work count for something. The functions of art have varied from time to time and place to place. There was a time in the Western world when the chief function of art was to teach. What is taught by an artist can have a profound impact on a society, and whether we like it or not every piece of art teaches in one way or another. Perhaps we could learn a lesson from the Chinese, for whether art teaches is not debatable. What is debatable is what we want to be taught through art.

Saturday, October 25

Wanda and I visited the market across the street from the compound to purchase insoles for our cotton-padded shoes. We needed more padding between our feet and cold concrete floors. After our trip to the market, we went to dinner. Wanda ate breaded pork chops, and I ate beefsteak and potatoes. At dinner we also found that the Bureau of Foreign Experts was sponsoring a trip to Datong, and I had to rush back to our room to secure money. I also had to deliver our employee's card so that the Security Bureau might grant us permission to leave the city.

We were to meet Tan Luying at the gate of the Friendship Hotel for an outing at the Summer Palace. Wanda and I were looking forward to spending an afternoon with our Chinese daughter, and when we saw the smile on her face we knew that she had been looking forward to an afternoon with us. We had a pleasant time together. We climbed the hills at the Summer Palace, and we visited out-of-the-way places in order to be alone together. It was important that we be able to talk without being overheard. Every time we go on an outing with Tan we are drawn to her a little more, and she to us. It is as though she were our daughter, as though she had always been our daughter.

It has occurred to me that our spending time with Tan might be dangerous, but I hope it does not turn out that way. I hope she is not hurt in the long run, and that we are not hurt for having accepted her so completely. Perhaps one must take risks; perhaps such risks are the ones that make life worth living. I am willing to gamble that all will turn out well. I know our lives have been made richer by our relationship with Tan.

Tan Luying had pictures of her family. She spent much of the afternoon talking about her family, and particularly about her father. It was as though she wanted us to know all about her that we possibly could. She is a fine young woman; Wanda and I agree on that.

Sunday, October 26

We waited for the bus that would pick us up for our trip to Fragrant Hill Park. As it turned out, the institute sent two buses and a car. One of the buses was loaded with teachers and students, all of whom were Chinese. The car was likewise loaded. Foreign teachers and their families boarded the other bus, along with a few Chinese teachers and officials, and then we were off to Fragrant Hill Park. The closer we came to the park, the more I realized what we were about to confront. The Chinese were traveling every available road leading to the park. There were thousands of them. Everywhere we looked we saw a sea of Chinese faces. In many places the roads were jammed. Policemen were trying to control the endless stream of those who were leaving the city for a final look at the beautiful red leaves on the trees covering the hill before winter robbed the park of its beauty. One could also see many foreigners among those traveling to the park. They too were going to get a final view before winter comes to Beijing.

The day was beautiful, and with four of my students Wanda and I climbed almost to the top of the hill that, as legend has it, defies the devil. With a student on each arm, Wanda enjoyed herself immensely. When we had almost reached the top, we stopped to have a picnic. As we ate, we noticed that even near the top of the hill there was a steady stream of people. After eating we decided that we had better return to the bottom of the hill and locate the others in our party. The path was steep and slippery, so we rested for a few minutes after eating before beginning our descent. The students were patient, kind, and courteous. It was one of those days that we will remember because we felt good about being at the park with my students. Before leaving for the Friendship Hotel, we visited the Temple of the sleeping Buddha, but we could not tarry and examine the Buddha closely. We were quickly swept by it in a great mass of humanity in which our movements were beyond our control. Once we had returned to the compound, Wanda and I agreed that we had enjoyed a remarkable weekend.

Monday, October 27

Since watching the film *Falling In Love* the other evening, I have been looking for a word that describes the Chinese attitude toward life, and I think I heard that word while en route to school on Monday morning. The Chinese are very *sentimental*. Perhaps because of the great emphasis they place upon the ideal existence, whether it has anything to do with communism or not, they are terribly sentimental. I remember saying my farewells to the student who served as my guide in Qufu, and I remember that she told me goodbye with tears in her eyes. I remember the young woman who came to ask me about mailing letters to the Americans she had met while she was serving as their guide in China. She talked about the American tourists, about how much she liked and missed them, with tears in her eyes. Such sentimentalism is not peculiar to the young women of China. I find it in the young men and in the older people as well. Somehow the Chinese have not become as emotionally hardened as have people from the West. I do not know how to account for that fact unless the answer lies in their idealism. It is refreshing to know people who express, rather than suppress, their emotions. Lu Zhibao once told me that the Chinese people conceal their emotions, but he has not observed them from the viewpoint of a foreigner.

I gave my students their first examination, an essay examination, and they were visibly frightened. One young woman became ill and had to leave the room. Because they are unaccustomed to making judgments and expressing their opinions, I asked them to write essays in which they did chiefly those things. Some appeared to be a bit lost from the outset; others did a fine job. One of the questions asked them to explain their feelings about death and to compare their feelings to attitudes toward death expressed in William Cullen Bryant's poem "Thanatopsis." Most of my students wrote that they agreed with the attitude toward death expressed in Bryant's poem. A few wrote that they were afraid of death, and some indicated that they had not given much thought to the matter. The majority explained that they considered death a part of a natural process to which all things are subjected, and that they had no particular fear of the process. Some of my students made a point of telling me that they did not believe in any kind of supreme being or a life after death. Others wrote that they did believe in a supreme being and a life after death. As for the latter group, their willingness to write such things probably indicates the extent to which they are willing to trust me. They would not express such beliefs to the Chinese teachers or to other Chinese students. One of the things the examination indicated is that my students are reading well, and I find that gratifying.

Wanda came home from work at six, and we had dinner in our room. Dinner consisted of a loaf of bread, peach preserves, fresh fruit, and hot milk with Lacovo (similar to Postum) in it. We then left the compound to see a production of Shakespeare's *Macbeth* in Chinese. I was excited about seeing the production, because I had a feeling that Shakespeare in Chinese would sound ridiculous. As it turned out, I was very surprised and very wrong. Shakespeare in Chinese sounds as natural as does Shakespeare in English. Furthermore, the production was superb. I have seen numerous performances of *Macbeth*. I have also taught the play many times. But I have never seen a more spectacular production of the play, even during the years in which Wanda and I attended the Shakespeare Festival at Stratford, Ontario, Canada. The acting was as convincing as any I had ever seen, and the makeup artist had made his characters look as much like Shakespearian characters as I have ever seen. Not one character looked Chinese. The theater was cold, unbearably cold, and we sat in a draft, but we endured the cold because the production was genuinely exciting. It surpassed anything we had expected.

Tuesday, October 28

It was a day for birthdays. Lucy Rosewell, a friend in Waco, Texas, had a birthday. Our daughter, Lynn DeNae, also had a birthday. Here in Beijing, however, it was the birthday of a fine young girl by the name of Marybeth Krumm, daughter of Don and Louise Krumm. Wanda and I debated what to get Marybeth for her birthday. One cannot purchase birthday cards in Beijing. After debating for several days, Wanda suggested that I write a poem and present it to Marybeth. I was reluctant to attempt writing a poem for a special event; most such attempts end in failure. Finally I wrote a few lines about being ten years old in Beijing, and about how forty years hence Marybeth will look back with fond memories to the time she was ten in Beijing. When Wanda and I went to dinner, we gave Marybeth the poem. Before dinner was over, Marybeth came to our table with two pieces of chocolate cake. She came to thank us for the birthday poem. We were pleased that Marybeth liked the poem, and we felt good about having contributed to her happiness on her tenth birthday.

The two girls who had brought me letters to mail to their American friends were back. They had written five more letters and wanted me to mail them. They had thought that I could mail their letters postage free through the American embassy, but I had to tell them that I actually paid for mailing their letters. They asked me how much it would cost to mail their five letters, and I told them that the postage would cost three *yuan* fifty. They were surprised and suggested that they hold the letters until they had enough money for postage, but I suggested that I mail the letters with the understanding that they would repay me when they could afford the money. It may be that their American friends will send money through me for the girls to buy stamps, for they surely know that the girls cannot afford stamps. Whether that happens or not is really immaterial in the long run. The girls miss their friends, and they have a very fine impression of Americans. Furthermore, my investment is a small one. The postage I have already paid has obviously produced much happiness. I have never seen so much happiness purchased at such a small price.

Wednesday, October 29

It was Wednesday morning in Beijing and Tuesday evening in Cleveland, Ohio, where the presidential debate was taking place. Although delayed by a couple of hours, the debate was heard in Beijing over the Voice of America. A shortwave radio three doors down the hall from my office brought in the debate poorly, but I listened anyway. I was pleased with the way Ronald Reagan conducted himself, with the way he answered the questions asked of him. I was pleased that he sounded confident and restrained. Many of the Americans in China want President Carter to win the election. Wanda and I are both Republicans, and that places us in a definite minority among Americans in Beijing. The Americans here share with the Chinese a misgiving concerning Reagan's proposal for a two-China policy, and they seem blind to the fact that such a policy is currently in operation. They are also worried over what they call Reagan's right-wing tendencies. They are afraid he will involve the United States in a war, but they fail to see that President Carter has gone to the other extreme and that as a result America has lost prestige throughout the world. I am not afraid of what Reagan might do, at least not as much as I am afraid of what four more years under Carter might do. While listening to the debate, I found it interesting that Carter had turned 180 degrees on some of the issues that had figured in his being elected four years earlier. The most obvious of those issues is the cost and size of government. In a few days we will know who will be the next president, and I am convinced that many Americans believe the solutions to present problems will require more imagination than Carter has demonstrated during his term in office.

Thursday, October 30

It was a day to celebrate, for exactly two months had passed since our arrival in Beijing. Some of the boxes we shipped before our departure for China had arrived, and one of the boxes contained soup mixes, candy, and napkins, the latter of which we have missed very much. I purchased bread and cheese from the delicatessen, and we celebrated by having dinner in our apartment. It was a good time to celebrate because we would leave the next evening for Datong. We would ride on a train all night, and the food on Chinese trains is not enticing. In some cases it is not even edible.

I was worried about Tan Luying. Earlier in the day, when I was in my office at the institute, she stopped by to see me for a few minutes, and from the way she conducted herself I was afraid she might be undergoing criticism for associating too much with foreigners. Prior to her short visit, I had not seen her for a week. I realized that my worries might be unwarranted, so I decided to wait a few days before saying anything. The classrooms are extremely cold now, and the dormitories are also cold. I fail to see how my students manage without becoming discouraged and ill. Tan returned to my office and began asking questions about her reading assignments, and I was surprised that she did because Chinese teachers were present. When the teachers had gone, she suggested that we review some of the Chinese lessons we had studied earlier. I wanted to ask her whether she was being criticized, but I knew she would not tell me.

One of the things I have noticed since class on Monday is that my students are asking more questions than they previously did. I attribute that to the examination I gave them. I believe the examination convinced them that they had better inquire concerning things they do not know. At any rate, something has happened to cause them to ask questions. One student stopped me after class and asked when I would be in my office. He has many questions, he said, and would like to discuss them with me.

Friday, October 31

The train station from which we will leave Beijing this evening was bombed last night. The official explanation is that a member of the People's Liberation Army was carrying dynamite in his luggage, but that may be a ploy to prevent undue alarm among the masses. It could have been an act of sabotage. The military in China, and particularly the army, is opposed to much of what is happening in the name of change, and for that reason opposed to the government as agent of change. The generals are well-off; that is, they live well, and they have power. If a bloodbath takes place because of China's new openness to the West, and particularly to the United States, it will likely be initiated by the military. One can hope that modernization will take place without violence, but hoping will not assure anything. China has had a feudal society for so long that many factions will resist change. The old people will resist, but the Communist Party will resist most of all. If my students are typical of young people everywhere, and I think they are, they will do all they can to bring change rather than resist it. They believe modernization is long overdue, and they believe freedoms enjoyed in the West should also be enjoyed by the Chinese people. Because of differences of attitude, particularly between the old and the young, modernization will not come easily.

In the afternoon I received a telephone call from Ambassador Woodcock's office. Wanda and I have been invited to visit Ambassador and Mrs. Woodcock at their residence on November 6, after which we will attend a reception hosted by the Woodcocks. Because the reception follows so closely the presidential election, I would guess the occasion is to celebrate President Carter's winning a second term and the consequent reappointment of Woodcock as ambassador to China. In the event President Carter does not win, the occasion will likely be used to announce Ambassador Woodcock's resignation. Either way, I think the reception is related to the election. The ambassador's secretary did not explain.

November

Saturday, November 1

We awakened in Datong, a city of 800,000 in Shanxi Province, not far from Inner Mongolia. Datong is a coal mining region, and fortunately so because the land is not very fertile. The population has to be supported by selling coal to other provinces as well as to other countries. In spite of its poverty, Datong is interesting. Once a center for Buddhism in China, the city was recently visited by the Tibetan lama. The Buddhist religion is still strong in Tibet, and it appears to be growing again in much of China.

Other things about Datong are exciting. For example, when our bus left the hotel for the cave temples of Yungang we found that traffic was heavy. People were on all sides of us as we approached the dining area. Everything (and everyone) was carrying coal. Coal was being carried on the backs of individuals. It was being hauled by wagons and carts. It was being hauled by trucks. It was being hauled in sacks on the backs of animals. It was being hauled in baskets mounted to bicycles. And we could see, at a distance, that it was also being hauled by train. From the way the coal was stacked on carts and wagons, I would say that each piece was being loaded and unloaded by hand. It was impressive, this never-ending string of human, beast, and machine working harmoniously to wrest coal from the earth. Coal is the lifeblood of Datong. To live in Datong is to be engaged in the life of a mining community.

The cave temples of Yungang, the Buddhist Caves, are situated in the north cliffs of Wuzhou Mountain, about sixteen kilometers west of the city of Datong. Hollowed out of the cliffs, these caves extend for about a kilometer from east to west. They contain more than fifty-one thousand statues and constitute one of the largest groups of stone cave temples in China. The excavating or building of the caves began fifteen hundred years ago, at the time of the Northern Wei Dynasty (A.D. 386-534). Five of them were built under the supervision of a Buddhist monk named Tan Yao during the reign of He Ping (460-465). Presently known as caves sixteen through twenty, the caves of Tan Yao were the earliest. Most of the other caves were built in the latter part of the fifth century, around the time the Wei capital was moved to Luoyang.

The majestic statues of Buddha were once instrumental in spreading religion and thereby helping to bolster China's feudal regimes. They are priceless relics that reflect the creative talents of the laboring people of ancient China. For more than a thousand years the Yungang caves were exposed to natural erosion and depredations wrought by people. Invading imperialist forces, in collusion with reactionary rulers of old China, caused enormous damage to the caves. Large stone pillars and statues were carried off, some of which can still be seen in museums around the world. I could still see the marks left by the axes and chisels. In most caves the walls are bare as far up as a human being can reach. Since Liberation in 1949, the Communist Party and the government have undertaken many repairs on the Yungang caves, and in 1961 the caves were listed by the state council among national monuments selected for special preservation. After visiting the Yungang caves, I felt that I had truly seen one of the world's great storehouses of ancient art.

On Saturday afternoon we visited a factory in Datong. Our Chinese guides hardly knew what to call the factory, or how to describe it, prior to our visit. Consequently, we were not sure what to expect. Some of our guides referred to it as a stove factory; others referred to it as a pot factory. When we arrived at the factory, I could see why they had been confused over what to call it. The factory, as we soon found, manufactures Mongolian hot pots. Beautifully done in brass and with elaborate designs, some of the pots cost more than one hundred *yuan* each. They are shipped to most parts of China and to some Western countries, such as France, where Mongolian hot pot is becoming popular.

After dinner we were taken to what was billed as an acrobatic performance, though only about a fourth of the performance had anything to do with acrobatics. In addition, we saw magic tricks, juggling acts of various kinds, and we enjoyed both vocal and instrumental music. The atmosphere for the entire performance was that of a circus in the United States in the forties. Clothing worn by some of the women performers was also reminiscent of clothing worn by American women in the forties. Held in a large hall packed with Chinese people, the program was exciting. It was exciting but long, and we left after three hours. As we left I could see that the Chinese were thoroughly enjoying themselves—so much so that I think they would have stayed all night.

Sunday, November 2

On Sunday we toured Huayan Temple. Some of the halls of the

upper temple were completed in the Ming Dynasty (1368-1644), and some of the wall paintings of the upper temple are from the Qing Dynasty (1644-1911). The five halls of the lower temple contain thirty Liao statues of ancient clay workmanship. Thirty-eight rooms of the temple are used for storing the sutras, sacred writings of Buddhism, which are carved on blocks of wood. A museum is located inside the temple, and all the relics excavated in the Datong area are on exhibit there.

At noon we boarded a train for our return to Beijing. It was time to turn our thoughts toward our reason for being in China, which in my case is to teach. When we arrived in Beijing at 10:00 p.m., I was eager to see my students.

Monday, November 3

I had enjoyed the trip to Datong, but I had missed my students. I have come to realize that I need them, that I depend on my encounters with them to give my life meaning, direction, and purpose. When I met with my class at 8:00 a.m., I felt good about being with my students. I felt that I belonged where I was, in the classroom with them, and I sensed that they had come to feel the same way about me. During the two months I have been with them, my students and I have developed a mutual admiration and a mutual trust, although a few of them have not entered into the relationship. Those who have not hold back because they are afraid, a condition brought on by the uncertainty of loyalties and friendships during the Cultural Revolution. Most of my students are willing to gamble that I will be fair and honest with them, and such a willingness is a tribute to them.

In class I turned back essays that I had collected and marked the week before, and I made another reading assignment. I talked about Edgar Allan Poe, explicating "Israfel," "Annabel Lee," and an excerpt from "The Cask of Amontillado." My students seem excited about Poe, but they still cannot accept the idea that American poems and stories do not exist exclusively for conveying political messages. They hardly know what to do with literature that is not directly related to politics. They often ask, "But where is the message?" They are accustomed to looking for "the message." As I explicated "Israfel," which some of them had experienced difficulty in reading, I could see face after face light up with excitement and joy. It was a gratifying experience for them as well as for me.

Tuesday, November 4

Tuesday began as most other class days, but it turned out to be one of the most enjoyable days I had experienced since my arrival in China. I had decided a day earlier that I would have to get out of my office and the apartment more; I still have not managed culture shock as well as I might have. For several days I had become increasingly aware that emotionally I had not accepted my new station in life or my new place in the world. I decided that I would have to break my routine and spend more time with people if I were ever to make the adjustment to being in China. I needed some form of security that was missing. Consequently, it was with this in mind that I went into the classroom and announced that I wanted to visit the national library in the afternoon, and that I was interested in having someone accompany me to act as interpreter. I told my students that I would be glad to take anyone who did not have classes in the afternoon. Much to my surprise, when I asked for a show of hands by those interested in accompanying me, only one hand went up. My immediate response was to be suspicious because of what might be said concerning the student who accompanied a foreigner to the library. I was a bit worried by the fact that only one student volunteered, but I was even more worried because the student was a girl. Because I was concerned that retracting my offer would instigate even more rumors, I requested that the student, Su Guifen, see me after class, at which time, I told her, we would agree on a time to leave campus. As it turned out, Su Guifen and I left the institute at 1:00 p.m. and rode a bus to the library.

As we caught the bus for Wangfujing Street, we began talking. All afternoon, until almost five o'clock, I asked questions of Su Guifen. I asked questions about her family, about her schooling, and about her aspirations, all of which she answered very candidly. I could tell that she was pleased with the interest I was showing in her. I even told her that she should feel free to avoid my questions if at any time she was embarrassed. She never stopped me, and she never avoided my questions. She was at ease, as though we had known each other all of our lives. She told me that she has two brothers and a sister, that she is the oldest of the children in her family, that she was enrolled in a language school when she was nine years old, that she left her family at that age to live at the school, that her home is in west Beijing, that her father is a factory worker, that she is twenty-five years old, that she taught in a middle school before coming to Second Foreign Language Institute, that she had once had a dream of going to America, that she has a boyfriend, and that she has no qualms about being assigned a job away from her family when she graduates. We talked about many things unrelated to either of us, things like crime, dating, and children. Throughout our conversation she was always interested in comparing what is happening in China to what is happening in the United States.

Su Guifen was helpful when we arrived at the library. She explained to the head librarian that I was a foreign teacher at Second Foreign Language Institute, and that I carried with me a letter of introduction from the school. She presented the librarian with the letter and secured a pass. Together we spent an hour or so looking through parts of the card catalog, in which she was invaluable because the filing system differs greatly from systems commonly used in the United States. Furthermore, the listings are in Chinese. Once I found that the library contained more American literature than I expected, Su Guifen arranged with one of the librarians to take me on a tour. I was excited because the library contains more than ten million volumes and more than half of them are from foreign countries. Our tour also gave Su Guifen her first opportunity to see library stacks. Chinese libraries, she explained to me, have closed stacks. Even foreigners are not allowed to visit the stacks, but with my letter of introduction and some persuasive talking on the part of Su Guifen, I entered the stacks of the library to wander among six large floors of books. It proved to be a rewarding afternoon, and before we left I was given a card to fill out in order to secure a library card for use on future visits.

When we had completed our tour of the library, we visited the shops in Wangfujing Street. Su Guifen purchased some mixed, dried fruit, and we shared that as we talked our way through shop after shop. Next we visited an ice cream stand and had strawberry ice cream. When we were finally ready to leave Wangfujing Street, Su Guifen purchased some dried meat to take back to the institute with her. All afternoon she spent her money on me, not allowing me to pay for anything. She was worried that I would be angry with her, but I told her that I would not be, even though I felt bad about using her money. She was satisfied. "The honor is all mine," she said. She wanted to see me safely home, but I assured her that I could find my way from the Beijing Hotel. She escorted me to the Beijing Hotel and then left for her bus ride back to the institute. I went home feeling good. Not only had I spent the afternoon with one of my students, but I had spent it with a sensitive and compassionate human being. I thought of Henderson in Bellow's novel *Henderson the Rain King*. I thought of Henderson's running around the airplane in Newfoundland, and I too wanted to run for I felt that I had found a new land, one that constituted a more solid ground of being than I had known in a long time.

Wednesday, November 5

More than ever I have noticed mountains of cabbage in the streets of Beijing, and in the fields outside Beijing. Cabbage is being moved into the city in every conceivable way. I wondered where it would go and how it would be used, but Su Guifen told me on Tuesday that every Chinese family will purchase a supply of cabbage for the winter in the next few days. She explained that her family stacks the cabbage in a pile in the courtyard and that they eat from the pile throughout the winter. "Vegetables are in short supply in winter," she explained, "but every family can eat cabbage all winter long." And they do eat cabbage all winter long. Cabbage is served in every imaginable form for breakfast, lunch, and dinner.

The election returns came. Early in the morning I heard on the Voice of America that because more Democrats had registered to vote Carter had a good chance of winning. The events of the day, however, proved the situation to be quite different. Not only did Reagan win by a large majority, but the Republicans gained a majority in the Senate for the first time in many years. They also picked up a number of seats in the House; estimates I have heard range from twenty to thirty-three. It was a day to remember because the American people were telling their politicians something about likes and dislikes, about what the people do and do not expect from government.

I have watched the news closely since coming to China. Being halfway around the world from America has given me an entirely new perspective on the American political system. Like many other Americans, I have always taken the American government as something that merely exists. I now see that the American political process has no equal anywhere in the world. No other government responds to the needs of the people so completely, and no other system is so completely under the control of the people. No other system contains such a delicate set of checks and balances, and no other system allows for such an orderly transfer of power from one person or one group to another. In America no danger exists of a coup or a revolution. No danger exists that the country will be taken over by the military. In America government is in the hands of the people, and I marvel at how well the system works. Furthermore, my Chinese students marvel at how well the system works. My students are awed by the fact that the American people elect representatives, and by the fact that the people can turn those representatives out for doing a poor job. The American political system can best be appreciated from a distance. We Americans are guilty of not seeing the mountain on which we are standing. When one views the mountain from Beijing, he stands in awe at the majesty of that mountain.

Thursday, November 6

It was our day to visit Ambassador and Mrs. Woodcock, and I was not sure what to say when we arrived. I had no idea how the ambassador was reacting to President Carter's defeat. On Wednesday I had gone to the embassy to listen to the election returns with other Americans. As I listened, I could make out that what had been happening in America was beginning to manifest itself in important ways. The liberals were obviously being defeated; the conservatives were obviously being elected. I interpreted the trend to mean that ours is no longer a youth-oriented culture, that the sixties generation had either grown up or had lost its power, that the decade of the seventies was more conservative than was the decade of the sixties, and that for Americans the future might contain a depth of meaning uncharacteristic of the past two decades.

The meeting with Ambassador and Mrs. Woodcock went well. Mrs. Woodcock was unusually congenial and made us feel at ease. She served cocktails, and we chatted while waiting for the appearance of the ambassador. Mrs. Woodcock talked about the election. She was obviously disappointed. When the ambassador arrived, I inquired of him concerning the sad shape of the automobile industry in America. He remarked that the industry is indeed in very bad shape, and that he could see no solution for the immediate future. He conjectured that General Motors will remain solvent, that Chrysler will fail, and that Ford may survive, depending on what happens to the car market for the next few months. When I asked about the possibilities of mass transit as a viable solution, the ambassador remarked that the American public is still not convinced. We talked for about half an hour. Then the ambassador and Mrs. Woodcock took us to a reception for American and Chinese scientists. I talked with eight or ten of the American scientists and found that they were pleased with the outcome of the election. I also realized that I had guessed wrong concerning the purpose of the reception. It was obviously not for the ambassador to announce either his reappointment or his resignation.

Friday, November 7

The day was difficult from the outset. One of my classes had returned from a month in the field as tour guides. I quickly learned that the month had not helped them academically. My other students can assimilate as fast as I lecture, but the students in class five cannot. They have missed the background lectures for the literature we are studying, and they have missed becoming familiar with my voice.

The day contained other problems. For example, I arrived at the school at about 7:45 a.m. to find that both the water and the electricity had been turned off. Halls, offices, and classrooms were cold. Early in the morning toilets were producing an odor that permeated the entire building. To make matters worse, I had promised my students that I would stay in the afternoon to answer questions concerning an examination I had turned back to them. I kept my promise. I stayed and met with my students. They appreciated the opportunity to talk with me about their exams and about literature, but the cold was penetrating. All afternoon I thought of our apartment in the Friendship Hotel, and I knew that when evening came I would be warm and comfortable.

Saturday, November 8

Before lunch Wanda and I went shopping at the market across the street from the Friendship Hotel; after lunch we went into the city. I had arranged for Tan Luying to meet us at the entrance to the Forbidden City. I realized that we had overscheduled for the day. After visiting the Forbidden City, we had to return to the compound, bathe, dress, and catch a bus. We were scheduled to have dinner with Wanda's fellow workers from the United States Department of Agriculture and the United States Department of Commerce. I had not calculated travel time in planning for the day, and we were running late. Also, I was coming down with a cold because of spending the previous day at the institute. I resented having to go to the dinner. I have had some difficulty in accepting the group with whom Wanda works. I have simply felt that they constitute an intrusion into our efforts to adjust to being in China. I have caused Wanda to worry over my attitude toward the job and toward the people with whom she works. I realize that she needs the job to keep her occupied. She works with interesting people, and they speak English.

As it turned out, the dinner was delicious. Everyone likely had too much to eat, but everyone joked and laughed, making the evening more tolerable than it would have been otherwise. Most of the people in the group want to end the job and return to the United States. They have not developed any strong attachments to China or to the Chinese people.

I felt guilty about the way we had hurried through the afternoon with Tan. We had met her at the gate to the Forbidden City and hurried restlessly through the afternoon. We visited the Bank of China as well as the monuments in Tiananmen Square, and then we hurried to the Beijing Hotel to get warm. When we tried to enter the Beijing Hotel, the doorman stopped Tan Luying and questioned her. She was referred to one Chinese guard and then to another. It did not occur to me that we had cause to be alarmed, but I later found out that some foreigners have taken Chinese women to the hotel for illicit purposes. I was furious because Tan was being interrogated, but I now realize that the Chinese were merely looking out for their own kind. After the interrogation Tan was allowed to visit the restaurant in the hotel with us. Once we were warm, we parted—Tan Luying for her home and we for our compound to prepare for our evening at the Sichuan Restaurant in Sichuan Street.

Sunday, November 9

We visited Zhoukedian, the site of the Peking Man Cave, about forty-eight kilometers southwest of Beijing. We had packed a picnic basket the evening before, containing enough food for Wanda, me, and Paul Mussen, a psychologist from the University of California at Berkeley. We had looked forward to the trip, but nothing seemed particularly stupendous about the site of the excavations, or about the museum where many of the artifacts are housed. After all we had seen in China, none of it seemed particularly startling or of great significance. What pleased me most was that the sun was shining.

I was tired, but I knew that Mao Zhiren was coming to visit us in the evening and that I should not count on any rest until late in the evening. As it turned out, Mao did not stay long. We talked about China, about the fact that campaign posters have been appearing on the sides of buildings at Beijing University, that students are actually campaigning to be elected as representatives to the People's Congress. Mao was excited, for he views the posters and the campaigning as the first step on the road to democracy in China. Mao believes that China will become a democratic country, and he wants to participate in the transition. Once Mao had gone home, Wanda and I prepared for bed. We were both suffering from colds, and we knew that in the week to come there would be no more space in China than there had been in the previous week. We knew that crowdedness would remain as one of the great facts of life in China.

Monday, November 10

In spite of my being tired, my class went well. We reviewed for a midterm exam, and I spent about forty-five minutes explicating and talking about Hawthorne's "Dr. Heidegger's Experiment." My students liked Hawthorne's story, and they were full of questions. Such behavior constitutes a remarkable improvement over their reluctance to ask questions when I began teaching them. I no longer have to retard the rate at which I talk to them. They can follow at a normal rate of conversation.

They have made remarkable progress in writing in English also. I feel good about the progress they have made, and I never miss an opportunity to tell them as much. I am convinced that praise is often the best form of motivation.

After class students stopped by my office to borrow books, and one young man came to ask if he could make copies of some of the poems I have written about China. In the afternoon, I returned to the compound to write letters, to work on a poem I have been trying to write entitled "Fragrant Hill Park," and to write in the journal I have been keeping since coming to China. The journal consists of my experiences in and impressions of China. It does not purport to be a record of historical or political facts about China. The so-called facts about China are elusive and obscure, even for the Chinese people. My impressions are subjective, but they are no less real.

Tuesday, November 11

After class I asked Su Guifen whether she had the afternoon free, and whether she might accompany me to the Museum of Chinese History, located immediately across Tiananmen Square from the Great Hall of the People. She said that she would like to accompany me, but that she would have to secure the permission of the dean. She suggested that she take a friend, another of my students, because of her poor knowledge of Chinese history. That way, she explained, I would learn more from what I was viewing. I told her that taking a friend was fine with me. I had brought my lunch to school because I could not stand the idea of eating in the school dining hall, which is cold, dingy, and very unpleasant. I ate bread and chicken soup, and I drank three or four cups of hot water. When Su Guifen and her friend arrived at 1:00 p.m., I was ready to visit the Museum of Chinese History.

After an hour of viewing artifacts from early Chinese history, I could tell that Su Guifen was bored. Pan Sulin, the friend, was also bored. I suggested that we cross the square and visit the Great Hall of the People, but my students were reluctant. As it turned out, we were told that for-eigners are allowed to visit the Great Hall of the People on Tuesday, Thursday, and Saturday mornings only. My students had been reluctant because they did not want me to be disappointed. As an alternative to visiting the Great Hall of the People, Su Guifen suggested that we visit a park near the Forbidden City. We followed her suggestion, and we enjoyed ourselves immensely. We visited a hall of mirrors for the fun of looking at various distortions of ourselves. We walked in the park and enjoyed several displays of beautiful flowers. One display of chrysanthe-mums was particularly impressive.

When we left the park, we went to Wangfujing Street. We inquired in the shops about tobacco pouches, but we found none. We purchased dried fruit. I had Su Guifen make the purchase while Pan Sulin and I looked for tobacco pouches. I told her to purchase two bags of the fruit, each weighing about a pound. We walked and ate dried fruit. We also visited an ice cream stand and ate strawberry ice cream. Late in the day we made our way to the bus stop in front of the Beijing Hotel, and when I bid my students farewell, Su Guifen handed me the sack of fruit that remained in her bag. I knew she was teasing me when she said that she could not accept it because of being criticized. I had no doubt that she would be criticized if the school officials ever found out, but I also knew their finding out was not likely. I persisted that she and Pan Sulin take the fruit back to school with them, and they finally consented. I felt good because their accepting the gift was a sign they had accepted me, not only as a teacher but as a friend.

Wednesday, November 12

The day was frustrating. The weather was cold, and I planned to stay near the heater in my office after class. But nothing turned out quite as I had planned. On the day before, Diane Stark had moved about ten Chinese teachers into the office for a meeting, and they formed a neat circle around the heater while I almost froze to death. Further, they had created such a disturbance that I could not do my work, and because they were occupying my office I could not hold conferences with my students. Tuesday had been very frustrating, and Wednesday was not much better. After class my students came in great numbers to check out books and to talk. Lu Zhibao came by and told the students to leave so that I might go home. I needed to be with Wanda. She was in bed with a virus, and I needed to carry lunch to her. I hated to walk out on my students, but I was glad to go home.

When I arrived at the compound, I went to lunch. I find that I am eating more than at any other time since coming to China, and I attri-bute that to the cold weather. After I had eaten, I took Wanda a dish of beef stew on rice. My effort was all in vain; she took a bite and decided that she could not eat. I wrote for a while and then visited the market across the street. I still wanted a tobacco pouch. I also wanted to find something appropriate for carrying food to Wanda, a container of some kind, and I looked for fresh fruit. I did not find the tobacco pouch, but I did find some dishes in which I could carry food to Wanda. As for the fruit, I decided that I would return to the compound for that. The fruit in the market was not good.

The store in the compound contained a large mob. Bananas were in stock, and the Chinese had turned out in great numbers to purchase them. Again I was reminded that crowdedness is one of the most frustrating things about China. Although conditions may be different in some parts of China, everywhere I have been is characterized by crowdedness. Nowhere can one be alone. Nowhere can one get off to himself or herself and meditate. Carl Sandburg may have been right in eulogizing the people, but Carl Sandburg never dreamed of the crowded conditions which exist in Beijing. He might have written a poem quite different from "The People" had he been a Chinese person living in Beijing in 1980.

Thursday, November 13

One of the deans, named Wang, came to the office to talk with Diane Stark and me. He talked with Diane Stark for two hours; or rather he listened to her talk for two hours. I knew that I would not talk with him until another day, so I turned to my work. I resented their occupying my office. My students will not enter under such circumstances. In this case, their talking prevented my having my Chinese lesson with Tan Luying. Stark had held a meeting with the Chinese teachers in the office on Monday, preventing my having my Chinese lesson at that time also. When she suggested that she would have another meeting, I told her that she would have to find another place, that she shared the office with two other teachers and therefore had no right to monopolize it. She seemed to understand. Again I was faced with having to handle the problem of crowdedness, and in this case I felt that my responsibility had to be directed toward my students.

In the afternoon I walked. Wanda was still in bed suffering from a virus. She was in considerable pain, and I felt that I had better entertain her as much as possible. After my walk we played cards for a while. Then we read, but mostly we relaxed. In the evening I was anxious to get out and go somewhere. I had tried to purchase tickets for a figure-skating event, but the tickets sold out while I was waiting in line. I had missed seeing the United States track and field team earlier, and in much the same way. Wanda hoped that she would be well enough to go to work the next morning, but I thought she was being a bit too optimistic. I said nothing; I thought I would let her find out for herself when the next morning came.

Friday, November 14

It was the last day of review for the midterm exam. My students were anxious. They were also full of questions. After class I went to my office, and students from all five classes began to show up with questions. Confronting the exam, they wanted to check the accuracy of what they had in their notes. The gathering of students overflowed my office, and we moved to a classroom. For an hour and a half I answered questions. My students were appreciative that I had taken time to help them, and I felt guilty that I did not have more time. My students are bright. They are perceptive beyond anything I imagined before coming to China. Not only will they perform well on the exam, but their diligence and conscientiousness will pay big dividends throughout their lives. I worry about excessive anxiety among my students, and I realize that examinations determine the future. For my students no such thing as a second chance exists.

In the evening Charles Wyvelle visited. I had invited him to discuss the possibility of my collaborating with him on a literary project for publication in the United States. I proposed that we do something new and different, such as a collection of interviews with Chinese writers. I thought living in China might give us an edge over the casual literary scholar who just happens to fly to China when he has an idea for a book. Also, I knew Chinese writers had become suspicious of well-meaning foreigners who drop by to pick up fragments of the culture in order to peddle them in the West. Our project would be different, I reasoned, and we had the advantage in that Charles already knew some of the writers.

After Charles arrived, we were some time in getting around to the topic of writers. First, Charles had a story to tell, a story about an old woman he watched get off the back of a truck not far from the compound the day before. She was ragged and thin, he said, and quite emaciated. When she dismounted, the truck driver saw her almost immediately. The driver and other Chinese gathered around her to shield her from the sight of Charles, the foreign onlooker. Charles was interested in the woman because he was convinced that she represented a situation similar to one that took place last winter, one that the government managed to handle without any adverse publicity. According to Charles, beggars came in great numbers to Beijing last winter. They came from provinces to the north. Since the end of the Cultural Revolution the government has publicized that all Chinese people have enough to eat, that for the first time all China is well off. Such propaganda the government deems necessary to encourage the Chinese people to work diligently toward goals of modernization. In the provinces north of Beijing last winter many people were starving in spite of the government's propaganda, according to Charles, and they came to Beijing in great numbers to beg for food in the streets. The police, in turn, rounded them up and shipped them home as systematically as they came. In doing so they avoided embarrassment for the government in the eyes of the Chinese people and in the eyes of the world press. The other countries of the world must be convinced that modernization is in progress. Otherwise they will lack confidence in both the Chinese government and Chinese trade.

We finally arrived at the purpose for which we met—to discuss the possibility of cooperating on a project concerning Chinese writers. We agreed to call together a group of young Chinese writers for a series of meetings on the state of literature in China. We want to collect firsthand information, and the way to do that is to get it from the writers themselves. In any event, the task will be difficult because Chinese writers must work in fear that they will say or do something that will antagonize the government. They must always protect themselves by saying nothing that might have international implications. Charles and I agreed that we could come up with a set of safeguards to protect those writers who cared to participate. Charles is known and respected by a few young writers, and they will be helpful in leading us to others. Before Charles left our meeting, I volunteered our apartment as a meeting place. We are optimistic about our project and will hold our first meeting as soon as Charles can arrange an acceptable time with the writers.

Saturday, November 15

I wanted to go to town and mix with the Chinese people. Wanda had to work. She had returned to work on Friday as she had wished. I left the compound around 10:00 a.m. Only once had I used the city buses on my own, and I realized that becoming lost is easy. I took bus number 322 to the terminal, which is near the zoo. I did not know the terminal for bus number 103 was nearby, although it was the bus I needed to take as far as the Beijing Hotel. Once I was that far, I could take bus number 4 to the Friendship Store and to the International Club.

When I arrived at the Beijing Hotel, I stepped from the bus and ambled down Wangfujing Street. I visited in shop after shop, and when the clerks could not understand my gestures, they would smile as I tried again. I spent three or four hours wandering around and making small purchases. I purchased a pipe, a tobacco pouch, a bag of candy, and several other things. I also visited a Chinese bookstore. I had not realized how many titles were available to the Chinese people. I then visited a bookstore for foreigners to examine titles available in the English language. The Chinese bookstore, I concluded, was the more impressive of the two.

What impressed me most about the day was what I saw from a window of the Friendship Bus on the way home in the evening. Darkness was coming rapidly, and at one place along the route to the Friendship Hotel I looked off at a distance to see thousands of what looked like crows (possibly grackles) perched in the tops of trees as though they were keeping watch over the city. The treetops were filled with these birds, and I wondered if they were waiting to descend and devour the leftovers of the Cultural Revolution. Outlined against the sky, the birds seemed appropriate to the mood of the times as well as to the place. I wonder if they are still there in the treetops looking out over the city. Since seeing them, I have been obsessed by the black birds in the treetops. They were an awesome sight.

Sunday, November 16

Sunday would be like any other day in that Wanda had to work. The U.S-China Exhibition would have another day like the one before it. Chinese and United States officials would walk through and inspect the exhibition in preparation for a grand opening on Monday. As for me,

Mao Zhiren was coming to take me for a tour of Beijing University, a tour that would prove to be boring and useless. Mao arrived half an hour late, and as it turned out he seemed to be in a great hurry to end our visit. We walked around campus. In late fall the barren landscape was anything but attractive. As for the buildings, we entered none. Realizing that he was in a hurry to end our tour, I asked him whether he might take me to a shopping area nearby to look for trousers. As the weather becomes colder, I will need more clothes for "layering." The department store had no trousers large enough for me. The best I could do was buy some pipe tobacco.

In the afternoon I wrote in my journal. I also completed a short poem entitled "In the Streets of Peking":

> It is dusk in Peking.
> The trees have all turned black.
> Thousands of crows have come
> to settle for the night
> along the boulevard.
> From the Friendship Bus
> I watch them watching me.
> I wonder where they were
> before the terror came.
> I wonder if they know
> about the death of Mao.
> Once again it is dusk in
> the streets of Peking
> and the crows are watching.

Writing the poem was not a great achievement, but it helped to make the day profitable.

Monday, November 17

I packed a lunch to take to school with me. I wanted to stay at school and grade exam papers in the afternoon, but I could not stand the thought of eating in the school dining hall. My students wrote for two hours; they had obviously prepared well for the exam. While they wrote, I caught up on chores, which I had deliberately postponed for the occasion. When my students had completed the exam, I went to my office to grade their papers only to find that other students were waiting in great numbers to see me. They had questions for which they wanted answers as part of their preparation to take the exam. We retired to a nearby classroom, and I answered questions for an hour and a half. At lunch time I dismissed the students and told them that I had work to do, that I had no more time to answer their questions.

In the afternoon I graded papers. My students, I discovered, wrote convincing answers to the questions I had given them. They knew the material. Some of them still have problems with the mechanics of the English language. Having them write is probably the best thing I can do for them, especially since I mark each paper closely. Perhaps they will learn more from going over the corrected papers than they would from reading more literature or listening to more lectures. As I anticipated, marking the papers went slowly. Chinese students do not make the same errors that American students make. In America a teacher can anticipate the performance of his students on an examination. Such is not so when Chinese students write in English. Only a few things are predictable, such as the fact that Chinese students will be confused by the function of the article in English.

Tuesday, November 18

I administered the midterm exam to another class of my students, and although I wanted to do some shopping in Xidan Street I decided that I would spend the afternoon at home grading papers. After lunch, I lay down for a rest only to find when I awakened that much of the afternoon had gone by. The day had begun strangely. Early in the morning I had gone to the car stand only to find that no one else was there—no foreign teachers, no drivers, and no cars. I waited, and finally a car came. The driver took me to the Second Foreign Language Institute. On the way to the compound, at lunch time, I was told a strange story about how an Australian man was attacked and cut to pieces the night before by a Chinese man. The attack took place while the Australian man was leaving one of Beijing's best hotels.

In the evening I thought about Qi Wenqin. She had come to my office in the morning to talk about her future as a Chinese teacher. I listened attentively. She is bored with what she is doing and would like to prepare herself to do something more exciting. I discussed with her the necessity of improving her proficiency in English as well as improving her interest in teaching as a profession. Qi is nearing forty, and she has begun introspecting, soul-searching. She has been at Second Foreign Language Institute for fifteen years, and she is locked into the system, as are the other teachers. She longs for status as a professional, but an atmosphere of professionalism is not to be found at Second Foreign Language Institute. It is not to be found, I am told, in most Chinese schools. When we ended our conversation, I lent Qi Wenqin a collection of essays on teaching English as a foreign language. Shao Jingfeng also dropped by my office. I lent her some books and talked with her. She was grateful that I would take time to visit with her. Shao Jingfeng has a beautiful smile. One smile from Shao Jingfeng says about all there is to say concerning genuine gratitude.

Wednesday, November 19

When Lu Zhibao came to see me, I asked concerning sixty *yuan* that I should have been paid. He went to the office of the paymaster and brought the money to me. It had been in the desk of the paymaster for several days and no one had claimed it. I dismissed the matter as bureaucratic blundering. When Lu returned with the money he had something he wanted to tell me.

The government, he said, had once again changed the rules concerning the giving of gifts involving foreigners. The law, he continued, simply states that a Chinese citizen is forbidden to give gifts to a foreigner or accept gifts from a foreigner. The law had not really changed. It had simply been relaxed for about two months, and I had begun to think that it might continue to be relaxed until it was ignored altogether. I listened as Lu explained the contents of an article in the morning edition of *People's Daily*. The government is trying to stop influence peddling, bribery, and corruption in general involving transactions between Chinese officials and foreign businessmen. Some Chinese officials are apparently accepting color television sets and various other gifts for arranging contracts with foreign firms. The result of such heavy-handedness on the part of the government will be a new scare among the masses. Knowing that this kind of thing happens in China, my students and fellow Chinese teachers have been cautious all along. They are aware of how easy it is to be caught in a trap when the pendulum swings.

When Lu had gone, I sat and thought of the bag of dried fruit I had given to Su Guifen and Pan Sulin. I realized that I could not convince them to accept such an offer again. I also stared at a pile of copies of *Chinese Literature* lying on my desk. The pile contained twenty-eight numbers of the journal, and I debated with myself what to do with them. One of my students had presented them to me earlier in the morning. The best thing to do, I decided, was to take them home and say nothing to anyone about them. I wondered whether the student who had given them to me was frightened. I knew that she would be lectured on the matter of giving gifts to foreigners in a political meeting for all students later in the day. I wondered how she would react to the lecture in light of her behavior. I also wondered whether she would worry that I might reveal to school officials that she had given me the numbers of *Chinese Literature*. My proposed project with Charles Wyvelle had not progressed, but I was still interested in assembling the material for an anthology.

Thursday, November 20

Earlier in the week I had met with a teacher and administrator named Wang. He is a curriculum coordinator and a dean or vice president. I can never be sure about titles for Chinese school officials; even the Chinese teachers are not sure. At any rate, Wang and I had talked about the curriculum in the English department, and I was still thinking about our talk. I was still wondering whether his reactions to my suggestions were as genuine as they appeared to be. I had been critical concerning what I saw as inefficiency in the curriculum as well as in the scheduling of classes. I had been both honest and critical, hoping that I might be of help. I felt then, as I do now, that I owe my students all the help I can give them.

After class Zhu Zheng stopped by my office. I had been critical concerning his handling of a request of mine for tickets that would allow my students to attend the American exhibition. My criticism had obviously been reported to him, as I intended that it would. Chinese bureaucracy is often used as an excuse for not getting a job done, and I find such excuses irritating. Zhu Zheng was apologetic. He explained that he had been in a conflict with the school liaison over who should solicit the tickets from the Chinese Committee for the Promotion of International Trade (CCPIT). Instead of resolving the conflict, they had apparently spent weeks bickering over whose responsibility it was to secure the tickets. In the meantime the CCPIT released all of the tickets, and the institute ended up with none. Such performances are typical; each Chinese does only what his job demands. On the other hand, when something comes along that does not seem to fit the system, no one knows how to react. In general the Chinese people are accustomed to being told what to do, and they are reluctant to do anything they are not told. The Cultural Revolution may be partly responsible. The Chinese are reluctant to assume responsibility that has not been clearly assigned to them because they may subject themselves to criticism when they do. They can hardly be blamed, although such behavior is extremely frustrating for a foreigner. I should have gone to the CCPIT for the tickets myself. As a foreigner, I think I could have avoided protocol. I felt sorry for Zhu Zheng.

Friday, November 21

It was the last day for administering exams, and I was wary because the class taking the exam had been absent for much of the term. They had been serving as tour guides in Beijing, Shanghai, Wuhan, and other places. They had attended only one or two of my lectures, and had done an equal number of reading assignments. To accommodate them I had designed an exam covering only the lectures they had attended and the reading they had been assigned. As it turned out, I was unduly alarmed. They wrote for two hours and seemed to enjoy it. Some wrote far more than I asked of them. They wanted to impress me with what they had learned. They obviously had been reading and studying, even while serving as tour guides. Once again they proved to me that they are eager to learn, that they are eager to please. The sixty hours I will spend marking their papers will be a worthwhile investment.

What pleased me most was that after class one of my students came to the office to apologize for not having followed my instructions. I had instructed all of my students to prepare to write an exam on four of ten questions I had assigned. When they came to class, I limited the four to two, and they wrote on the two. My apologetic student felt that she was better prepared to write on one of the questions I had not assigned than she was on one I had. She had taken the exam the day before, and answered the questions she knew instead of the ones I asked, and she was worried. I could tell that she had undergone a sleepless night over what she interpreted as an attempt to deceive me. I praised her for her honesty, and she in turn promised to write the essay I had assigned. I told her that I would accept both the apology and the essay, and that I admired her courage and honesty.

Saturday, November 22

Although Wanda and I had been to see a Chinese movie the night before, I had to rise early and mark papers. The paper grading had progressed slowly, and I knew I would have to concentrate on the papers if I was ever to return them to my students. I graded until noon, and although I had been grading for five days I still had not completed the second of five sets of papers. The papers are interesting. They tell me much about my students. They tell me things that I could not find out in any other way. They tell me, for example, what my students hold as valuable and sacred. They tell me what my students think about authority, responsibility, love, war, and other such topics.

In the afternoon I went for a walk. Walking in the direction of the zoo, I stopped and visited in shops along the way. I visited shops that I had not seen before. I purchased tea and nuts for a bridge party in the evening. It was good to be outside, and I was looking forward to the bridge party. Some of my students were supposed to accompany me to the Old Summer Palace, but one of them called to explain that they could not come. I had hoped that my students could explain the significance of the Old Summer Palace. But the explanation and the trip will have to wait for another day. My students are being confined to the institute for important political meetings. They are preparing to elect representatives to the People's Congress, and their first opportunity to participate in a democratic election is important to them.

Sunday, November 23

In the afternoon I met Tan Luying and her brother Luke at the exhibition center. I met them at 1:30 and it was almost 5:00 before we left the exhibition. We examined numerous exhibits, and I took them to the office of the director of the agricultural exhibits, where Wanda introduced them to her supervisor. Wanda escorted the three of us to a lounge where we enjoyed a long conversation and cokes. It was an enjoyable afternoon, one which Tan Luying and her brother will remember for a long time.

In the evening Mao Zhiren came to visit. We talked about the elections at Beijing University. Mao explained that thirty-two candidates from Beijing University are running for positions in the People's Congress and that only five of them will be elected. Mao sees the election as a victory for democracy in China. The election also has government officials in Beijing worried, he says, because they are afraid "election fever" will spread throughout China.

They are worried because the government has authorized elections and because those officials who would suppress them cannot afford to antagonize the government. They are worried because the process, if it spreads, threatens to revolutionize China's political system and in doing so replace the present one with a system based on competence and willingness to serve the people. Such a system would make the government accountable to the people, and many of the cadres, particularly the uneducated and unqualified ones, are opposed to that. Mao Zhiren predicts that it will come. "It has gone too far to be turned back," Mao contends.

China is about to be changed in another way. Heretofore, the Chinese people have not paid a tax on income, but that is about to change. Wanda and I have recently received forms from the municipal government on which to file our income. As I see it, the tax is directed at foreigners. Foreign businessmen are coming into Beijing and establishing offices. Numerous directors of joint-venture companies now live in the Beijing Hotel. They operate in Beijing in order to escape paying taxes, and the municipal government has decided to take advantage of that. Likely, the tax will affect teachers minimally, if at all. But it is a nuisance, and that is the biggest disadvantage as far as foreign teachers are concerned. Also, many foreigners object to giving Chinese officials any more information than is absolutely necessary. They are afraid of how that information might be used.

Monday, November 24

I lectured on transcendentalism to my class. After that, I went to see Zhu Zheng. Wanda had succeeded in getting about seventy tickets to the exhibition, and I wanted him to know about that. Zhu Zheng immediately invited me to his house. He was pleased because Chinese teachers had finally been granted permission to have foreign teachers in their homes without first seeking written permission from the authorities. Zhu Zheng was exercising his new right by inviting me to his house. We used my visit to talk about the lack of freedom and privacy in the lives of the Chinese people. We talked about politics and elections. We talked about Chinese schools. Zhu Zheng is a perceptive man as well as a dedicated teacher, but he cannot afford to oppose the system. Such behavior is far too dangerous. He must work slowly, bringing about improvements where he can without alienating officials.

Zhu Zheng talked briefly about the Gang of Four. Our talk was timely; the trial began last week. As far as most foreigners are concerned, the trial appears to be a great propaganda venture for the government. After the trial, or because of it, the government hopes to put the Cultural Revolution into the background and at the same time gain psychologically in the form of motivation toward modernization on the part of the Chinese people. On the other hand, the Chinese people have become accustomed to blaming everything wrong with their society on the Cultural Revolution. I doubt that they can let go of what is probably the most effective scapegoat they have ever had. As for the Gang of Four, indictments were brought against them last week. The Gang of Four is being charged with persecuting more than half a million people, approximately thirty-five thousand of whom died as a result. The indictments are intended particularly for Jiang Qing, the widow of Mao Zedong, along with six others from what is known as the Lin Biao clique. The press has already pronounced them guilty, and consensus among both foreigners and Chinese seems to be that they will be judged guilty in court and sentenced, although opinion also indicates that they will not be sentenced to death. If such proves to be true, one can surmise that they will be more valuable as political prisoners than as corpses.

Tuesday, November 25

I lectured on transcendentalism to another class. The students in class three seemed more equipped to handle the abstractions involved than Monday's class had been. I learned on Monday that I would have to make adjustments, and my students in class three profited from more details, explanations, and illustrations. They went away satisfied. After class I asked Su Guifen about accompanying me to Xidan Street to purchase some Chinese trousers. We agreed on Thursday afternoon as the time to go, but little did I realize I already had a commitment for Thursday afternoon. Thursday will be Thanksgiving Day in America, and on Thursday afternoon Wanda and I will be having Thanksgiving dinner in the home of the Lenahans. Wallace Lenahan is an attaché who works out of the American embassy. The trip to Xidan Street will have to be rescheduled.

The trial of the Gang of Four continues. On Friday evening millions of Chinese people viewed a pre-taped program in which Jiang Qing and others were presented their indictments. The trial is being covered on radio and television. The government is concerned that the masses watch the first real attempt to display a legal system which will, as the Chinese people have been told, guarantee fair representation under the law for everyone. Although the courtroom manner of the judges and the prosecutors is reminiscent of a Perry Mason episode, the Chinese people are obviously impressed. They have never before seen such a display of legality, and they are hopeful that the establishing of a legal system will really serve as the beginning of fair representation under the law.

Wednesday, November 26

On Tuesday night I had stayed up late grading essay exams. At 8:00 a.m. on Wednesday I turned the essays back to class four. I then lectured on transcendentalism, and they responded enthusiastically. After class they gathered around my desk with questions. They were excited because they realized they were learning. As soon as I could, I slipped away and went to my office. I had acquired another two dozen tickets for the exhibition, and I was eager to tell Zhu Zheng. Because Zhu Zheng was not available, I gave the tickets to Qi Wenqin. Combined with those I had given Zhu Zheng earlier, we had about ninety tickets, but we were still short of enough for all students and teachers in Grade 77 to attend the exhibition. Another fifteen or twenty would have been enough, but I was told that I could have no more. Most of my students will be able to attend, and they are happy about that.

On the way to the institute in the morning, Jeanne Lonnoy had asked if I might be interested in returning to the compound at 10:30 instead of waiting until noon. She could tell that I was tired. I had graded the last few papers for Wednesday's class while riding in the car, and had recorded the grades shortly before reaching the institute. My students did not know that I had come so close to the deadline. Exhausted from lecturing and grading exams, I went home at 10:30 to rest.

Thursday, November 27

The trial goes on, and there is no doubt that Jiang Qing will be convicted. Surely she thinks the world has caved in about her. She either refuses to answer the questions directed at her, or contends that she does not know the answers. Evidence is piling up rapidly to the effect that she is guilty of the charges presented in the indictment. On Wednesday, November 26, a member of the Gang of Four turned against her and testified that she was the one responsible for a plot to topple the late premier, Zhou Enlai, and China's strong man, Deng Xiaoping, by making an insinuating report to Chairman Mao about them. Also on Wednesday Wang Hongwen, another member of the Gang of Four, turned state's witness. He told the court, in Jiang Qing's presence, that the Gang of Four met in October of 1974 to plot the defamation of Zhou and Deng, and that it was Jiang Qing who called them together for the purpose of preventing Deng from becoming first vice premier.

An outsider hardly knows what to make of the trial. I have surmised that Mao was senile and insecure in his dotage. He was apparently paranoid about being ousted and possibly assassinated. He set out to eliminate those who were attempting to usurp his power, and he had reason to be paranoid because a number of government officials and army generals realized that he was no longer capable of making rational decisions. In his efforts to save himself, Mao Zedong spawned the Cultural Revolution. He had been accepted as a god by some of the Chinese people, and he had reached that stage in his paranoia at which he had come to see himself as a god. As a god, he thought he could do no wrong. The result was that he divided those in power and threw China into ten years of hell. Yes, Mao Zedong himself engineered the Cultural Revolution.

Friday, November 28

Because it was Friday I finished my lectures (the fifth) on transcendentalism. I was pleased when, after class, one of my students stopped me in the hall and expressed her appreciation, as well as that of her classmates, for what she called my approach to teaching literature. By her comment I took it that she was referring to the fact that I use a philosophical approach, examining the ideas about which a writer writes and how he or she goes about expressing those ideas. The approach has always made sense to me. That is, I have always felt that essentially two things are worth looking for in a piece of literature: what a writer says and how he or she says it.

I decided that I would go to town and purchase some trousers. I went to Xidan Street accompanied by two of my students; I had never been there before. We visited in the department stores until we finally found trousers large enough for me, and I purchased them. We found an ice cream store and enjoyed a dish of ice cream. We wandered in the shops in Xidan Street and talked until my students had to return to the institute. The weather was nice, and I relished the sunshine. I had been grading papers for days, and because of that I especially enjoyed being in the streets. Being out on such a warm and beautiful day was gratifying, for I knew that Beijing would not see many more days of such weather. In the evening I returned to the compound feeling the best I had felt in many days.

Saturday, November 29

News from Foreign Agencies and Press (November 29, 1980) reports Friday's trial session in this way:

Chen Boda, a creator of the Red Sun cult around Mao Tse-tung, appeared in court Friday barely able to walk and admitted he ordered the persecution campaign against the late head of state Liu Shaoqi.

Chen, 76, the apparently ailing ideologue who reputedly acted as go-between linking the Gang of Four led by Mao's widow, Jiang

Qing, and the generals of the late defense minister Lin Biao, also confessed complicity on two other counts of persecution against party and state leaders.

He admitted he has responsibility in making use of a pamphlet found in Tianjin in 1967 as an excuse to go after the "bosses behind the scenes"— meaning leaders like Deng Xiaoping, Marshall Zhu De, Ye Jianying, and others. He also admitted approving a report falsely accusing former Vice Premier Lu Dingyi of rebellion and saying Lu should be "handed to the Red Guards for trial." (p. 1)

When the indictments were brought in, several days earlier, Chen was charged with persecuting 84,000 people in eastern Hebei Province, 2,955 of whom reportedly died. These charges were not brought up in Friday's court session, indicating that Chen will be back in court in the near future.

Sunday, November 30

Wanda and I went to Tiananmen Square to visit the Chairman Mao Memorial, but our trip was in vain. Lu Zhibao, who was supposed to have made the necessary arrangements, did not show up. It made little difference, for we found that the mausoleum is not open on Sundays. In the afternoon ten of my students showed up at the gate of the Friendship Hotel, and we bicycled with them to the Old Summer Palace. We looked at the ruins of what was once a grand palace, that is, before it was burned to the ground. We visited the museum there, and we took pictures of my students standing in front of some of the ruins. It was an unusual sight—something like the ruins of ancient Rome or ancient Greece. To me the ruins represented the grandeur that was once China. When we returned to the Friendship Hotel, a number of the students took packages containing Mao badges from their pockets and presented them to Wanda. They presented her with Mao badges of various shapes and colors; they obviously wanted to please her. I had announced in one of my classes that Wanda was interested in collecting Mao badges, and my students took advantage of the opportunity to make Wanda happy.

December

Monday, December 1

Mostly I graded exams, as I had done for several days. But two things happened that pleased me. First, while I was at school one of my students, Liu Liming, came to see me concerning her examination paper. We went through her paper word by word, and I explained what was wrong with her paper as we went along. She was pleased that a teacher would show so much interest in her work. It took us at least an hour to go through the exam, but when we were done she was happy. She learned much in the hour we spent together.

Second, Tan Luying came to help me with my Chinese lesson. As it turned out, she was unusually talkative and we never got to the lesson. Tan wanted to talk about Chinese young people, and about friendships between teachers and students. What she was trying to tell me was that I should not be disappointed when my students do not meet my expectations as friends. She seemed overly concerned about my feelings, and I explained to her that I had learned much about student-teacher relationships in the twenty-one years I had been teaching. I explained to her that I had long ago stopped expecting the same kind of friendship from my students that I expected from my colleagues and neighbors. Realizing that I was realistic about such things, she changed the topic. She talked about her family, and she talked about the United States. She talked for more than an hour, and when she stopped I was ready to return to the compound to grade another batch of exam papers.

Tuesday, December 2

While preparing for work in the morning, I listened to a Voice of America broadcast on the radio. What I heard was interesting. According to the broadcast, Chinese educators and government officials met in Beijing a few days ago and agreed that modernization cannot take place unless Chinese education improves much more rapidly than it has. The matter poses a challenging dilemma, one about which I have talked with some of the teachers at the institute. In short, the intellectuals, those who could change the system, are afraid to make decisions that might result in their being criticized. They remember very well what happened to intellectuals during the Cultural Revolution. They remember what happened to the schools, and they will not subject themselves to punishment, harassment, and degradation again. As my Chinese colleagues tell me, Chinese education is in transition along with the country, and they prefer to wait and see what happens before they identify with any change or policy concerning change. The result is that the entire system of education is drifting. The gains that must be made in education for the country to modernize are being postponed, and modernization is consequently being pushed further and further into the future. Sooner or later someone must take a chance. Someone must gamble rather than play a safe game. If they do not, those officials who met in Beijing the other day will meet again in the future and conclude that modernization did not come because the system of education did not change.

Following my morning class I talked with a number of Chinese teachers. I talked with Zhu Zheng about shipping household effects home at the end of the year, about spring vacation, and about other things. I talked with Lu Zhibao about my contract, which should have been signed days ago, and about our aborted visit to Mao's tomb. I talked to Qi Wenqin about when I might plan on going home at the end of the year, about the schedule for the spring semester, and about my assessment of what to expect in the way of China's relations with the United States while the Reagan administration is in office. In the evening, Wanda and I went to see a nine-act play entitled *A Cloud Who Waits for the Return of Her Husband*. Based on Chinese myth, the play was interesting, but Wanda and I were both glad when we could return to the compound and retire. In China even theater can be tiring.

Wednesday, December 3

After class, two of the Chinese teachers, Shao Jingfeng and Cheng Yu, came to my office. They wanted to talk about their students as well as about their roles as teachers in the English department. They began by explaining that their students seemed bored, and that their students were missing class in great numbers. At first they pretended they did not understand what was wrong, but eventually they admitted they were bored with what they were teaching. They had been studying such things as the education of Navajo Indian children. We talked about the controversy that had recently arisen in every meeting held by the Chinese teachers in the department—whether they should spend their time acquiring greater proficiency in the English language or whether they should spend their time learning about methodology in teaching. They argue over the issue, so I have been told, every time the teachers meet, but they never resolve the issue. They merely argue. I spent an hour or so talking to Shao Jingfeng and Cheng Yu about teacher training, and about the necessity of having a structured approach to learning teaching methods, evaluating materials, and other such things.

Thursday, December 4

On the way to the institute, early in the morning, I witnessed an accident. A young boy was hit by a city bus. He looked to be ten or twelve years old, and he was obviously in great pain. He grabbed at his leg as he limped to the curb. Once there he collapsed. Our car did not stop; the driver did not so much as slow down. I wanted to examine the boy, and possibly to help him in some way, but our driver seemed not to be interested. As a foreigner, I could do nothing.

In the evening Wanda came home from work disappointed. She had suspected that something was wrong at the exhibition for some time, but she had not known what it was. On the day before her job was to end, she found out what was wrong. She learned that the construction company that had prepared the center for the exhibition had been guaranteed the contract before the bids were let. She also learned that the Americans who were responsible for setting up the exhibition had taken payoffs from the construction company receiving the contract. The payoffs were sizeable, and her faith in a number of the people she had been working with was shattered. I too was disappointed, for I had met and socialized with all of them. She also learned that a number of the people employed by the United States Department of Commerce to work at the exhibition were using embassy shipping privileges (avoiding customs inspection) to ship pieces of furniture and other private purchases to avoid paying duty. Wanda was glad that her job was ending, for she felt that she could not be comfortable with such a group of people.

Friday, December 5

In the morning Qi Wenqin came to see me and inquired whether I might write a letter to the officials at the institute stating my opinions concerning the future of Sino-American relations under the Reagan administration. The request was prompted by the fact that the government officials in Beijing, and the school officials at the institute, have been newly upset by a speech recently made in Singapore by Ray Cline, Reagan's Asian affairs advisor. To dismiss Cline's speech as merely insensitive would be a mistake; it was mindless. In his speech Cline said that the Carter administration had made a bad deal with China when relations were normalized at the beginning of last year. Cline said that in return for recognition of China the United States should have demanded that China return to civilized behavior, that China announce a policy of non-force toward Taiwan, and that China free its market forces and open up the country to the outside world. Dismissing China as too weak to be a worthwhile ally, Cline stated that the Reagan administration would have to review the present United States relationship to China. The Beijing government is upset over Cline's speech and expects problems ahead in Sino-American relations. As for Qi Wenqin's request, I can only express my viewpoint, for I do not represent any government or government agency.

In the afternoon I attended a tea party for freshmen at the institute. I was the target of hundreds of questions, on every imaginable subject. The students asking the questions seemed to enjoy themselves, and I had two hours of fun trying to answer their questions. I drank far too much tea, and I ate far too many sweets, but I enjoyed talking with the freshmen.

Saturday, December 6

Wanda and I were scheduled to be at the Chairman Mao Memorial Hall at 9:00 a.m. We would finally see the body of Chairman Mao. We met two of my students at Tiananmen Square. A crowd of four to five thousand had met to pay their respects, and it was not surprising to see many soldiers among them. For many military men Mao is still a great hero. The old generals who served under Mao will not let the younger soldiers forget that Mao was once a military hero. We filed past the glass-enclosed remains of the late chairman. A line formed on either side of the glass enclosure, and as we passed the body complete silence prevailed. We looked upon the remains of a man who had been deified, a man who had ruled China with an iron hand from the time of Liberation in 1949 until his death in 1976. Lying there under glass, he did not look much like a ruler. On the contrary, he looked small and insignificant. I wonder what China would be like today had the war for Liberation turned out differently. Mao Zedong kept China in a feudal state while the remainder of the world changed, and that his memorial is modeled on that of Abraham Lincoln may not be a fitting tribute to either man.

After we toured the Chairman Mao Memorial Hall we crossed Tiananmen Square and toured the Great Hall of the People. For this tour Chinese people pay forty *fen* (about U.S. 25¢); foreigners pay five *yuan*. In our case, the tour was worth what we paid. The Great Hall of the People, built in eleven months, is an impressive engineering feat. Besides containing thirty meeting halls, which amounts to one for each province, it contains an auditorium which seats ten thousand and a banquet room which seats and serves five thousand. The meeting rooms, or halls, are well furnished and decorated with arts and crafts from all provinces. The art alone was impressive enough to make our tour worthwhile.

In the afternoon Wanda and I visited the Evergreen People's Commune with a group of foreign experts from the Friendship Hotel. We visited two peasant dwellings with piles of cabbage stacked like cordwood outside the doors. We toured the nursery school and the kindergarten, where we were entertained by the children. We toured the commune hospital and examined the acupuncture room as well as the gynecology department. We toured large greenhouses where we were introduced to Chinese intensive agriculture. The mammoth greenhouses and hotbeds in which food is grown all winter long were impressive. In the evening we went to dinner with Ed and Gail Grejda at the Xinqiao Restaurant. It was the kind of evening that we would like to repeat now and then.

Sunday, December 7

We attended church for the first time since arriving in China. The Beijing Christian Church is located in Xidan Street. It contains a sanctuary seating about five hundred people, and I was surprised to see that at least four hundred of the seats were filled. I was also surprised to see that approximately half of the congregation consisted of young people, many of whom were of college age. When we entered, we were given hymn books printed in English. We sang from those while the Chinese people sang in their own language. The sermon was based on Matthew 10:35-45, and I expected that it would contain concessions necessary to practicing Christianity in a Communist country. I was wrong. A young

Chinese-American interpreted for us, and I was amazed that the same sermon could have been preached in almost any Christian church in America. The sermon was direct, sincere, and honest. It was the story of Christ's being crucified that man might be saved from sin. I had heard the story many times in American churches.

In the afternoon Wanda and I went Christmas shopping at the Friendship Store. When we grew tired of shopping, we went to the International Club and enjoyed hot tea while waiting for the Friendship Bus to make its evening run from the Friendship Store to the Friendship Hotel. It had been a good day, and we were looking forward to early retirement.

Monday, December 8

Wanda and I awakened to our first snow in Beijing. The streets were icy, and on the way to the institute I saw many bicycle wrecks as well as stranded buses. Because the trip took two hours, twice as long as usual, I arrived an hour late for my 8:00 a.m. class. Nevertheless, when we in the car arrived I met with my class for fifty minutes and talked about Thoreau. Then I met with He Jiang, dean of the English department, for a conference. I wanted to talk with him about the system of education in China in general and about the program at Second Foreign Language Institute in particular. I wanted to find out whether he had a realistic understanding of the problems involved in both cases, and after we had talked for a while I was pleasantly surprised to find that he did. He Jiang was open and candid. He was frank about the failures of Chinese education as he understood them. He was also frank about causes for the failures as well as possible cures. He admitted that government bureaucracy has a stranglehold on education, and that little improvement will be made until that stranglehold is broken. He agreed with me that students spend too much time studying Communist ideology and too little time studying the essential subjects.

I was also open and frank with Dean He Jiang. I was critical of the system in general and of inefficient scheduling of classroom time in particular. I criticized the way foreign experts are recruited and suggested alternatives. All in all, I think Dean He Jiang and I developed a healthy respect for each other. At least he learned that I am interested in educating the youth of China.

The news bulletin *News from Foreign Agencies and Press* (December 4,

1980) contains an article which begins: "China bluntly warned President Elect Reagan not to resume official links with Taiwan Wednesday, and indicated it might sever diplomatic relations if the incoming administration ignored Peking's advice" (p. 1). The Chinese government is still angry over Ray Cline's speech in Singapore. Since his speech, Cline has apparently suggested that Reagan might send representatives to Taiwan to strengthen United States-Taiwan relationships. Another article in the same paper begins: "Dutch Ambassador Jan Kneppelhout was summoned to the Foreign Ministry in Beijing today to receive a stiff Chinese protest over the Dutch government's decision to permit the sale of two submarines to Taiwan" (p. 2). The same article ends with: "Some diplomatic sources in Peking suggested the strong reaction of the Chinese to the Dutch submarine sales could also be an oblique warning to the United States of Peking's official displeasure if there was an increase in American arms sales to Taiwan" (p. 3).

Problems between the United States and the People's Republic of China are growing. Today I released my letter to Qi Wenqin, who immediately took it to school officials. I tried to make a case for why I think the United States and China need each other, and consequently for why I think the Reagan administration will take seriously the possibility of even stronger ties with China.

Tuesday, December 9

For two hours class number two and I looked at Thoreau's "Life without Principle," but two hours was not enough time. For more than an hour I answered questions, and when I looked at their books I discovered that my students had devoured Thoreau's essay. They had examined every word closely, had marked their books extensively, and had formulated provocative questions based on what they had read. For them, as well as for me, class was a pleasure.

I met with Gong Weiling, a student from class one. She had many questions about Emerson and Thoreau, questions which took me more than half an hour to answer. I also spent an hour or so with Qi Wenqin going through a document prepared by the Ministry of Education proposing a loan from the World Bank for the purpose of upgrading education in China. Qi Wenqin had translated the document into English and asked me to work with her in drafting a final copy. I found the document pleasing because it stressed education in the humanities as opposed to education in the sciences. It singled out jurisprudence and economics for special emphasis. I was encouraged that someone in the Chinese bureaucracy was finally examining priorities in education.

In the evening Wanda and I went to see a Beijing Opera (Peking Opera). As our first exposure to Beijing Opera, we saw *The Fourth Son of the Yang Family Visits His Mother*, one of the "forbidden" operas. It was the first performance of *The Fourth Son of the Yang Family Visits His Mother* since the Gang of Four outlawed it during the Cultural Revolution. The Chinese people loved the performance. They applauded enthusiastically. Although one needed to know both the story of the Yang family and the Chinese language to appreciate the opera fully, we knew neither. But we enjoyed the elaborate costuming, the acting, the singing, and most of all the instrumental music. I have been told by my students that opera does not appeal to young people in China, and that it does not was made evident in this case by the lack of their presence. Foreigners supposedly do not care for it because they do not understand it. I concur with the latter part of the statement—that they do not understand.

Wednesday, December 10

My students were in a good mood. They were excited about Thoreau, and they were full of questions. I lectured for an hour, and then we looked at Thoreau's "Life without Principle." The class proved to be as excited about Thoreau as had the classes which came before it. Qi Wenqin, who is always concerned about my welfare, came by the office to talk about final examinations. She asked whether I might consider giving no final since my students confront about eight exams in their other courses. I agreed to postpone or suspend all exams until the spring term. For me, not giving exams means about sixty to seventy fewer hours of paper grading. I gladly accepted her offer.

In the evening Billy Vigneault came to visit. Billy has been very helpful in matters of exchanging money. Since his job at the exhibition is over, Billy and his Polish wife, Ella, will leave Beijing on Saturday. They will spend two or three days in Hong Kong before returning home to the United States for Christmas. Billy's next assignment is in Saudi Arabia, and he hopes to find a way of avoiding it. He wants to return to Bonn, Germany, in his work for the United States Department of Commerce. He previously spent four years there and wants to return. As for Ella, she wants her husband to stop traveling. Ella wants to settle down, own a home, and have children.

Thursday, December 11

We awakened to snow, the second snow of the week. As before, the streets were icy, and traveling to work took two hours. On the way to work I watched many bicycles fall. In most cases the bicyclist would get up, kick his bicycle, remount, and go on his way. As I watched this happen repeatedly it reminded me of the history of the Chinese people. I had the impression that the entire history of China was being acted out by the bicyclists in the two hours it took us to travel to the institute. As one bicyclist after another fell, I observed what appeared to be dogged determinism, but I saw very little use of ingenuity or foresight to prevent the falls.

The weather did not improve. At 11:30 a.m., I looked up Jeanne Lonnoy and we took a car back to the compound. In spite of the weather, at 2:00 p.m. Wanda and I took the Friendship Bus to Wangfujing Street. We visited several shops, all of which were crowded. The weather was bitter cold, and everywhere we went a few thousand more Chinese were spitting and blowing their noses on the sidewalks and floors. I had never seen so many people without handkerchiefs, but I had been told that handkerchiefs were usually considered bourgeois. We spent a cold and depressing afternoon in Wangfujing Street. When 5:00 came, we were happy to board the Friendship Bus and head for home.

Friday, December 12

Since coming to teach at Second Foreign Language Institute, I had often wondered about boy-girl relationships on campus. On one of my trips to Wangfujing Street, I had asked Su Guifen whether she had a boyfriend. She confided in me that she had a boyfriend, but she asked that I not tell anyone because students are forbidden to date. She also confided in me that she believed in love and would eventually marry someone she loved. She knows she is not conforming to Chinese customs and beliefs when she advocates and practices such things. As she explained, the Chinese people do not marry for love. Love plays little or no part in the typical husband-wife relationship. As for marriage, it is an acceptable arrangement for getting on in Chinese society. Marriage partners are usually friends of the family and therefore must meet family approval. The test of marrying anyone who is not a friend of the family lies in convincing the family that the proposed marriage partner is worthy and industrious. Admittedly, from a practical standpoint such arrangements have their advantages in that divorce is rare in China. On the other hand, Chinese married couples expect little of what is known in the West as marital bliss.

I asked Jeanne Lonnoy about the fact that dating is not allowed among college students, and she explained that not dating is one of the conditions a student agrees to when he or she is admitted to college. I also asked her about premarital sex and pregnancies that occur out of wedlock. As for premarital sex, she explained, there is little. As for pregnancies that occur out of wedlock, they are terminated by abortion. Furthermore, such abortions are performed at great expense to the pregnant woman in that she is allowed nothing to kill pain that might accompany the abortion. Suffering pain is part of the humiliation to which she is subjected; it is a lesson to her as well as an example to others. I have noted that a striking difference exists in maturity between American and Chinese young people, and although there are likely other reasons for it, the distance between the sexes maintained by Chinese young people is surely a contributing factor.

While sitting in the restaurant of the Beijing Hotel in the afternoon, I thought of Joseph Conrad's story "Outpost of Progress." I have thought of Conrad's story several times since coming to Beijing, and likely because it is a story about two men who leave a highly developed civilization to live in a wilderness and what they do in an effort to retain their civilized ways. Like these men, foreigners in China cultivate little habits they brought to China with them in order not to lose touch with their sense of what it is they consider to be civilizing. For example, Ed Grejda has the sports section of his hometown paper mailed to him every week, so he can sit and read it each Sunday morning as he was accustomed to doing in Pennsylvania. As for Wanda and me, we have our nightcap every evening before retiring, just as we did at home in Texas. These little habits vary from foreigner to foreigner, but all foreigners seem to cultivate them as links with the past, as links with home, and as links with what they consider to be a more advanced civilization. Such habits are merely psychological props, strategies necessary in adjusting to a culture very different from one's own.

Saturday, December 13

Radio Beijing carried an interview in English. From the University of Pittsburg, the man being interviewed was a teacher at a university in Shanghai. I was curious about how he would answer the questions asked of him, and I was curious about how politically sensitive the questions might be. I was also curious concerning how his teaching experience in China did or did not correspond to mine. When the interview ended, I was convinced that the professor from Pittsburg had been candid, and in that respect he may have made a contribution toward improving conditions for foreign teachers in China.

The teacher being interviewed was asked about culture shock, and his response was that all Americans who come to China to teach go through it. He also explained that he and his wife attempted to reduce the effects of culture shock by attending classes in Chinese language and culture before coming to China. He explained, however, that their daughter had suffered greatly, particularly as a consequence of attending a Chinese school. He was asked about socializing, about social life in general. He observed that socializing was difficult because his Chinese colleagues were reluctant to socialize with foreigners, and especially with Americans. As he pointed out, they suffered in the Cultural Revolution. They are still aware, he said, that such a thing could happen again. They are afraid. They are courteous and congenial, but they know that to fraternize with foreigners is to take a big risk.

The professor from Pittsburg teaches American literature. The interviewer asked him to comment on his students, and to compare them to students in the United States. His response was that Chinese students are more dedicated, that they take education more seriously, and that they work harder. He also pointed out that teaching them literature is difficult because they are completely ignorant of the cultural and intellectual history of the Western world. His observations about this, as well as about most other things, concurred with mine. For thirty years China isolated itself, but that isolation did not merely close the Chinese people off from the modern world. In those thirty years the history of Western civilization was completely eradicated from the minds of the Chinese people. Those who once knew about the West have largely died off, and among the younger people only abysmal ignorance exists. The experience of the professor from Pittsburg very closely resembled my experience, and when his interview ended, I was pleased he had shared with me his experiences as a teacher in China.

Sunday, December 14

Last Sunday we went to church in Xidan Street with the American linguist Kenneth Pike and his wife. Professor Pike was in Beijing to lecture on linguistics at First Foreign Language Institute. Today we went to church with Clara Roesh, a conductor from New York. Clara is here to conduct Chinese performances of Western operas. She will go home in January, but we hope to attend one of her performances before she goes.

The church in Xidan Street is exciting. I am impressed by the sincerity of Chinese Christians. Today we heard another sermon that could have been preached in any of thousands of pulpits throughout America. It was a sermon filled with enthusiasm, motivated by sincere belief in the urgency of living a Christian life. The sermon contained no concessions to political concerns; on the contrary, it subordinated everything else to the message that Christ was crucified and the consequent importance of being a Christian.

Presently Beijing has three churches. A city of eight million, it contains one Catholic and two Protestant churches. The church in Xidan Street is the newest of the three. It opened its doors about the time Wanda and I arrived in China, and this morning almost all the five hundred seats were filled. The Chinese people are curious about religion. It was outlawed during the Cultural Revolution, but in 1978 the government took a more liberal stand. Some Chinese people are examining the possibilities concerning religion. But most remain both cautious and afraid.

The history of Christianity in China is intriguing. At the height of the Christian missionary movement, less than one percent of the Chinese population was Christian. Then came Liberation, followed by the Cultural Revolution. Christians declined in numbers; religion of all kinds was outlawed. My students are typical of their generation, and most of them make clear that they believe in no religion. In fact, they dismiss religion as nonsense and superstition. At the same time, I have noticed that they are intellectually curious when I present them with ideas about religion in my lectures. They respond verbally the way they have been taught to respond concerning matters of religion, but they have a sense of honesty and intellectual curiosity that will not let them be satisfied with what they have been taught.

As for the church in Xidan Street, announcements this morning were encouraging. For example, the church will celebrate Christmas with Christmas services. The church will conduct Bible-study classes throughout 1981. Outlawed and burned during the Cultural Revolution, Bibles are once again being printed in China, a fact which excites the pastor at the church in Xidan Street. Finally, one of the announcements made this morning came as a great surprise to me, for I expected that such announcements would be several years in coming. The announcement was that Nanking Seminary will open its doors and begin classes in February. Those in the congregation interested in preparing themselves for the Christian ministry were encouraged to see the pastor and make arrangements for taking the entrance exam. Considering what happened during the Cultural Revolution, Chinese Christians are acting boldly. They know that the price they may be called on to pay for their boldness is no less than their lives, but the minister who preached this morning, Qi Tingduo, did it with a confidence exceeded only by his winsome smile.

Monday, December 15

I lectured to my students on Walt Whitman. The second hour of class I spent talking about such poems as "There Was a Child Went Forth," "I Hear America Singing," and "Give Me the Splendid Silent Sun." My students and I looked at the poems together, and I illustrated my generalizations by drawing examples from the poems themselves. I talked about Whitman's use of grammatical parallels, and about his use of the device known as a catalog. I talked about the line as a unit of both sound and sense. I talked in general about his free-verse prosody.

More than the ideas of Thoreau, the ideas of Whitman strike a chord of familiarity in my students. After class one young woman came to me and pointed out that much of what Whitman advocates is synonymous with the philosophy of Karl Marx. I could not disagree; the two contain some striking similarities. But I pointed out to her that some basic differences also exist. Gong Weiling, the young woman, had obviously read her Whitman assignment closely. She explained that she had found Whitman's poems to be the most interesting and beautiful poems she had ever read. "Although Whitman failed in his attempt to appeal to the American masses in his own time," she said, "he addresses the conditions of life in China at the present." She was impressed by Whitman's desire to be poet of the masses.

I announced to my students that Wanda and I would attend church in Xidan Street on Sunday and that anyone caring to accompany us was welcome. To see if any of my students accept the invitation will be interesting, and if they do, to see which ones accept will be even more interesting.

Tuesday, December 16

On the way to the institute, Lisa Wichser observed that in the heavy fog of the morning Beijing looked like a city at war, a bombed-out city. She made the observation while we were passing a construction site near the zoo. It was an apt observation. Anyone riding through the streets for the first time at that hour would have no way of knowing the piles of rubble found at construction sites throughout the city had anything to do with construction. Neither could they distinguish that shells of buildings were actually under construction as opposed to having been destroyed. Yes, it was an apt description, for in early morning Beijing looked very much like a city that had recently suffered the ravages of war.

Recent news concerning a shake-up in the government seems to be related to the trial of the Gang of Four. Before the trial, Mao Zedong's widow, Jiang Qing, released a statement to the effect that the government in Beijing could not afford to go through with the trial because too many people in the government were in danger of being implicated, including some of the highest officials. At the time, it appeared that the Chinese people viewed her statement as no more than an effort to save herself. Near the end of the first week of the trial, surprisingly enough, the newspaper *People's Daily* and Radio Beijing (Radio Peking) both announced that Party Chairman Hua Guofeng will retire when the People's Congress meets next summer. The trial of the Gang of Four could turn out to be more significant than anyone in either the East or the West has imagined. It could turn out to be a trial of the Chinese government. Ironically, the

Chinese government appears to be confronting its own Watergate scandal, if not something worse. The extent of the scandal has not been revealed to the people, but if the trial continues, protecting those involved in atrocities committed during the Cultural Revolution may prove difficult.

Wednesday, December 17

The day was exciting, but not so much because anything exciting happened. Rather the excitement came in the form of information. For example, I was told after class that the vice president in charge of construction in Beijing had been dismissed from his position. I could not help but wonder whether his dismissal was related to the trial of the Gang of Four.

After my morning class I talked with Cheng Yu. When her father died during the Cultural Revolution, he was vice chairman of the People's Congress. Before that, he was a general in Mao's army. But prior to being a general in Mao's army he was a general in Chiang Kai-shek's army. Cheng Yu's father met Mao in a secret meeting that took place in Shanghai in 1946, at which time Mao shared with Cheng Yu's father plans for Liberation, which finally took place in 1949.

Through her father Cheng Yu and her family have been acquainted with the government, and the people in it, for many years. She knows the story of the government from inside, but at the present time she has little confidence the government will remain stable. She confided in me that the Chinese people generally lack confidence in the stability of the government. Like Cheng Yu, they can say little about what they think except among themselves, and even that is dangerous.

Cheng Yu told me about an incident that took place at Second Foreign Language Institute when she was a student there. She made the mistake of telling some of her classmates that Jiang Qing was a dancer in Shanghai before becoming Mao's wife. For that revelation Cheng Yu was incarcerated at the school. She has a story to tell, but she does not know how much of it to tell me. She knows that I would like to work with her in writing that story, but she is afraid for herself and her family. She is presently weighing the possibility, trying to determine how much of the story can be told without endangering her own well-being as well as that of her family. She will likely decide that the risks are too great, but I hope she will take the risks because case studies are needed to document the maze of abstractions and generalizations the West has been given concerning recent Chinese history, particularly that of the Cultural Revolution.

A rumor is about that the *yuan* will soon be devalued. Shops and stores are filled with buyers, and foreign experts are concerned over what devaluation might do to their incomes. Another rumor is that the *yuan* will soon be allowed to float in the world money market. If that happens, it may lose more than half of its value. That China has problems with inflation is not a rumor, but what inflation will do to a controlled economy remains to be seen.

Wanda found a new job today. Tomorrow she begins as secretary to a firm that is scheduled to begin construction of a large hotel located between the city and the airport. The hotel, she was told, is to be modeled after the Hyatt-Regency in Dallas, Texas. Construction plans call for the most elaborate and sophisticated hotel in all of China.

Thursday, December 18

The trial of the Gang of Four has been postponed for at least four days. Explanations in the press are that the government wants to make sure the trial does not result in reprisals against Hua Guofeng. On the other hand, speculation is that Hua Guofeng is not happy about the idea that he will soon retire. When Hua Guofeng's coming retirement was announced, the front page of *People's Daily* carried an extensive article calling for purging the government of the old guard, of those people in the government who were appointed by Mao. The timing of the release of the article will increase doubts among the Chinese people concerning the stability of their government. Calls in the press for purging the government have come before, but this time the call came when confidence in the government was already low. Concern over government stability has already led to what is referred to in Beijing as the biggest Chinese migration in the history of China. Chinese people are fleeing to the West in every way they can and for every reason they can. They are finding study abroad to be a particularly suitable way of escaping China. The trial of the Gang of Four, if it leads to implicating government officials, could also lead to a tremendous power struggle, and such a struggle could be catastrophic for the Chinese people.

Friday, December 19

Rumors concerning devaluation of Chinese currency remain in the air. Estimates pertaining to the amount of devaluation range from 50 to over 100 percent. Afraid of the effects of such rumors, the government has repeatedly denied it has any plans for devaluation. In the meantime, prices in Beijing are rising rapidly, as they are elsewhere in China. Whether Chinese currency is devalued or not, the government will have to cope with the spiraling cost of inflation in some way.

Tan Luying came to my office, and we studied Chinese. Lu Zhibao came for advice concerning what to do in preparing for his trip to America to study at Georgetown University. Qi Wenqin came, and from her I requested an interpreter to accompany Wanda and me to the theater on Tuesday evening. Zhu Zheng came and asked if there was anything he might do for me. Cheng Yu came and presented me with a Christmas card. I presented Christmas cards to each of them. I also presented to Tan Luying a copy of *Weeds and Wildflowers*, a thin volume of poems I had published in 1975. When Shao Jingfeng came, I talked with her about housing and religion. She had heard in a report on television that the recently completed high-rise apartment buildings along the main street in Beijing are unoccupied because of engineering flaws. According to the report, electricity and water supplies are inadequate, the problem of garbage disposal was never considered, and the buildings were not designed to accommodate the thousands of people who are supposed to live in them. Whatever the reasons, some of the buildings completed six months ago are still not occupied.

As for religion, I talked with Shao Jingfeng about the experiences Wanda and I have had in the church in Xidan Street. Her response was twofold. First, she said she failed to understand how America could be the most advanced country in the world and at the same time one of the most religious. How Americans could accomplish so much and believe in superstitions at the same time, she told me, remains a mystery to the Chinese people. Second, she indicated that she would like to visit the church with us and see for herself what happens when "people practice religion," but an obvious fear came to her voice as she said it. Although I told her we would be glad to have her accompany us to church, I doubt that she will ever go. Her fear is no less than that of my students.

Saturday, December 20

I visited the Bureau of Foreign Experts to pick up tickets for the

Chinese play *Teahouse*, the cast for which has recently returned from touring Germany. I had previously made arrangements for reserving the tickets, but someone bungled. The tickets had all been sold. Following my visit to the Bureau of Foreign Experts, however, the day went well. After lunch, Wanda, Gail Grejda, Bronwin Maas, and I took the Friendship Bus to the Friendship Store. From there we took a city bus to Xidan Street and went shopping. After dinner the Grejdas came to our apartment and played bridge. It was an enjoyable evening, and we made it last as long as we could. When the Grejdas went home, I read from the Bible, which has become a custom of ours. Then Wanda and I went to bed.

Sunday, December 21

My cold, which had been nagging at me for several days, was worse. In spite of my being ill, two of my students were supposed to meet Wanda and me at the church in Xidan Street, and I was determined that I would not deny them their first opportunity to attend a church service. As it turned out, I stood at the church entrance for half an hour waiting for the arrival of my students; I was too cold to stay any longer. As I learned later, they had gone to the wrong church. When they realized they were at the wrong church, they had made their way to the Xidan Street church, but managed to arrive only ten minutes before the service ended.

The Christmas service in the church in Xidan Street was filmed by a Canadian television company. The church had been beautifully decorated with poinsettias, and at the front of the church stood a large and elaborately decorated Christmas tree. The church was filled, and people were standing in the aisles. I was pleased to see that a large number of those attending the Christmas service were of college age. Pastor Qi preached his first Christmas sermon in twenty years with tears of joy in his eyes. He preached on the story in Matthew of the three wise men and their visit to the manger in Bethlehem. "That star," he said, "should be the star of China." I was moved by the sermon, and I was pleased that once again I heard no concessions because of the fact the church had been closed for twenty years. I was glad to be present at the first Christmas service held in the Xidan Street church in twenty years. I felt that I was participating in one of the most significant events in modern Chinese history.

Monday, December 22

My cold had grown worse from standing in the weather at the entrance to the church. I was miserable, but I decided that I would teach my class anyway. As I had planned, I lectured on tendencies and trends in modern American literature. Although I knew much of what I said would fly over the heads of my students, I reasoned that I had to begin somewhere and fill in as we studied American literature for the remainder of the year. After class I was presented with Christmas presents by Qi Wenqin and by some of my students.

I returned to our apartment in the compound and began writing letters. In a short time the phone rang. Tony Trimarchi, a teacher from Syracuse, New York, called to say that he was bringing a young Chinese man to see me. Although I did not feel like talking, I thought the matter might be urgent. As it turned out, the young man and I talked for about two hours. We talked about efforts he had made to enter a number of American universities. He had written to more than a dozen but had heard from none of them. When I asked him about writing follow-up letters, he reminded me that each postage stamp for sending letters abroad cost him a day's wages.

We also talked about his family and the Cultural Revolution (or rather we whispered because of his fear that we were being overheard). He told me how his family suffered because of being Christians. He explained that one of his uncles was tortured to death. He whispered slowly and cautiously, afraid he would be found out and reported. He was especially afraid he would be punished for talking with a foreigner about religion. All of the older members of his family, he said, have advised him not to apply to foreign universities, not to talk about religion, not to associate with foreigners, and especially not to visit a church. They have cautioned him that a sudden shift in government policy could prove embarrassing, that his activities and acquaintances could turn out to be extremely dangerous. In spite of warnings by his family, he persists in going his own way. I think he believes that the New Testament he carries in his pocket will protect him. I admire him for his willingness to take risks in hopes of living a better life.

Tuesday, December 23

It was the day of the Christmas party for Grade 77. I had managed to borrow and copy a tape of Christmas carols. I had also managed to borrow a Christmas tree from Gail Grejda, who had purchased it for a Christmas party at the International School. My students had pushed desks aside and decorated two classrooms. They had also duplicated copies of Christmas carols, some of which I had given them. When time for the party came, students gathered in great numbers into one room. With Patrick Cassidy leading, we sang carols. I gave a short speech on Christmas in America, after which I read for them "The Night before Christmas." The school supplied us with large wicker baskets filled with sunflower seeds, peanuts, and candy. Because the water had been turned off, we had no hot water with which to make tea. When the party began, we could not burn the lights on the Christmas tree because the electricity had been turned off. Much to my surprise, the electricity came on about an hour and a half after the party started.

From the outset I could tell that some of my students were greatly moved by the party. They took turns gathering around the Christmas tree, each fingering decorations on the tree as though the decorations had special meaning. Many of my students had never seen a Christmas tree before, and they were so impressed that they took turns standing in front of the tree to have their pictures taken. At 5:00 p.m., the students were still not ready to stop partying, but I had to return to the compound. My cold had finally caught up with me. My muscles had tightened up, and I was dizzy. When I reached the compound, I went directly to the health clinic. After that, I went home and went to bed.

Wednesday, December 24

On Wednesday morning, I got up to go to the institute as usual. My head ached, my sinuses were completely blocked, and my chest hurt. I soon realized that I could go nowhere. After calling Patrick Cassidy and asking him to notify Qi Wenqin and my students of my illness, I went back to bed. Furthermore, I stayed in bed all day.

When Wanda came home from work, we had decisions to make. We were scheduled to be at an embassy party at 4:30. We were also scheduled to leave on a three-day trip to Jinan at 9:00. I knew that I would not go to either, but I planned to convince Wanda that she should go without me. As it turned out, I only partially succeeded. We cancelled the Jinan trip, but Wanda went to the Christmas party at the embassy. When she returned, I convinced her that she should attend a Christmas Eve party at Ken and Bonnie Martin's apartment. I saw no reason for her to be miserable on Christmas Eve. I had no choice but be miserable. But she had a choice, and there was really nothing she could do for me. Wanda enjoyed Christmas Eve, and I was glad.

Thursday, December 25

When I arose in the morning, I felt that I would not stray far from my bed, but I was determined not to ruin another day. We had to make a decision whether we could be present at a Christmas dinner in the home of William Davis, a United States agricultural counselor. We opened our presents and had tea. Feeling better, I told Wanda to call the Davises and inform them that we would be to their house for dinner. I reasoned that I could dress warmly, and I expected that the counselor's house would be heated well.

The house was drafty and cold, but I was pleased to be out of our apartment. I was pleased to be in the company of other Americans for Christmas dinner. We talked with the Davises, with the counselor's assistant and his wife, and with a young man who is in Beijing under the auspices of the United Nations, supervising programs in Chinese schools sponsored by the United Nations. We spent much of our time talking about China, and I was particularly interested in what insights the others might have regarding the trial of the Gang of Four, the proposed devaluation of Chinese currency, the present status of Sino-American relations, and a number of other issues. They had no new insights, but when we sat down to dinner all agreed that we liked the Chinese people very much while deploring the political system. We also agreed that there will be no turning back now that the Chinese people are enjoying a few freedoms. Any attempt to turn back will meet great resistance from the people. The road ahead will not be easy. China will be anxiety-ridden for a long time to come.

Friday, December 26

My cold persisted. In the mail we received six or seven letters from home, including a card containing a poem by our good friend Marvin Ludwig, the president of Defiance College, in Defiance, Ohio. I plan to write him soon about the possibility of his finding someone to sponsor

Chinese students so that they might attend Defiance College. He will be sympathetic, and he will find someone to sponsor Chinese students if it is possible. I plan to write Bowling Green State University also. As for Baylor University, I hope the administration will consider entering into a teacher exchange program in addition to sponsoring Chinese students who wish to study at Baylor. China needs help in education, and I hope the missionary spirit of Southern Baptists will come through in the form of assistance toward educating Chinese young people. Such could be the most significant missionary effort any university has ever undertaken.

Ed and Gail Grejda came to our apartment, and we spent an enjoyable evening playing bridge. Ed and I won, and I was particularly happy about that because Wanda has often been disappointed in me for not taking my bridge playing more seriously.

Saturday, December 27

Wanda and I went to town to exchange a cap she had purchased for me a day earlier; the cap was too large. We visited the typewriter repair shop in Wangfujing Street to pick up a typewriter we had taken for repairs about two weeks earlier. We then purchased a few things at the Friendship Store before returning to the warmth of the Friendship Hotel. The wind in Wangfujing Street is very cold this time of year, and the shops are as cold inside as they are on the outside.

After lunch in the dining hall we checked to see if we had received any mail. As it turned out, Mary Margaret Stewart had sent us the newsletter of the English department at Baylor. More importantly, she had included a letter from the archivist and head of special collections in the Ohio University Library, Athens, Ohio. I was both surprised and pleased to find that the letter contained a proposal for establishing a J. R. LeMaster Collection at Ohio University Library consisting of my personal papers, correspondence, manuscripts, and other materials related to my being a writer. I need such an arrangement, for I have not done the job of preserving and storing I should have done over the years. Part of the reason, and perhaps much of it, is that I have never really come to view myself as a writer. Now that I have published ten books, three or four dozen critical articles, and approximately four hundred poems, I suppose I should accept the fact that I am a writer. But I am afraid of success. I am afraid that if I can ever sit down and say that I am a success I will never get up and work as though I had a world to conquer. I much prefer to work. I enjoy working. I receive no enjoyment from idleness.

In the evening Wanda and I went to the home of Evelyn Hydro for a Christmas party; Evelyn is secretary to William Davis. While there, I met and talked with Theodore Liu. He informed me that he is retiring from foreign service and will return to Washington, D.C., in three weeks. We talked about education in China, and about the fact that many Chinese students are applying to universities in the United States. Several universities, he explained, have each accepted one or two Chinese students. They plan to experiment with these before admitting more. They want some indication that Chinese students can do acceptable work in United States universities, and some indication that Chinese students can adjust to life in America.

I also talked with the United States press coordinator in Beijing. His remarks interested me. For example, he said that the trial of the Gang of Four, the current elections, the recent lifting of a government ban on religion, and a number of other liberalizing trends in China all constitute an effort to appeal to President Carter and to the government in Washington by addressing human rights issues advocated by the United States. "These are direct and somewhat extreme measures," said the press coordinator, "designed to win the favor of the U.S., and they have been taken for no other reason." Perhaps he is right. If so, I hope the overtures succeed. If such proves to be the case, President Carter will have made a sizeable contribution not only to China, but to the free world.

Sunday, December 28

We went to church in Xidan Street, where I expected to see a dramatic after-Christmas decline in attendance. I was surprised when I looked around the room and found that most of the seats were filled. Wanda and I were without Wen Yee Chin, our interpreter, so we could not understand the sermon. But we sang the hymns as usual, read the scripture passages for ourselves, and took communion. We were especially pleased to take communion because we had not done that since leaving Texas in August. After church the minister extended us a hearty handshake, and I was pleased because I had wanted to meet him. I would like to interview him. I am eager to talk with him about the church in China, about innovations taking place in worship, and about his expectations concerning the future of the church.

After church we took the typewriter back to the repair shop in Wangfujing Street. When I took it home from the repair shop on Saturday, I had hoped to catch up on some correspondence, but within an hour the typewriter had quit working again. I have discovered that having an electric typewriter repaired in China is probably the most difficult thing to do next to communicating. But I am more optimistic about communicating in the future than I am about typewriter repairing. At the rate the Chinese are learning English, I will not be surprised if China constitutes the world's largest English-speaking community outside the United States in another decade. Somehow I am not that optimistic about the rate at which they are learning to repair electric typewriters.

Monday, December 29

I got up and put on my peasant's underwear, which looks more like a jogging suit than it does underwear. It is at least as heavy as a jogging suit. Then I put on Chinese trousers, which I had purchased especially large to accommodate "layering." The trousers proved to be too small around the waist, but I wore them anyway. I went to the institute heavily dressed, and for the first time I wore a cap in my office as well as in the classroom. Staying well in Beijing in winter occupies much of one's time. In order to stay warm I left the institute early and returned to the compound. Once I had warmed myself, I went to the Bureau of Foreign Experts to claim a refund for the Jinan trip and to check on the possibility of seeing Lao She's play *Teahouse*. I was fortunate on both counts; I picked up my refund and tickets to the play. I am reading the play, which I find a bit confusing. It covers much Chinese history and involves a cast of almost sixty characters. I am eager to see it performed.

The battle with the typewriter continued. I recruited a Chinese-American by the name of Wu to communicate my message concerning the typewriter to the repairman. Because Wu speaks both Chinese and English well, I feel that I may be making progress in my efforts to have the typewriter repaired. Wu seems knowledgeable about such things, and he suggested that the problem might lie in the electrical converter necessary to convert 220 to 110 volts. The more I thought about his suggestion, the more I realized that he was likely right. Perhaps the battle with the typewriter will end soon.

Tuesday, December 30

On the way to the institute the morning before, the driver of the car in which I rode referred to me as "the famous professor" as soon as I sat down in the seat beside him. I had been puzzled by such a remark; I certainly had not solicited such behavior on his part. Further, I had not done anything of particular note. But while en route to the institute on Tuesday morning, Lisa Wichser commented that she had seen an article written by me in an "underground newspaper," as she called it. I had written no such article, but I recalled that I had written a letter for Qi Wenqin to take to the school officials. The letter was about why I thought the Chinese government should be optimistic concerning Sino-American relations under the Reagan administration. The school officials had apparently liked the letter; they had had it published in an information sheet, a newsletter, for cadres. The driver had apparently heard about my statement, or had read it for himself. At any rate, he knew a bit of English and wanted to talk. We talked about his family and mine. He had apparently liked my statement on what I thought to be the future of Sino-American relations, for he seemed very pleased to be talking with me. Lisa informed me that she had not liked the letter, so we dropped the matter.

The trial of Jiang Qing has ended. All that remains is the sentencing, and the prosecutor is calling for the death sentence. Prior to the trial the government seemed to be committed to almost any sentence, but two things have happened to affect that attitude. First, Hua Guofeng is expected to resign his position as chairman, and Jiang Qing may have done inestimable damage to a number of others presently in power. The friends and colleagues of Hua Guofeng will do all they can to silence her once and for all. Second, China is trying to appeal to the United States' stand on human rights, but what will President Reagan's position be? A clear signal from Washington could make a difference. I believe that a clearly stated document from Washington pertaining to human rights would take precedence over internal incidents or decisions in determining the fate of Jiang Qing. In the meantime China waits for the sentencing of Jiang Qing, the former first lady.

The institute sponsored a dinner and dance for its foreign teachers to celebrate the coming of the new year. Chinese officials and teachers attended, along with teachers from the United States, Canada, Japan, Egypt, England, Germany, France, Belgium, and a number of other countries. We enjoyed a typical Chinese dinner, with many courses, after which the floor was cleared for dancing. During and after dinner, I engaged a newly married Chinese teacher in conversation. I asked her about marriage customs in China. She told me that Chinese couples do not exchange rings; there is no wedding band. She also told me that the woman does not take the man's name at marriage; she retains her family name. Because both members of the married couple must work outside the home, she continued, they share house duties equally from the time of the marriage. If they do not live with their parents, she interjected with a smile, they frequently go home to visit and to enjoy a good meal.

Wednesday, December 31

My students responded enthusiastically to Stephen Crane's *Red Badge of Courage*. Before class Lu Zhibao had come by my office, and while he was visiting Su Guifen came. Because I wanted to give her a book, I asked her to return when I was not busy. I felt that she wanted to talk, that she had something to tell me, and as it turned out she did. She returned shortly after 11:00, but because a Chinese teacher was present Su Guifen could not talk freely. Cautiously, she informed me that she was leaving the department to participate in a cadre training program. Once she has undergone training in the program, she will become a teacher. When I asked about her decision, she said the alternative was to be appointed to China International Travel Service as a tour guide. Su Guifen taught in a middle school before coming to the institute, and she did not enjoy being a teacher. It was obvious that she had chosen the cadre training program because she considered it the lesser of two evils. She does not like the idea, but neither does she like the alternative. As the teacher visiting Diane Stark commented when Su Guifen had gone, "China has population problems, and a strictly controlled economy is necessary. The happiness of one person is really not very important."

January

Thursday, January 1

On New Year's Eve Wanda and I had gone to dinner at the Minzu Restaurant with Ed and Gail Grejda. After dinner we had retired to our apartment and talked until about 1:00 a.m. Engrossed in conversation, we were not aware of the new year when it came. On New Year's Day we slept late. Because the weather was extremely cold we ventured outside only for a short walk. In the afternoon we slept and read. We read *Time, Newsweek*, and the *Beijing Review*. The latter was full of information about the Gang of Four, and *Time* contained an article concerning the disappearance of Hua Guofeng. We also read mail from home. We had received half a dozen cards from family, friends, and colleagues. In the evening, we were joined at dinner by Rita Clarke, Eunice Stronacn, and the Grejdas. We had an enjoyable evening, and after dinner we returned to our apartment feeling good about the new year.

Friday, January 2

When I arrived at the institute I was in for a surprise. Fifteen of my best students had been pulled out of my classes and assigned to the cadre training program, and I was angry about that. When I walked into the classroom I met a strange mixture of my students. I immediately inquired of my students concerning the unusual mixture of faces as well as empty chairs. "There has been a shake-up," one student volunteered. I learned that most students had been assigned to new classes. I found it hard to believe that a week and a half before final exams my classes had been subjected to a reorganization, and especially that it had been carried out without my knowledge or consent. But it had been done and I could tell that my students liked it no better than I did. I still do not know what brought about the shake-up. When I asked Shao Jingfeng about it after class, she explained that students sometimes have difficulty getting along together, especially after they have studied together for a long time. Shao Jingfeng remained elusive and did not explain what had caused the shake-up. Neither did my students explain. Nor did the usual classroom manner prevail. They would no longer ask questions or talk in class. Something drastic had taken place since I left them two days earlier. Once again they seemed suspicious of each other. Whatever the ordeal to which they had been subjected, they were not talking, and before the class ended I realized that much of my work during the semester had been undone. I felt sorry for them. I wanted to strike back at the system because of the emphasis on indoctrination instead of education. I wanted to hit someone or something, but I knew that any effort on my part to strike back would only make life more difficult for my students. "I must wait," I told myself. "I must wait."

After lunch I tried to relax, but I could not. I took a walk and thought about my students. "Even this will pass," I told myself. Whatever brought on the shake-up, I was convinced, had political implications, and I was discouraged that what I had thought to constitute an improvement here and there had really changed nothing. Changing the system to emphasize education in place of indoctrination will be slow in coming. Too many people have vested interests; too many must serve the party and in doing so promote their own selfish interests.

Saturday, January 3

Because I had missed classes during my illness, and because of the rearrangement of classes, I knew that some of my students had missed lectures on Stephen Crane as well as lectures on background material for the twentieth century. I had some catching up to do, and with that in mind I scheduled classes for Saturday morning. I had been promised that my students would be free to attend my lectures on Saturday morning, but when I arrived at the institute, I found that one class had a reading lesson scheduled for the same time I was to lecture. At 10:00 a.m. I lectured on Stephen Crane, but I knew I would have to find a time to lecture to class three on background material for the twentieth century. The appropriate time for some of my students would be the next Friday, which would also be the last day of class for the semester.

Once we were in the classroom the lecture went well. My students were overcoming their "hangdog" look of the day before. They were eager to learn, and once again they asked questions. Upon leaving the institute at noon, I walked across campus with two girls from class five. I inquired regarding what had prompted the shake-up, and their reply was that a classroom was needed to accommodate a newly created teacher training course. I failed to see the logic in beginning a new teacher training course two weeks before the end of the semester. I also failed to see how a classroom would be freed. According to the girls, even the Chinese teachers view the whole thing as a big mistake. I hope that at the first of next week I will get to talk with some of the school officials about what is supposed to be accomplished.

The morning was strange in a number of ways. At class break, around eleven o'clock, I went to my office to smoke my pipe and have a cup of tea. When I unlocked the door and entered, I found Qi Wenqin standing over Patrick Cassidy's desk. I likely would not have thought much about finding her there, except that I had experienced a similar incident once before. On that occasion I had unlocked the door and entered to find a Chinese man going through the desks. On both occasions I had shown up when I was not supposed to be on campus, and in both cases I had little doubt concerning why the Chinese were in my office. Qi Wenqin, I realized, has an obligation to the school officials. She must act as intelligence gatherer and informer. Her position as leader for Grade 77 demands such behavior, and she is good at her job. She accepts her responsibilities completely.

Sunday, January 4

We planned to visit another church, one in Dongdan Street, but Wanda did not feel good when the time for church came. We stayed home to let her recuperate from a stomach problem, but by the middle of the afternoon she was feeling better and we took a walk. Walking was a pleasure because we had done little of it since the coming of cold weather. The walk made her feel much better. Once more I was reminded that a foreigner must be preoccupied with his or her health in China. Staying healthy is a daily concern demanding much time and energy. The Chinese are also preoccupied with staying healthy. Many have phobias about their health; they observe exact temperatures and dates for adding and discarding layers of clothing.

In the afternoon I also had a meeting with an eighty-year old Chinese man named Wang Jingxuan. Charles Wyvelle had arranged for him to meet with Morag and Don Stauffer, and with me. Wang Jingxuan had been educated in the United States as a Lutheran minister. After his education he taught in a seminary in Hong Kong for twenty years. When Liberation came, however, he would not renounce his country or the

Communist Party. He was dismissed from his teaching position in the seminary in spite of the fact that he had never met a Communist or read any Communist literature. His dismissal took place in the fifties when Senator McCarthy was conducting his famous hearings and the cold war between the United States and the Soviet Union was generating heat waves. At the same time the Soviets were moving men and equipment into the People's Republic of China. When Wang Jingxuan was relieved of his job as teacher in the seminary, he was given a job of translating Christian literature, but he says he was isolated, that he could not fellowship with other Christians because he was considered dangerous. He left Hong Kong with his family to serve as pastor in the Chinese countryside.

At the time he returned to China, explained Wang Jingxuan, the Chinese people were encouraged to practice their religion. Zhou Enlai, he said, was a man who saw the value of religion; Wang had nothing but praise for China's former premier. When the Cultural Revolution came, Wang was not persecuted, for he had never spoken out against the government. As a result, he was assigned a job translating confidential government documents at a military installation. After the Cultural Revolution he was assigned a teaching job in Beijing and has remained at that job. He does little teaching now, but he continues to be paid as a teacher by virtue of belonging to the school as his work unit. Such is common practice in China.

I was curious about how Wang rationalized his decisions concerning communism with the idea of being Christian. At first I was impressed that I was listening to a tired old man who had sold out to the Communist Party, but I soon realized that such an explanation was far too simple. Wang had spent his life thinking about his decisions. In each instance in which he had confronted a decision, he had weighed the alternatives carefully. After an hour or so of listening to him, I realized that he was not confessing any guilt on his part, but that he believed his decisions to have the sanction of God himself. While talking, Professor Wang often used the expression "God's will." Rather than feeling that he sold out to the Communists, he views his entire life as a fulfilling of God's will. As he said, he chose to be silent in order to survive. He chose not to speak against the government in order to have an opportunity to preach and teach.

There is a certain logic to Wang Jingxuan's story. To have martyred himself would have done nothing for his family or to further God's kingdom on earth. He now reads his Bible and talks to other Chinese people about Christ and Christianity. He teaches those who will lend an ear. He seems to be a man of compassion as well as of Christian commitment. The more I listened to his story, the more I found that I could not condemn him. He has survived, and all the Christian martyrs in China, both before and during the Cultural Revolution, might have done better to stay around to help with reestablishing the church after the conflagration instead of heroically going out in a blaze of fire to prove that they were right and the Communists were wrong. Oh, martyrs of the past, where are you now that you are needed? What did your martyrdom do to prevent an entire generation of Chinese young people from being brought up atheist? Would it not have been better to have worked in silence touching one life at a time? Would that not have made a greater contribution to the Kingdom of God in the People's Republic of China? I salute you Wang Jingxuan, old man that you are, because you accepted the difficult way. May you live the remainder of your life in peace.

Monday, January 5

The old lady who brings the hot water to my office made her morning rounds. I made myself a cup of tea and settled in to do some work before my 8:00 a.m. class, but Su Guifen interrupted. It had been one week since she was transferred to the cadre training program, and she stopped by to express her gratitude for my teaching. To show her gratitude she presented me with a beautiful hand-painted card duly inscribed with "To Dear Professor LeMaster, with sincere respect, a pupil, Su Guifen, January 4th, 1981, Peking, China." She apologized for not bringing me a more expensive gift, but I was moved by the card. Considering her standard of living, the card had cost her much, and the spirit in which she gave it was invaluable. I was impressed that I had touched the life of one of my students deeply, and that in itself would have been reward enough. I usually handle such things calmly, but in this case I choked up with emotion. I realize that there are many Su Guifens among my Chinese students, and I have come to admire them.

Back at the Friendship Hotel I settled in to write in my journal, but

Lu Zhibao came. He wanted to talk, although he seemed to have difficulty in finding words. He had come to bid me farewell and to express his gratitude for the relationship we had enjoyed. He said he thought we had much in common, and that although he was to leave for America in six days he wanted to stop and tell me he appreciated me. I assured him that the feeling was mutual. Lu invited me to visit in his home and have dinner with him and his family before his departure for America, and I accepted. Finally, I told him to say what he felt, what he had come to say, and when he said it his face lit up with a smile. He had come to say, "I like you, and I appreciate our being friends."

Lu Zhibao had apparently not had much practice in expressing his feelings. Like his Chinese colleagues, he had kept his distance because of not knowing who could be trusted. But this time Lu gambled, and the fact that he did told me much about his need to trust and be trusted. Perhaps he discovered something about himself, about his emotions, and I hope it will make a difference for the rest of his life. When he had gone, I sat and thought about the hour or so we had spent in conversation. "We touch each other's lives in strange and unexpected ways," I told myself. In the case of Lu Zhibao what I had believed for many years proved valid. What I believed then, as I do now, is that none of us ever lives his life for himself or herself. Each of us lives his life for others, and in that sense there is no such thing as a private life. We are always accountable to and for others—even to and for those we do not know.

Tuesday, January 6

I took time from our study of literature and talked to my students about applying to American universities. I did so to inform them rather than encourage them. I talked to them about costs, about money and scholarships, about the nature of curricula in American universities, and about other considerations pertaining to applying to a university in the United States. After my talk, some students came to see me with specific questions. I did not encourage them, but I gave them the information as objectively as I could. I have several students whom I would like to see have an opportunity for a good education, but they will probably not have that opportunity in China.

I sent for Qi Wenqin, and when she came we talked. I told her that I did not appreciate the fact that students had been pulled out of my classes and reassigned without my having been informed. She apologized and explained that the students were protesting to the administration over having been reassigned. According to Qi Wenqin, the students protested the reassignments when they took place and had protested every day since then. The protesting, I knew, would avail my students nothing. The reassignments would not be revoked.

Qi Wenqin and I also talked about the winter trip which would take place during the latter part of January and the early part of February. Sponsored by the institute, the trip would include Xian, Chengdu, Kunming, Chongqing, and Wuhan. It would also include two or three days on the Yangtze River. I told Qi Wenqin that I would like an additional week in order to visit Guilin, Guangzhou, and Hong Kong. Not only was she willing to grant me an additional week, making vacation for Wanda and me a month long, but she volunteered to try to convince school officials that we should have an interpreter paid by the institute to travel with us. Qi Wenqin talked about schedules for the coming semester and about a number of other school-related matters. When she went away I felt that much had been accomplished, that we had understood each other concerning a number of issues pertaining to the second semester.

Wednesday, January 7

I received a letter from Wang Jingxuan as a result of our talk on Sunday. In his letter he asked many questions about me, about the Lutheran Church in America, and about my knowledge concerning Lutheran missionaries in China before Liberation. The letter was cordial, and I could tell that he wanted to talk further. I too am interested in talking. When the letter came, I had already sent word by Charles Wyvelle that I would like to pursue the conversation we started on Sunday. I want to know more about Wang Jingxuan's life, more of what happened to him between Liberation in 1949 and the end of the Cultural Revolution. I want to find out how many case histories he has stored away in his memory of specific instances of persecution and death. I want to know more of the details concerning how he managed to escape such things. I want to know what he thinks about the present position of the government concerning religion. There are many things I want to know from Wang Jingxuan.

I had lunch with Lu Zhibao, his wife, and their nine-year old son. The meal consisted of nine dishes prepared by Lu Zhibao himself. Other than having visited for about two hours in Zhu Zheng's flat I had never been in a Chinese home, so I had little idea about what to expect. Before my visit Lu had apologized for not having a fine home, but he characterized his home as typical. The apartment in which Lu and his family lived contained a small kitchen with a gas burner for cooking. It contained a sitting room with chairs, tables, chests of various sizes, and a bookcase. The bedroom contained a large double bed, a wardrobe, and beautiful, double windows through which the sun was shining. The dining room contained a table, chairs, a small cabinet, a single bed, and two or three large chests. I was impressed by the cleanliness and orderliness of Lu Zhibao's home. The home reflected a sense of pride as well as good taste.

During lunch we talked about a broad range of topics. Because Wanda could not be present, I conveyed her regrets to Lu and his family. We then talked about our families, our backgrounds, our work, his coming year studying in the United States, and the remainder of my year teaching in China. Conversation came easily and naturally, and we enjoyed ourselves. By 2:00 p.m. I was feeling anxious about my preparation for the next day of classes. Lu Zhibao walked with me as I returned to my office and collected my things. He walked with me to catch a car for the Friendship Hotel. When we parted, I felt good about having visited in Lu Zhibao's home.

Thursday, January 8

Shao Jingfeng came by my office with forms to be signed. Qi Wenqin and I had a conference. Two of my students stopped by to talk about studying in America. The morning passed swiftly, and I was preparing to return to the Friendship Hotel when a young Chinese teacher for whom I had previously marked two essays came to see me. He wanted to talk, but he did not want to talk in my office. I could not tell whether he was afraid of being seen with me or whether he was suspicious that the office of a foreign teacher might be "bugged." At any rate, he suggested that we talk in his classroom.

When we arrived at his classroom, he thanked me for the three hours I had spent in marking his essays. Then he asked if he might assist me as tour guide, interpreter, or in some other way. I could tell from the time he began talking that something big was coming. As it turned out, he proposed that I adopt him as a special student in order to teach him the English language. In return, he volunteered that he would do anything I requested as long as it was in his power. Realizing that he was a teacher and not a student of mine, he had decided before talking with me that the adoption proposal was the only conceivable way he might secure help in studying the English language. Because his plea for help sounded desperate, and because I did not want to hurt him, I told him I would help him as much as possible after winter vacation, but I also told him that my first responsibility was to my students. The young teacher, whose name was Spring, was obviously pleased.

What bothers me about Spring is that there are tens of thousands of young people like him in China. Furthermore, I have found that a familiar pattern persists in such relationships. Although he did not bring up the subject, what Spring wants is to go to the United States. He wants me to assist him in gaining entrance to a university in the United States. He is serious about learning the English language, and he works very hard at it, but he does so because he sees the English language as his passport to the United States. I must explain to him that I have no secret formula for getting him to the United States. Like all other Chinese who want to go, he has no money and no way to earn more than forty or fifty *yuan* per month. Like many others with whom I have talked, he is obsessed by a dream and has no way to turn the dream into a reality.

Friday, January 9

I went to the institute to teach my last class of the semester. Once again I lectured on the backgrounds of twentieth century American literature. But before class began Su Guifen came to see me. She borrowed books to read over winter vacation. Zhang Li also came to borrow books. After class Qi Wenqin and I discussed the grades I would assign my students for the semester. We discussed the winter trip that Wanda and I will take. She told me that we may not have an interpreter during the week after we depart from our traveling group, so I requested official letters from the institute pertaining to travel arrangements, living accommodations, and other such concerns.

In the evening Wanda and I went to the theater in the compound. We saw a Chinese film entitled *Love for the Sky and Hatred for the Sea*, and although it contained some beautiful scenes of Taiwan and Hong Kong the film was abominable. It was a prime example of how poor art can be when it is made to serve as propaganda for the state. About how the Chinese living in Taiwan are presumably longing to return to the mainland, and are being prevented from returning by the Chinese Nationalist army, the film was a terribly naive distortion of the facts as well as an insult to cinema-goers in the People's Republic of China. As with other Chinese films, *Love for the Sky and Hatred for the Sea* was sentimental, but it was also blatant propaganda. Even if it were shown nightly in every theater in Taiwan, I doubt that one Chinese person would return to the mainland to trade his life in Taiwan for the one he would have to live in the People's Republic of China.

Saturday, January 10

Articles in the new issue of *Beijing Review* (January 5, 1981) admit that Mao Zedong engineered the Cultural Revolution, but the same issue contains an article by Zheng Bian entitled "The Trial Doesn't Involve Chairman Mao." Zheng Bian writes, "As regards Chairman Mao, he only committed mistakes in his work and his intention in launching the Cultural Revolution was to prevent the restoration of capitalism" (p. 4). But the trial of the Gang of Four makes clear that Chairman Mao was interested in saving himself. Although old and senile, he refused to step down and surrender his power to anyone younger, to anyone who could carry on effectively. The same issue of *Beijing Review* contains a long article (unsigned) entitled "Distinguishing Crimes from Mistakes," which is a weak attempt to justify Chairman Mao's mistakes. The government in Beijing is greatly concerned about how rapidly the demise of Chairman Mao can be accepted by the millions of Chinese who for many years worshiped him as god and hero. And now that Chairman Hua is about to be "washed out" the government is even more concerned because praise for Chairman Mao has been redirected by the masses in the form of praise for Chairman Hua. As a Chinese teacher told me the other day upon hearing that Chairman Hua had not only resigned but that he had disappeared, "The Chinese people are crushed; they had placed their faith in Chairman Hua. From what they have read and heard about the trial thus far, the Chinese people must surmise either that Chairman Hua is a criminal masquerading as a great humanitarian and statesman, or that he is being framed by the government. Regardless of which alternative they believe, the result is a tremendous credibility gap." As the Chinese teacher explained to me, "The Chinese people do not know what to believe. They have lost confidence in their government, and they are terribly frustrated." In spite of efforts by the press to build confidence in the government, the Chinese people remain frustrated. Inflation is hurting the Chinese economy, and articles such as one recently appearing in the *International Herald Tribune* (January 3-4, 1981), entitled "China's Leaders Call for Austerity to Fix Serious Fiscal Imbalance," add significantly to that worry. The Chinese people are concerned about economic instability, about governmental instability, and about signs that a power struggle in the government could lead to dark times in the future. Economically, the man in the street is suffering, and government rhetoric pertaining to belt-tightening causes many Chinese people to think more about the Cultural Revolution than they would otherwise. Such is particularly so because they have become accustomed to listening to promises from the government concerning a brighter future.

Sunday, January 11

On Saturday night Wanda and I went to the Minzu Restaurant to have dinner with the Grejdas. After dinner we played bridge and talked. What we enjoyed most was sharing information about our children, our relatives, and our homes in the United States. We seem to have much in common with the Grejdas, including the fact that Ed and I both worked our ways through college. As for Gail and Wanda, they have similar tastes, enjoy shopping together, and enjoy talking with each other about everything from cooking to buying clothes.

Once again we went to church in Xidan Street. Wen Yee Chin interpreted for us, as she had done before. After the church service, I asked her to inquire of the pastor whether I might have a conference with him. I told her to tell him that I would like to talk about the church, both in Xidan Street and in all of China. He asked that I come to the church office on Wednesday afternoon. That will make for a busy day because Charles Wyvelle will take me to the home of Wang Jingxuan on Wednesday morning.

Monday, January 12

Even though I had no classes, I had to go to the institute to deliver our passports and security papers in order that the institute might secure permission for us to travel during late January and early February. While I was at the school, I also picked up some cotton rationing coupons. I talked with Qi Wenqin concerning a number of things, including the printing of a course outline for my students. She asked me whether I might consider lecturing for two hours each week during the spring semester to Grade 78, but I declined. I declined because I knew that accepting would anger other teachers. I explained to Qi Wenqin that I would not interfere with another teacher's classes, that I would not appreciate another teacher who interfered with my classes. I would object bitterly if someone else attempted to do my job, or if he or she interfered with my doing it.

When I returned to the compound, I visited the health clinic, after which I took some medicine and lay down. When I awakened, I felt the best I had felt in several days. I took a long walk. I walked for an hour and a half, thinking about my students, about living in China, and about Lu Zhibao. Early in the morning Lu Zhibao had stopped by to tell me he would leave for the United States the next morning. He was emotional about leaving. I gave him our Waco address and phone number and he promised that he would get in touch with us once Wanda and I had returned to the United States. Because I had not presented him with a gift, I tried to give him ten *yuan*. Although overwhelmed by the gesture, he refused the money.

Tuesday, January 13

For the first time since coming to China I was involved in an automobile accident. When it happened the driver had just left the compound. We had traveled no more than a hundred yards when I looked up to see that we were rapidly approaching the rear of a truck. No sooner had I looked up than we hit the truck, caving in the front of the car in which I was riding. Because I had thrown myself into a horizontal position, bracing myself against the back of the front seat, I managed to escape injury. Fortunately, I was the driver's only passenger.

When the accident happened, I was on my way to meet Wanda for lunch at the Xinqiao Restaurant, and in spite of the accident I arrived early. I sat in the lobby and waited while reading a copy of the January 9, 1981, issue of the *International Herald Tribune*. On the center of the first page I read the headline "Deng Meets Resistance to the Ouster of Hua." By Michael Parks, the article discussed the fact that a power struggle is taking place in the government, and that the opposing parties are rapidly polarizing. According to the article, old party members, senior army commanders, and the intelligentsia are now clearly in support of Hua Guofeng. All three groups are opposed to the changes which have been taking place. As for Deng Xiaoping, he is counterattacking with a massive campaign of rhetoric. He knows that he must have the backing of the Central Committee, which meets next month, if he is to continue on the road to modernization. According to Parks, that meeting could go either for or against Deng: "The shape of that meeting, as well as its timing, depends to a large extent on the reaction of senior party, government, and army officials to the decisions of the top leadership, informed Chinese sources said Wednesday." Hua Guofeng has been busy trying to undermine Deng Xiaoping and his new policies, and Deng has accused Hua of "openly leading minority factions trying to overturn the party's new policies." Whatever the case, all of China can expect a conservative backlash soon.

Wednesday, January 14

In the morning I went to visit Wang Jingxuan. We talked about Christianity in China. We talked for three hours, freely and candidly. When we broached the topic of Christianity and the Chinese government, I expected Wang would talk less freely, but to my surprise he did not. He explained that Marxist philosophy is unilaterally opposed to religion of any kind, and he agreed with an observation of mine that the government presently allows the Chinese people to practice religion because the damage has already been done. A generation of people who have known nothing of religion will not sweep the country with a religious revival. But the fact is that the government may have miscalculated. Among the young people in China, and half of the population is under twenty-six, there is a sense that something crucial is missing from life. Some of them suspect that what is missing may be related to religion. As Wang Jingxuan pointed out, the present government favors the Buddhists and the Muslims; it discriminates against the Christians. The government is afraid radical ideas will come into China through radical Christian sects, and the solution lies in tolerating no foreign importations of religion. Missionaries are not allowed. At least Christian missionaries are not allowed.

Wang Jingxuan made clear that he does not have great hopes for the future of Christianity in China. The old pastors have almost all died off, and no new ones exist to take their places. Given that fact, the government is expecting Christianity to die because of a lack of interest. The government also fears that opening China up to Christian missionaries again would result in imperialist tactics as well as political interference in Chinese affairs. Wang reminded me that China has never been a Christian country. Only one book, he said, has ever been written on Christianity by a Chinese person. Further, China has never produced a religion of its own, and in that sense China has never been a religious country. As one looks back over the history of China, one cannot help but agree with Wang Jingxuan that Christianity has never been a strong force in China.

In the afternoon I visited Pastor Qi Tingduo at the church in Xidan Street. With Wen Yee Chin interpreting, the session proved to be informative. Pastor Qi explained that the church in Xidan Street began sixty or seventy years ago as a London mission. Over the years it passed through the hands of several denominations before becoming the Beijing Christian Church, a part of the Chinese Christian Church, in 1958. It was in 1958 that all denominations were eliminated. The Catholic church became the Catholic Patriotic Movement, and all Protestant sects were replaced by the Protestant Three Self Movement. When Pastor Qi trained for the ministry in the thirties, Beijing boasted four seminaries, including one at Beijing University. In 1952, however, only two seminaries were left in all of China, one of which was in Beijing and one in Nanking. In 1962 the two combined into one, located in Nanking, and during the Cultural Revolution it closed its doors.

Pastor Qi explained that in China church and state are not separate, and that members of the Communist Party often attend church on Sunday mornings to observe. "The members of the church," he said, "always know who they are and consequently go out of their way to shake hands with the party members as well as to thank them for allowing the church to reopen." As for church support, Pastor Qi explained that the Xidan Street church receives rent money from what was once church property. The government confiscated the property in 1958. The government rents the property out and gives 35 percent of the income to the church. At one time the churches in Beijing had large property holdings. They owned and operated schools, convalescent homes, hospitals, and other enterprises. They owned residential property as well as commercial property. The Buddhists were the wealthiest. "Now," said Pastor Qi, "the government practices capitalism with what was once church property."

When I asked Pastor Qi what he thought about the future of the church in China, he smiled and said he was optimistic. He said the youth are beginning to come to church because of "the appeal of Christ's love." He also said he envisions steady growth in church membership over the next several years, provided that the government remains stable. Once again I was made painfully aware that in countries like China the stability of the government determines almost everything in the lives of the people.

Thursday, January 15

Although I had no classes, I went to the institute at the usual time. I went to inform two of my students that large boxes from the United States had arrived for them, and that I had the boxes in my apartment in the compound. The boxes were from a California woman for whom the students once served as tour guides. But that was last fall, and the woman has sent them things ever since. I also went to talk with the personnel in the experts' office at the institute. Ed and Gail Grejda would like to accompany us on our winter trip, although Ed teaches at Beijing University. Beijing University has scheduled an inferior trip for them, and Ed has refused it. The present difficulty in their accompanying us lies in working out reservations at such a late date. We leave on January 24. Officials in the experts' bureau agreed that Ed and Gail might accompany us provided that Beijing University handles the scheduling of accommodations for them. Also, Beijing University will have to reimburse the institute for the cost of the trip. The side trip we plan to take, including visits to Guilin, Guangzhou, and Hong Kong, will have to be paid for by Ed and Gail themselves. Whether Ed and Gail accompany us on the trip depends on the cooperation of Beijing University.

Friday, January 16

I returned to the institute early in the morning to inquire concerning details regarding whether or not Ed and Gail might accompany us on our winter trip. While I was at the institute I also met with some of my students who had questions about language and literature. I also found the two students for whom the boxes had arrived from California. The students came to my office with bags, as I had requested. I had opened the boxes, containing clothes and books, and had transported the contents to my office. I impressed upon the two students the importance of being careful because the gifts came from a foreigner. I told them to protect themselves above all else. I cautioned them against leaving any gifts from foreigners where they might be found by fellow students or cadres carrying out their usual task of snooping and informing. They appreciated my talking with them.

After a strange intrusion into my office by two men who claimed they had come to repair the heater, I went looking for Qi Wenqin. I could not find her, but I managed to talk with Shao Jingfeng. After talking with Shao Jingfeng I found two students who were willing to take me to the home of Qi Wenqin. She was pleased to see me, so pleased that she sent immediately for Zhu Zheng and had him make Chinese noodles for me. The noodles were to serve as a symbol of friendship and hospitality, and Zhu Zheng brought me a mammoth bowl of them. I convinced him that he should share the noodles as a token of friendship; he happily obliged. I could not have eaten them all. Chinese noodles are not my favorite food; they are loaded with leeks and other things that my stomach will not tolerate. But I ate my portion of the noodles and complimented the cook on preparing a fine dish. I was happy when I had finished my noodles and could go out into the fresh air.

When I had completed the noodles, Qi Wenqin accompanied me to talk with the officials in the institute's bureau of experts. For some time I explored with them the possibility of having Ed and Gail accompany us on the winter trip, but I got nowhere. The bureaucracy is too deep. Not enough time remains for securing approvals which must come from party committees, school committees, and government committees. Even if the accommodations could be arranged, not enough time remains to solicit necessary approvals. The only alternative seems to be that Ed and Gail meet us in Hong Kong for a few days. I thanked the officials and returned to my office to read from Theodore White's book *In Search of History* until I could catch a car and return to the compound. On the way home I was alone in the car with the driver, and he spoke no English. I laid my head back on the seat for almost an hour and thought about the four and a half months I had been in China. I thought about the Chinese people and the lives they must live. I thought about my students. I thought about the future of China. I thought about the present crisis in the government over the ouster of Hua Guofeng. And finally, I thought about our friends in Texas. When the car arrived at the Friendship Hotel, I was still thinking. I was thinking about what it means to be an American teacher in Beijing.

Saturday, January 17

When I talked with Wang Jingxuan the other day, he told me about some of the atrocities Japanese soldiers committed on the Chinese people during the war between Japan and China. Because he was in the war, he observed the atrocities. He told me about a Chinese village in which, when the villagers heard that the Japanese soldiers were coming, five hundred of the women in the village threw themselves into wells and took their own lives. Wang Jingxuan is an old man of eighty, and I thought he might have been exaggerating, but recently I have come across the following in Theodore White's book *In Search of History*:

> The names of the villages (Liushe, Wangjiazhuang, etc.) are meaningless 100 miles away, but in some, every single woman without exception was raped by the soldiers in occupation. In villages whose occupants had not fled quickly enough, the first action of the Japanese was to rout out the women and have at them; women who fled to grain fields for hiding were forced out by cavalry who rode their horses through the fields to trample them and frighten them

into appearance. (Warner Books, 1978, p. 90; rpt. of Harper & Row edition)

As for the Chinese men, they were stripped of their clothes and hitched to carts to serve as beasts of burden. Like the animals they were replacing, they were driven through the mud, writes White, until they either died or were driven mad. It is little wonder that the Chinese people hate the Japanese.

Meng Su is a young Chinese teacher at First Foreign Language Institute. On her way to the Friendship Hotel the other evening, she was hit by a bicycle rider. In spite of the fact that she was in great pain, she made her way to the Friendship Hotel and had dinner with Tony Trimarchi, Wanda, and me. She then returned to her school to visit the doctor. The doctor in turn sent her to the hospital. The doctor at the hospital found that she had broken her ankle in three places and ordered that her ankle be placed in a cast. Because she was ordered by the doctor not to put any weight on her ankle, upon being released to go home she inquired about crutches only to be told that the department issuing crutches closes at 5:00 p.m. Meng Su hobbled her way to a bus stop and from the bus stop nearest where she lived to her home. The story of Meng Su's ankle might be of little significance except that it is typical of how the Chinese bureaucracy works. Even in the same building the people in one work unit seldom know what is happening in another work unit. It does not occur to the Chinese to coordinate their work, schedules, or activities with those of another work unit. Each unit is both a work unit and a political unit, and the remainder of the world, including the remainder of China, seems to be irrelevant.

In the afternoon Wanda and I visited the mosque in Niu Jie (Ox Street). Located inside the southwest gate of the outer city, it is the largest and oldest of the mosques in Beijing.

Built in the eleventh century, during the Northern Song Dynasty, the mosque contains six paintings, located in the main hall, which date from the eleventh century. Rows of pillars divide the main hall and at the farthest end from the entrance is a pulpit. As the worshiper enters the hall he faces the direction of Mecca. In the courtyard are located ancient tombs of followers of the Moslem faith, some of which date back as far as the thirteenth century. The neighborhood surrounding the mosque is inhabited largely by the Hui, a national minority who subscribe to the religion of Islam, and the government has built a special school and hospital for them. The mosque in Niu Jie is well attended; Islam seems to pose less threat to the government than does Christianity.

Sunday, January 18

When Sunday morning came, I was eager to go to church. I was eager to see what the controversy in the government over the ouster of Hua Guofeng might do to church attendance. Although the news of the controversy has been published in newspapers and magazines in the West, the government is trying to keep any details from the Chinese masses. Last week a new issue of *Newsweek* showing a statue of Mao being pulled down appeared on the stands. The issue was on sale for only about thirty minutes. The copies of *Newsweek* all disappeared. Shortly after that, all copies of all newspapers and magazines from the West disappeared and have not been seen on the stands since then. Too much is being printed about the crisis in China's government, and such news must be kept from the Chinese people. The crisis in government does not appear to be widely known among the Chinese people. At least church attendance was little affected. I have believed for some time that church attendance will serve as a barometer of fear among the Chinese because the Chinese people are still suspicious of having been granted the opportunity to worship. When they are threatened, one of the things they will do, I believe, is to stay away from church. Another thing they will do is to stay away from foreigners. To identify with either in a time of crisis would make the Chinese person suspect. He or she would be suspected of capitalist leanings, and possibly of political subversion. The next few weeks will be interesting as the drama of a power struggle is played out in the government.

Monday, January 19

I was to be paid for the month of February in advance in anticipation of our winter trip. Because we planned to visit Hong Kong, I had asked that I be paid in Hong Kong dollars. But when I arrived at the institute, no one was there. I sat in my office and waited, for I had requested that two of my students come for some of the books and clothes which had been shipped to me. I had some sweaters with me, and when they came I encouraged them to take the sweaters immediately so I would not be caught with them in my office. When they left, they were carrying books and clothes in bags, and I felt good about getting them out of my office. I felt good that the students had been able to receive the books and clothes through me. My students and I were breaking the law, and penalties for such violations, I have been told, are severe. The books and clothes will be taken home by the girls when they leave for vacation, and I will be glad when that has happened. Their rooms in the dormitory are subject to search at any time. As one of my students told me, "There is no privacy." She also told me about the danger of associating with a foreigner. "They will think you are passing government secrets to the foreigner," she said. "You must not be seen alone with a foreigner."

At about 9:00 a.m., Qi Wenqin came with the money. We talked about my classes, and about the schedule for the coming semester. I volunteered to teach a special section of literature to accommodate those students who were transferred into teacher training programs. I volunteered knowing that I would likely have to meet them in the afternoon. Qi Wenqin seemed very pleased that I would do the extra work. After she left, I continued my reading of White's *In Search of History*. It is a powerful book, a penetrating book, and it appeals to my interest in Chinese intellectual history. Perhaps what appeals to me most about it is that it is not merely an account of many dry facts and statistics. In White's book history walks across every page. Sometimes it even runs.

Tuesday, January 20

Although I had had no classes for several days, I returned to the institute. When I arrived at the car stand, the driver put me in a car and did not wait for other foreigners. I have never had that happen while going to the institute, but it has recently happened upon returning to the compound. For several days, I have been quietly ushered into a car upon arrival and hauled away. I have become a bit paranoid because it appears to be an attempt to isolate me. Either someone has decided that I am unusually important and need protection, or that I am a political threat and should be isolated. I cannot imagine another reason for the treatment I have been receiving. The way I am being treated may account for the driver who sometime back addressed me as "the famous American professor." Whatever the reason, I am sure the Chinese will not tell me.

Later in the day I tried to make a telephone call to Hong Kong. I did not expect to complete the call easily, for my previous efforts to use the telephone in Beijing had been frustrating. I made three calls, amounting to forty-four *yuan* fifty and requiring two hours of my time, before I succeeded in reserving a room at the Imperial Hotel of Hong Kong. I should have been happy that I was finally successful, but I could not overcome my disgust for the inefficiency of such a system. Finally, I found that I could dismiss the matter from my mind by rationalizing that my telephone experience was typical. In China everything one does takes a tremendous amount of energy and time. That anything gets done is a miracle.

Wednesday, January 21

I lay awake much of the night thinking about a lecture I had given to Rita Clarke's classes the day before. It was supposed to be a lecture on modern American poetry, but it turned out to be a lecture on the intellectual milieu of modern America. Furthermore, I had used poems to illustrate my contentions. Much of what I had to say flew over the heads of my Chinese audience, but I frequently saw a face light up as if to say, "Although I cannot completely follow what you are saying, I understand enough to know that I like what I am hearing." My lecture was not an anti-Communist diatribe, but it was an effort to place the current poetic tradition squarely in support of a democratic society.

I had expected that my lecture would be attended by a number of cadres, party officials, and school officials whose responsibility it is to protect the good name of the school as well as good Marxist philosophy. I was not disappointed. The fact that party officials were present changed nothing that I had to say. If anything their presence egged me on to say things that I might not have said before a different audience, even in a Chinese school. As it turned out, the students who were present were pleased. When I began, I had to push aside enough microphones to clear a space on the desk for my notes, and when I ended I received a hearty round of applause. They had obviously understood more than I had expected of them. They had appreciated me more than I had deserved. The lecture had given me an opportunity to say a few things about dignity, respect, and the value of the individual human being. It had given me an opportunity to comment upon the nature of man and the relationship of the individual to the state. Some of the party members present likely found what I had to say a bit subversive, but the students loved it. The future of China belongs to its young people; only they can make China a better place in which to live.

Yesterday was the day of the inauguration of Ronald Reagan. While reading Theodore White's book *In Search of History* yesterday, I realized that the biggest decision to be faced by the new president might not have to do with measures to heal an ailing economy. The biggest and most important decision might be that of who will replace Leonard Woodcock as ambassador to China. During the thirties and forties we blundered time after time in dealing with China. We supported the incompetence of Chiang Kai-shek. We interfered in a civil war and drove Mao Zedong to an alliance with the Soviets. We brought thirty years of hardship and suffering upon the Chinese people by our shortsightedness in dealing with both Chiang Kai-shek and Mao Zedong. The result of our short-sightedness was a war in Korea and another in Vietnam, both of which were unnecessary. I hope President Reagan will not be as shortsighted as was President Roosevelt and the presidents who followed him. I hope President Reagan will examine the potential for peace in the free world through strengthening China. I hope President Reagan will examine the possibility of an alliance with China as a means of checking Soviet hegemony. The Chinese government must be changed, for it is presently little more than a continuation of a system of old Chinese warlords. Such a government will not suffice in the twentieth century, but we Americans cannot change the Chinese government by abandoning China. Only through embracing China is there hope of maintaining a balance of power between East and West and thereby assuring peace in the next decade. Yes, the decision President Reagan makes about an ambassador to China may prove to be one of the most important decisions a United States president has ever made. It is a decision to be made for the entire community of nations.

Thursday, January 22

I visited the dining hall in building number two and looked through a copy of *Time* while drinking a pitcher of tea. I visited the clinic and picked up some medicine. I thought about China, about my students at Second Foreign Language Institute, and about problems in the United States economy. I wrote a letter to Paul Mussen, a friend at the University of California at Berkeley, explaining that I frequently agonize over China—over the Chinese people. I agonize because I do not see bright prospects for the future. The government still consists of people with minds from China's feudal past. They are people with warlord mentalities; they still see the world as a fiefdom. At least they still see China that way. Until Chinese government officials acquire a new mind-set, a more modern mind-set, China has little possibility of entering into the modern world. Furthermore, I am beginning to doubt that the Chinese way of seeing the world can be changed gradually or peacefully.

The sentencing of Jiang Qing has been postponed for a second time, and the reason is quite obvious. The split in the government over the Deng-Hua controversy has affected the judges who are to make the decision. Those who favor Hua want the death penalty; those who favor Deng want life in prison for Jiang Qing. The drama surrounding Hua Guofeng's ouster may work itself out in the sentencing of Mao's widow. If Hua has his way, Mao will not continue to be discredited; rather the new policies of Deng will be revoked. If Hua does not have his way, Deng's policies will remain in effect; Mao will continue to be discredited; Mao-appointed officials in the government will be purged; and Jiang Qing will receive a life sentence as opposed to a death sentence.

Friday, January 23

I awakened with such ambition that I washed my socks and underwear in the bathtub once I had taken my morning bath. I performed a number of such domestic chores in the morning, but after lunch I settled in to outline my course in American literature for the second semester. For two weeks I had been thinking about a plan or format, but it was not until Friday, January 23, that I was ready to commit my plan to paper.

At lunch I sat with Tony Trimarchi. He told me a story concerning a Chinese mother who had been forced to abort her second child at six months. She had committed the crime of becoming pregnant the second time, and the state frowned on that. After efforts to shame her into an abortion failed, her work unit insisted that she have an abortion. She resisted stubbornly until her work unit and that of her husband cut off their meager salaries and starved them into submission. They have one child to feed, so in the long run the Chinese mother had no choice but submit.

Saturday, January 24

At 9:00 a.m., we began our winter trip. When the train left the station at 9:50, we were all aboard, all thirty-one of us. The ride to Xian, the first leg of our journey, took twenty-two hours, and for the first time I slept well on a train. All day long we rolled west, while bearing south, and all day long I observed the Chinese countryside. Once again I admired the mountains, which were terraced and farmed from top to bottom. I admired the miles of railroad track tunneled under huge mountains, the trestles over rivers and ravines, and the Chinese people who were out working in cold weather.

Once we arrived in Xian, the largest city in China in the Middle Ages, we were taken to the Renmin Hotel. After breakfast we were taken to the neolithic exhibit at Banpo Village. Six thousand years old, Banpo Village is about seven kilometers east of Xian, provincial capital of Shaanxi. This ancient settlement, Banpo Village, was discovered by construction workers in 1952. The largest such discovery in China, and the best preserved, Banpo Village once belonged to a maternal clan. At the site we saw unearthed foundations of houses and recessed fire pits. We saw a communal cemetery, earthenware urns for burying infants, and many other artifacts.

After lunch we visited the Greater Wild Goose Pagoda, which is located within the compound of the Monastery of Grace in the southern suburbs of Xian. Built in 684 by Emperor Gaozong of the Tang Dynasty to honor his mother, the monastery was destroyed late in the Tang Dynasty, and although the present structure was built in the Qing Dynasty it was built in Ming style. Inside the wall of the compound stands the sixty-four-meter high Greater Wild Goose Pagoda, built in 652. A masterpiece of Buddhist architecture, the pagoda was built to house Buddhist sutras brought from India by the Tang Dynasty pilgrim, traveler, and scholar Xuanzang (602-664). Xuanzang went to India to study Buddhism and returned with 657 volumes of Buddhist scriptures. It was inside the Greater Wild Goose Pagoda that he translated them into a Chinese version consisting of 1,335 volumes. Finally, we visited the Shaanxi Provincial Museum, where we saw stone tablets containing many of the Chinese classics.

We ended the day by watching the sentencing of Jiang Qing on television. Receiving a compromise verdict worked out by the Deng-Hua factions in the government, Jiang Qing will have two years in which to undergo what the Chinese call "re-education." If she does not respond to indoctrination efforts and mend her ways, she is to be put to death at the end of two years. For the present, it seems, Jiang Qing should be content that the ghost of Mao haunted the trial from beginning to end.

Sunday, January 25

Early in the morning we visited the museum which contains the buried sculpture legion of Qin Shi Huang, located about thirty kilometers east of Xian. Qin Shi Huang (259-210 B.C.) was the emperor who unified China and built the Great Wall. He devoted thirty-six years and used seven thousand conscripted laborers in building his magnificent tomb near Xian. The tomb still stands at the foot of the slopes of Mount Lishan, facing the Huishui River as a magnificent underground city containing walls lined with copper. The tomb contains a throne room and seats for officials as well as a treasury of jewels and other valuable objects. Although much excavating remains to be done, the three vaults which have been excavated have drawn worldwide attention. Upon being excavated, vault number one yielded six thousand life-size warriors and horses of terra cotta arranged in battle formation. The warriors wear helmets and armor; they also carry swords, javelins, bows, arrows, and crossbows. The horses are hitched to chariots in teams of four. Three rows of seventy warriors make up the vanguard, followed by the main body of the army consisting of thirty-eight rows of troops.

Vaults two and three are equally impressive. In 1976 nearly a thousand terra cotta soldiers were found in vault number two, which contains four separate units of chariots, cavalrymen, archers, and foot soldiers. Vault number three is a building resembling a gallery; it contains sixty-nine terra cotta warriors with defensive weapons and a wooden chariot pulled by four horses. Ten thousand pieces of weaponry have been unearthed from the three vaults, and experts predict that excavating the entire tomb of Emperor Qin Shi Huang will require the efforts of another two generations. The terra cotta legion of Emperor Qin Shi Huang reflects the power of China's first emperor, and as I viewed it I could not help but think of the present power struggle in China's government. I could not help but wonder whether the task of ruling China has changed much since the time of the first emperor.

Monday, January 26

At the foot of Mount Lishan we visited Huaqing Pool, which was once a winter resort for emperors. The resort is famous for its hot springs. Discovered three thousand years ago, the hot springs have a regular flow and a constant temperature of 109.4 degrees Fahrenheit. More than a thousand years ago Tang Dynasty Emperor Xuanzong spent his winters at the hot springs with his favorite concubine, Yang Guifei. Living in luxury and debauchery, Yang Guifei was pampered and spoiled. For example, she was fond of fresh litchi fruit, as Chinese legend has it, which was grown far away in Sichuan Province. According to the story, the emperor ordered couriers to travel day and night without rest to carry fruit to Yang Guifei.

Chiang Kai-shek was captured at Huaqing Pool in the famous Xian Incident of 1936. While the Japanese intensified their invasion of China, Chiang Kai-shek was bent on waging a civil war instead of fighting the invaders. In December of 1936, he flew to Xian to plan his military campaign against Yanan, the center of the revolution. He ordered the suppression of a large, patriotic student demonstration. Two of his generals, Zhang Xueliang and Yang Hucheng, were reluctant to carry out the order and tried to persuade Chiang to form a national, united front for resistance against the Japanese, but Chiang would not cooperate. Feeling that they were left with no recourse, they arrested their leader.

On December 12, 1936, troops commanded by Zhang and Yang arrived at Huaqing Pool to arrest Chiang, but Chiang fled. He was finally caught while hiding in a rock crevice halfway up Mount Lishan. Forced to negotiate with Zhou Enlai, Chiang Kai-shek agreed to accept a united front against the Japanese invaders. I wonder how the fact that Chiang Kai-shek was such a self-serving rascal was concealed from the West for so many years.

In the afternoon we visited the Bell Tower and strolled in the streets of Xian. About 9:00 p.m. we boarded a train for Chengdu in Sichuan Province. We knew that we would ride all night and well into the next day, but we were looking forward to seeing the "breadbasket" of China. We were also looking forward to warm weather; snow had fallen throughout most of our stay in Xian.

Tuesday, January 27

When we awakened in the morning our train was rolling across the lush farmland of Sichuan Province. Arriving in Chengdu at about 2:30 p.m., we checked in at the Jin Jiang Hotel. In the third century the feudal kingdom of Shu made its capital at Chengdu, and earlier, in the second century B.C., a local official named Li Bing had the Dujiangyan irrigation system built. The system is still very much in use. In the southwest suburbs of Chengdu is a park shaded by giant cypress trees and spacious buildings which form the temple dedicated to Zhuge Liang, a Chinese statesman of the third century. He helped establish the state of Shu and served as its prime minister. In doing these things he contributed greatly to the unification of southwest China as well as to its economic and cultural growth.

Wednesday, January 28

For about an hour and a half we rode in buses before arriving at the Dujiangyan irrigation system, a remarkable feat of hydraulic engineering. The irrigation system is as impressive as it is large, and along the road one's eye is taken by the beauty of lush, green fields. Also, everywhere one looks along the road he sees produce being hauled into Chengdu. Never in my life had I seen such large heads of cabbage and cauliflower. Some of them looked to be as large as bushel baskets. The vegetables all looked fresh and crisp, unlike the vegetables one sees in Beijing in January. But like Beijing, in Chengdu and the surrounding area every available inch of soil appears to be utilized.

After visiting the irrigation system, we visited the cottage of Du Fu, an eighth-century Chinese poet. Du Fu made his reputation as a poet by writing about China's poor people. He wrote hundreds of poems on his favorite subject, and consequently has been immortalized through the centuries. We walked in a beautiful park surrounding the cottage of

Du Fu, who is remembered for the splendor of the park. On the other hand, for a time in his life he was extremely poor. Because he felt a great empathy with the poor, he did much through his poetry to raise consciousness concerning their plight.

Thursday, January 29

Mount Emei is located about 155 kilometers from Chengdu in Sichuan Province. We rode in buses for most of the day, stopping for lunch about noon. Because the roads were narrow and crowded, we could not travel far in a day in the countryside. But the things we saw made the trip enjoyable. For example, we saw many ancient water buffalo being worked by peasants in the fields. We saw thousands of acres of lush, green vegetation. We saw many people in the fields with their pails spreading human fertilizer. We saw a funeral procession in which the casket containing the deceased was elevated high on a cart, and the immediate family was pushed along behind the cart in wheelbarrows. We saw bridges under construction on which both men and women were engaged in pouring concrete pilings. We saw mammoth rivers and terraced mountains. We saw irrigation systems everywhere in an obviously prosperous province. In the towns and villages the streets were always crowded—a reminder that in China there is no escaping the masses.

At some point in our trip I began thinking that what I was viewing was essentially like what Thomas Jefferson once advocated as the best direction for the future of America. What I saw was a kind of existence in which the rhythms of life for the individual are in harmony with those of nature, and I must admit that it did not all appear to be bad. In that existence men, women, and children work in the fields; they appear to live simple but unimaginative lives. I wonder what produces happiness in such an earthbound existence.

We saw tea bushes terraced high on at least a thousand hills, and below them fields were plowed for the growing of rice. From our bus window, it all appeared to be unreal. It appeared to be some kind of magical fairyland which exists only in dreams or in the fantasies of one given to daydreaming. But the daydream ended when we arrived at our lodge, a lodge where Chiang Kai-shek once stayed to plan his war against the revolutionary Chinese rather than concentrate on fighting the Japanese invaders. In place of negotiating with the revolutionary forces, Chiang was willing to take his chances with the Japanese, even though they slaughtered tens of thousands of his countrymen. It was history of sorts, our sleeping in the lodge where Chiang had stayed at the foot of Mount Emei, but not history of the best kind. My wife saw a large rat in our room just before we were ready to retire.

Friday, January 30

It was our day to climb Mount Emei. We visited two Buddhist monasteries and observed a Buddhist ceremony, but other attractions on Mount Emei were more rewarding. The mountain range itself was breathtakingly beautiful. The rich forests are inhabited by many kinds of wildlife. A species of goat antelope and the silver pheasant both live on Mount Emei. It is also the home of about 280 species of butterflies and many monkeys. The mountain range is carpeted with azaleas, ancient gingko trees, dove trees, and many other flowers and trees. What proved most interesting, however, were the people who live on Mount Emei. High up the sides of mountains, many fields appeared to be totally inaccessible to human beings, but the peasants terrace and cultivate them. I noticed that those who work on the sides of the hills wear a special shoe, a shoe with large spikes in the bottom, to assure safe footing. As for us, we climbed about four miles up Mount Emei. We reached the halfway point and were content to stop there.

Saturday, January 31

When we headed back toward Chengdu at 7:00 a.m., I was still trying to evaluate some of the experiences I had undergone on Mount Emei. I meditated on them as our bus made its way along the narrow roads. I wondered about life in the Buddhist monasteries we had visited. I wondered about the pool of blood I had seen when I looked down a toilet hole at one of the monasteries; I wondered whether or not it had involved an abortion. I wondered about a Buddhist ceremony we had witnessed, a ceremony performed by four decrepit old men. As Louise Krumm had commented later, it was a worship service without worshipers; it therefore seemed pointless and empty. I wondered about the isolated and desolate lodge where we had spent two nights, sharing our room during one of them with a huge rat. I wondered whether foreigners would frequent the lodge once they found that they would have no heat and no hot water.

As our bus moved us along the roads, I also wondered about my students back in Beijing. I missed them and felt my time might be more profitably spent with them in the classroom. As I thought of Mount Emei and my students interchangeably, I observed the countryside, and of what I observed four things impressed me most deeply. First, it was the time of year for weddings. We passed a number of wedding processions in which the participants were carrying the marriage bed and household effects of various kinds to the new dwelling place of the bride and groom. Second, many babies were being carried on the backs of their mothers, and some of them looked to be between fifteen and twenty months old. It was as if the people in the countryside had not heard of the government's effort to bring the population under control. Third, I was impressed that almost always the most beautiful of the young women were engaged in carrying buckets of human manure into the fields to fertilize the crops. I wondered about the relationship between the job and being beautiful, and I surmised that the job could be a form of punishment, or an effort to produce a measure of humility in the worker. Fourth, I watched the peasants as they worked their ancient water buffalo. I decided that this slow, bulky creature sets the pace for living in the countryside. The accommodations he negotiates with nature, I decided, establish the pattern for such accommodations negotiated by the peasants and their families.

February

Sunday, February 1

Our train ride from Chengdu to Kunming would take about twenty-five hours, and we were under way by 6:00 a.m. Wanda and I shared a compartment with Ken and Bonnie Martin. In order to make time pass rapidly, we played bridge, and after a lunch of bread, ham, and beer we took a nap. During much of the afternoon I watched the countryside. A sharp contrast to the fertile valleys of Sichuan Province, the mountains through which we were passing seemed to be poor in almost every way. Mud dwellings blended in with the landscape, and one could not overlook the meager lives that the peasants in the mountains live. All afternoon and all night we passed through the mountains, and during the night I lay awake wondering how the Chinese people have survived in such drab and desolate surroundings. I wondered whether they are as afraid of the government as the people in Beijing are. I wondered whether they could afford to worry about the government, given their gaunt and haggard faces. Although our train would carry us through and beyond the poverty of the mountains, and although we would arrive in Kunming in the morning, I knew that what I had seen in the mountains would continue to haunt my memory as though I had experienced a bad dream.

Monday, February 2

Located in Yunnan Province, Kunming has a history dating back two thousand years. It is a plateau city with an altitude of almost two thousand meters and a population of more than 1.5 million. The population of Kunming includes people from several national minority groups such as the Hui, the Yi, and the Bai. As a result of this mixture of population we saw a delightful contrast in clothing as well as in skin tones and facial features as we walked in the streets of Kunming. Endowed with charming scenery and a mild climate, Kunming is known as the "city of eternal spring." Even in February we could not help but be impressed by the scenery. We could not help but be impressed by the parks, by wide, tree-lined boulevards, and by Western architecture. In Kunming we saw more Western clothes than we customarily saw in Beijing, and the atmosphere was more relaxed, perhaps because of the climate.

In the afternoon our group went to West Hill, but I stayed behind to have my hair cut and to wander alone in the streets and parks of Kunming. I wandered for most of the afternoon. I observed men and women purchasing fruit, vegetables, meat, and bread from street vendors. I observed children at play. I also visited in a department store. Nowhere did I observe the sadness that I had seen in the faces of the mountain people. Life in Kunming seemed to be marked by an even tempo, and I was pleased to see that.

Tuesday, February 3

When we arrived at Stone Forest, we found that there are two such forests, a little one and a big one. We visited the little one before lunch; after lunch we visited the big one. The Stone Forest does not consist of petrified trees; it consists of huge stones which stand as tall as, or taller than, giant trees. According to our Chinese guides, the tree-like stone formations were shaped as part of a seabed, but more likely they were left behind when a glacier moved through the area thousands of years ago.

Stone Forest proved to be a spectacular display of nature's handiwork, but two other things also proved very interesting. With the temperature approaching eighty degrees, one could see beautiful flowers and flowering trees everywhere. I saw the largest camellias I have ever seen. I saw beautiful wildflowers that looked like marigolds and flowering trees resembling the mimosa trees which grow in central Texas. I saw a hedge like forsythia, and it too was beautiful. The second thing I found interesting is that the women and girls of one of the national minorities were selling their needlework in the area of the Stone Forest. The little girls of ten to twelve were ragged but cute. They were also shy, for when I tried to take a picture of some of them they turned and ran. I was told later that they were of the Yi nationality.

Wednesday, February 4

We visited Golden Hall, which is located in a northeastern suburb of Kunming. Golden Hall was built in 1671, and its beams, pillars, arches, roof, tiles, and window frames of cast bronze are unique. We saw about two hundred tons of cast bronze at Golden Hall, including several sculptured pieces.

After viewing Golden Wall, we visited Kunming Botanical Gardens, and in the afternoon Wanda and I walked to the center of town, which was three to four miles from our hotel. We toured many shops and stores before returning to our hotel tired and hungry. On our way back to the hotel, a beautiful, young woman stopped us to practice her English. A member of a local dance troupe, she offered us tickets so that we might see her perform. She was disappointed when we told her that we would leave Kunming before her performance was to take place. She wants very much to study dance in America, she told us.

Thursday, February 5

It was the beginning of the lunar year, the Chinese New Year, and the people of Kunming were celebrating. As had been the case throughout the night, hundreds of thousands of firecrackers were being set off in Kunming. The streets were filled with revelers and sightseers. Much wine was being consumed, and the people of Kunming were obviously enjoying themselves.

Early in the morning our group went to visit Hot Springs, but I stayed behind to think, to reflect concerning the people of Kunming and Yunnan Province. Because our train would leave at 4:00 p.m., I wanted to do some final walking and reflecting. Based upon what I had seen and heard in Kunming, my thoughts led to these conclusions. First, the people in Kunming are looser, freer, than are the people in Beijing. The reasons may be that the population contains members of a number of national minorities, that Yunnan Province was little touched by the Cultural Revolution, and that Yunnan Province is far removed from the center of government in Beijing. Whatever the reasons, the people in Kunming and Yunnan Province are not as "uptight" as are the people in Beijing.

Friday, February 6

Our train rolled northeastward toward the Yangtze. It would be colder in Chongqing, but I was looking forward to seeing my students. Our trip would not end for several days, but at least we were headed in the right direction. The land appeared to be poorer the farther we traveled from Kunming. In the mountains the huts of the peasants were made of clay, and the peasants themselves were ragged. Somewhere on our way through the mountains my eye fell upon a young woman of about eighteen who stood gazing over the back of a water buffalo and into a stream of water. Even the noise of our train did not awaken her from her trance; she never looked up. I wondered about her preoccupation. Could it be that she was thinking of the flow of the water toward some river beyond the mountains? Whatever her thoughts, she looked lonely and sad.

We had a four-hour delay in Guiyang, where we enjoyed breakfast and a rest. We encountered no surprises until we left our train at about 9:00 p.m. in Chongqing, once headquarters for Chiang Kai-shek and the Kuomintang. When we left our train, the natives gathered around in great numbers. And when we boarded our buses, they gathered around several hundred strong. When they surrounded our buses and pushed their faces up against the windows to stare at us, our guides were uneasy. We were hurried from the station as quickly as possible. Later we were told that Chongqing had only recently been opened to foreigners, and that most, if not all, of those who had stared at us so intently had never seen a foreigner. It was about 10:00 p.m. when we finally arrived at the Renmin Hotel in Chongqing. Wanda and I had something to eat and retired early, for we would leave our group at six the next morning with Ken and Bonnie Martin in order to arrive in Hong Kong on February 11 or 12.

Saturday, February 7

Excited about our coming boat trip down the Yangtze River, Wanda and I were awake at 5:00 a.m. From the English department at Second Foreign Language Institute, Shao Jingfeng was to accompany us as far as Wuhan. We boarded the boat at 6:45, and at 7:00 we were on the way. For most of the day we watched the river, the river traffic, and the Chinese people. Again we were the center of attention; the Chinese on the boat had apparently not seen foreigners either. Our first day on the river was relaxing, and we played bridge with the Martins as we watched the river from a glass-enclosed deck. All day the river was covered by heavy mist, but that did not bother us because we knew the next day would be the important one. During the next day we would pass through the gorges.

When evening came, our boat docked at Wanxian, and we went ashore to purchase some oranges as well as to explore the city. After climbing many steps to enter the city, perhaps a thousand or more, we found that everything had closed for the night. The streets of Wanxian were dark and practically empty. In that respect Wanxian proved to be unlike any American city I had ever seen on a Saturday night. After purchasing oranges and tangerines from a street vendor, we returned to our boat to retire. Upon docking we had taken on many new passengers. The boat was crowded, and many men, women, and children were sleeping on the floors of halls and corridors. I went to bed thinking about the faces I had seen in the halls and corridors. From where had so many people come? Where were they going?

Sunday, February 8

For us it was Sunday on the Yangtze. Our boat was underway by 4:00 a.m., but we did not stir until about 7:00. By that time we had passed through the first of three of the largest and most beautiful river gorges in the world. After breakfast we were on deck to watch the river as we passed through the second gorge, and we passed through the third shortly before lunch. We missed much of the third, because we had to eat lunch early in preparation for leaving the boat at 12:30 p.m.

We docked about forty kilometers from Yichang, where we were met by a van from China International Travel Service. We were taken to a hotel in Yichang and were allowed time to take a walk in the city. The people of Yichang gathered about us two and three hundred strong everywhere we went, because they had not seen many foreigners. Although the largest dam in China is under construction at Yichang, it is not a city that I would care to stay in for long. It is far removed from anything of interest, and the city appears to be dull. Fortunately for us our train left the Yichang station at 9:00 p.m., and we were on our way to Wuhan.

Monday, February 9

We had breakfast before we left the train in Wuhan at 10:00 a.m. Breakfast consisted of fried eggs, bread, jam, hot milk, and hot coffee. The eggs tasted good, but they were floating in grease. By lunch time, I was becoming ill. After lunch I felt worse; I had no recourse except to retire to my hotel bed. Little did I know that twenty-four hours would pass before I would feel like stirring again. More than two weeks of Chinese food had devastated my stomach. I had learned shortly after arriving in China that my stomach would not tolerate a steady diet of Chinese food, but while we were traveling there was no alternative. Hong Kong would be our next stop after Wuhan, provided that we did not have to stay overnight in Guangzhou, and I was looking forward to some Western food. I had even counted on getting to Hong Kong without any stomach problems, but nothing turned out as I had planned. Even as I lay in my hotel bed ill, I was comforted in believing I would soon escape Chinese food.

Tuesday, February 10

When I awakened I realized that I was more ill than I had been the day before. I obviously had an infection. Wanda inquired at the hotel desk concerning a doctor, but the response was not encouraging. Fortunately, Bonnie Martin had brought along some penicillin, and I began taking that. I stayed in bed until noon. Then we had lunch, and I lay down again. Wanda and Bonnie spent the morning shopping, and Ken wandered in the streets of Wuhan.

Our train was scheduled to leave the Wuhan station at 2:40 p.m. and arrive in Guangzhou the next morning at 7:30. We had been warned that no sleeper compartments would be available. Confident that sleepers would be made available for "the foreigners," we went to the train station anyway. We were sold tickets for hard seats, and that meant we would ride with the masses. We traveled with the masses, and one such experience in a lifetime is more than enough. As elsewhere, spitting and snorting never ceased. Peelings from fruit and various kinds of garbage were carelessly thrown onto the floor and allowed to accumulate. Cigarette smoke was so thick that one could not see from one end of the car to the other. As we rode into the night, I became more ill, and I began to wonder how we would ever find a doctor since we could not communicate with the mass of Chinese.

Once I became nauseous and realized that I might faint, I found that we were sitting near a Chinese man who spoke a little English. He was kind enough to talk with train officials about my condition and request consideration. I do not know what he told them, but it worked. Around midnight we were taken to the dining car, where I was given a bed made of folding chairs. I was placed between two tables with my legs passing underneath and out the other side of one. Wanda and the Martins sat in chairs and rested the tops of their bodies on tables. We settled in for the remainder of our ride to Guangzhou, but even better fortune eventually came our way.

Six hard sleepers became available at about four o'clock in the morning, and we welcomed an opportunity to lie down, even for a short time.

Wednesday, February 11

When we arrived in Guangzhou, we were met by a security officer who wanted to check our travel permits. We showed him our permits and left the station in search of the offices of CAAC (Civil Aviation Administration of China) and China International Travel Service. At CAAC we purchased tickets for our return trip to Beijing on February 16. Again I was disgusted by what I considered a high level of inefficiency. Purchasing our plane tickets took two hours. Nor was China International Travel Service any more efficient. We wanted to purchase train tickets from Guangzhou to Hong Kong, but we waited for an hour and a half only to be sold tickets for the following day.

Almost half of the day was gone before we made our way to a hotel, where we checked in to stay until the next morning. The remainder of the day was fairly routine except that not far from the hotel we encountered beggars working in the streets. The beggars were aggressive, and we were surprised because we had encountered no beggars in China prior to visiting Guangzhou. The government admits that China is poor, but it also emphasizes that the Chinese people are proud. The government stresses in its propaganda that enough food exists for everyone, and that life in China is the best it has been in many years. Regardless of government propaganda, beggars work the streets in Guangzhou.

Thursday, February 12

It was the day Wanda had been waiting for, a day of "passage" in more senses than one. As for me, I have never been greatly attracted by large cities. I like a quiet and orderly life; Wanda likes the noise and confusion of large cities. We met Ken and Bonnie Martin at the train station in Guangzhou at 7:30 a.m., and by 8:30 we had cleared customs. We were on our way to Hong Kong, and Wanda was as excited as a ten-year-old child.

It was already past noon when we checked in at the Imperial Hotel in Hong Kong. Having missed breakfast, we left the unpacking for later and began looking for a "uniquely American" place to eat. Not far from our hotel we found a McDonald's restaurant, and when we entered we found Ed and Gail Grejda, whose winter vacation had also brought them to Hong Kong. After lunch Ed, Gail, and Wanda went shopping while I visited the Star House (a travel agency) to purchase tickets for a trip to Macao. Once I had purchased the tickets I returned to the Imperial Hotel to eat. I had not recuperated from my illness, and I tired very easily.

Friday, February 13

We took a jetfoil to Macao early in the morning. The ride was pleasant, and when we arrived we were approached by a young man who wanted to sell us a tour of the six-square-mile peninsula known as Macao. We accepted his offer, and the tour proved to be the most exciting event of the day. We visited an old Catholic church and cemetery. We toured an old fort, which dated back to the thirteenth century. From the fort we looked across the Pearl River at the People's Republic of China. In another place we examined the barbed-wire fence separating Macao from the People's Republic of China. Our guide told us that Macao had recently petitioned for admission to China, but that the petition had been denied. We also examined a Vietnamese refugee camp.

Macao is a very old and run-down city. Compared to those in Las Vegas, even the gambling casinos are fifth rate. But Macao is a place of beautiful flowers. Flowers may well be the city's greatest attraction. As Gail Grejda said at dinner, "Macao is not a place one would go back to."

Saturday, February 14

We spent Valentine's Day in Hong Kong. After a morning of shopping, we returned to McDonald's for lunch. After lunch we took the Star Ferry and left Kowloon for what is known as the Hong Kong side. We spent much of the afternoon wandering in the small streets on a hill above the Pearl River. Many of the vegetable, fruit, and meat stands reminded me of those I had become accustomed to in Beijing. Furthermore, sanitary conditions appeared to be just as bad as those in Beijing. Some shops sold beautiful cut flowers, but cut flowers are plentiful in Hong Kong. We foreigners noticed them because we had come from Beijing, and we appreciated being out of the cold weather for a while. Wanda and I walked until we wore ourselves out; then we took the Star Ferry back to Kowloon and returned to the Imperial Hotel for a rest before preparing for dinner.

Sunday, February 15

The night before, we had eaten dinner at Lindy's Restaurant. We had enjoyed our dinner immensely, for we knew that in a matter of hours we would leave for Beijing where the food we ate for the next few months would be inferior. After dinner at Lindy's Restaurant, Wanda and I had walked in the streets. While walking, we decided that we did not care for Hong Kong. The people in Hong Kong are generally rude and unfriendly. Almost everywhere one encounters hucksters, salesmen, and pimps; in Hong Kong what I call "humanity" is paper-thin. Known as "economic animals," the people of Hong Kong are passionate without passion; they are lovers without love.

On the morning of February 15 we went to the Holiday Inn on Nathan Road for breakfast. We enjoyed the best breakfast we had eaten since leaving Texas six months earlier. Then we went shopping. I purchased a cloisonné bowl for the dining table at our home in Waco. Wanda purchased some agate beads. We wandered in and out of shops and finally went to McDonald's for lunch. Already the humidity was bad. In the summer months, when temperatures are high, Hong Kong must be unbearable. Regardless of the weather, it was Sunday, and we were spending our last day in Hong Kong, so we decided to spend our last few hours taking a tram ride to Victoria Peak. Early the next morning we would have to leave for Guangzhou, where we would board a CAAC plane for Beijing. As for me, I had had enough of vacationing; I wanted nothing more than to return to my students.

Monday, February 16

We enjoyed a light breakfast, checked out of our room, and took a taxi to the dock where we would board a hover ferry. At 9:45 a.m. our hover ferry left the dock. It was a pleasant journey of two and a half hours, a journey during which I watched the many kinds and numbers of ships we passed. While watching I also reflected on the significance of our vacation. Our vacation had been good, but Wanda and I were both ready to return to Beijing and resume our duties. It was during vacation that we realized how much China had affected us. For example, I felt guilty about spending money in Hong Kong. I resented Wanda's purchasing gifts. I resented what we were spending for food and lodging. China, I realized, had conditioned me for something other than the comfortable life we had enjoyed before coming to China. Two days in Hong Kong passed before I could adjust my thinking—before I could accept that our lives lay outside of China and that we would return to our lives in another four months.

The last day in Hong Kong had been particularly enjoyable. When we took our tram ride to the top of Victoria Peak, the mountains were covered by a heavy mist, and the parks were filled with beautiful flowers. Nothing had seemed quite real, but I was likely drawing parallels to the harsh realities of living in China. I thought about our last day in Hong Kong as our hover ferry skipped across the water as though it were a giant water bug.

When we arrived at the border between Hong Kong and China, we stopped and took on an armed escort. The next time we stopped would be in Guangzhou. When we picked up the armed escort, I was reminded of what the young man who had carried our luggage to the taxi in Hong Kong had said. He had asked us what we thought about living in China, and we had given him an evasive answer. He had responded with this: "The difference between living in Hong Kong and in China is that in Hong Kong you are free." When we arrived in Guangzhou, I was convinced of the accuracy of his observation. Nevertheless, we were happy when our CAAC plane had completed our fifteen-hundred-mile flight from Guangzhou to Beijing. We were even happier when our taxi ride from the Beijing airport to the Friendship Hotel ended at 11:00 p.m. We were welcomed home by the attendants on our floor, and we entered our apartment for the first time in almost a month.

Tuesday, February 17

It was a good day, a calm day, and I spent much of my time reading and answering letters. The mail had accumulated while we were gone, and I knew that catching up on correspondence would require several days. Particularly pleasing was a letter from Memphis State University Press concerning reviews of my new book entitled *Jesse Stuart: Kentucky's Chronicler-Poet*. According to the letter, my book is being well received, and that is especially good news because I worked on it over a period of ten years.

Wanda and I unpacked and put things in their proper places. As we did, we felt that we were creating order, and order was something which had been missing from our lives for almost a month. We looked forward to a schedule of work, a routine which marks activity as meaningful because it has a place in one's day. Wanda was so excited about order and routine that she called her supervisor to ask whether she might return to work a day early.

Wednesday, February 18

Although I had no intention of returning to work before February 23, I took a car to the institute because I had a number of things to discuss with Qi Wenqin. I wanted to arrange an exam for a student who had missed one because of illness. I wanted to arrange to give a lecture to class number four because those students had missed one of my lectures near the end of the semester. I wanted to discuss my schedule for the coming semester. But most of all, I wanted to see my students.

I met with Qi Wenqin and handled details concerning the exam, the lecture, and my schedule. I also encountered my students in the halls and elsewhere. Wherever I met them, they rushed up to me and shook my hand or put their arms around me expressing their happiness that I had returned. As for me, I felt good on each such occasion. I felt that perhaps I was making a difference in their lives. I felt good about being back at the institute. I felt good about the coming semester, and I hoped that it would prove to be as successful as the first semester had been.

In the afternoon I worked on four different poems, but I did not get far on any of them. I concluded that they needed more thought. As I worked I realized that they were largely without provocative imagery and that the language was the language of third-rate prose. But in each of the four cases I had a beginning, something committed to paper. I knew that over the next few days my mind would continue working the poems, shaping them. When the thinking had been done, I hoped to end up with poetry.

Thursday, February 19

Nothing seemed to go well. Even the car was unusually late in arriving at the institute. At noon I returned to the Friendship Hotel and went to lunch. After that, Wanda and I took a nap; we were still exhausted from traveling. While Wanda slept, I lay awake much of the time thinking about the young man in Hong Kong who had carried our luggage to the taxi when we left the Imperial Hotel. I thought about his remark that in China one does not have freedom. I thought about many things I had seen and heard during our trip, and I thought about my students. I thought about two of them who are scheming to go to school in America, not realizing that what they are planning will not work because the institute must grant permission before they can be issued visas. I thought about the student who says she is afraid to talk with me in my office because she might be accused of passing state secrets to me. I thought about the fact that the life of each student is closely monitored, that each must account to the school for everything he or she does as well as everywhere he or she goes. I thought about the fact that students are obligated to inform on each other, as is the case in all work units. Yes, I realized the significance of the statement made by the young man in Hong Kong, and I knew that he was aware of the importance of his statement. He had moved to Hong Kong from China; he did not grow up with the freedom he has in Hong Kong, and I was made aware of how precious that freedom is to him.

I also thought about an article I had read in a Hong Kong newspaper about massage parlors. In Hong Kong, as in many other places, massage parlors are fronts for illicit sex. In some Hong Kong massage parlors, masseuses are young Chinese women who have newly arrived from the mainland. They are smuggled into Hong Kong and issued false documents along with promises of freedom and good jobs. But once they are in Hong Kong they are faced with the alternatives of becoming prostitutes or returning to the mainland. Many of them want to escape China so desperately that they will do whatever they must, including becoming prostitutes, until they can find a way of improving their lot. What they do not realize is that the chances of improving their conditions are very slim. Some of them commit suicide. Some find a way to escape those who have enslaved them. But most of them find that they have merely replaced one form of slavery with another, and that the new form of slavery is more demeaning than the old one. In most countries justice for the oppressed is hard to come by, but in Hong Kong what could be a paradise becomes a hell on earth for young women eager to escape the oppression which comes from living in a Communist state. As for the newspaper article, it confirmed what I had suspected concerning massage parlors and prostitution in Hong Kong.

Friday, February 20

Snow had fallen in Beijing. The streets were slippery. I procrastinated about starting for the institute because I did not have to be there until 11:00, at which time I would deliver a lecture. I wanted to talk with Shao Jingfeng and Qi Wenqin. I had purchased a calculator in Hong Kong for Shao's son, and I wanted to give her that. Also, I wanted to invite Qi Wenqin and Zhu Zheng to have dinner with Wanda and me. They had been married while we were on our winter trip, and Wanda and I wanted to congratulate the two of them as well as wish them a long and happy life together. For Chinese people, both of them had experienced unusual marriages. Both had spouses who cheated on them, and in both cases the cheating had resulted in divorce. Now they appear to be happy as husband and wife. Each has had some extremely difficult years, and I wish them the best in their new venture.

At school the office was quiet. I sat and thought about how best to organize a number of activities for the new semester. At 11:00 I lectured on the backgrounds of American literature, and at noon I went home to the compound.

Saturday, February 21

On February 16, 1981, the news bulletin *News From Foreign Agencies and Press* printed a UPI news release dated February 16. The text of the release may be significant to the future of Sino-American relations, and for that reason, I will reproduce the text:

Outgoing ambassador to China Leonard Woodcock said Monday he is confident President Reagan will not bow to pressure from some advisers to re-establish formal relations with Taiwan.

Woodcock, whose resignation is effective at the end of the week, was asked on NBC's "Today" show whether he trusted Reagan to stand by the Peking government in the face of pressures by some advisers, including some of his transition team, who have expressed displeasure at the unofficial relations with Taiwan.

The Carter administration formally opened relations with mainland China in 1979 and ended formal relations with the nationalist Chinese government on Taiwan.

"I understand there have been such sentiments voiced, but it's not possible to have relationships with two Chinas," Woodcock said. "American policy under Republican and Democratic administrations has always been there is one China; . . . the eminent good strategic sense of that relationship, I'm sure, will prevail with this administration and succeeding administrations."

Woodcock said the Chinese were not too concerned about Reagan campaign statements critical of the Peking government because they will judge the administration by its actions, not by campaign rhetoric.

He also said the Chinese were encouraged by the administration's recent pledge to stand by the previous administration's December 15, 1978, normalization communique.

Woodcock said although the Chinese welcome the administration's "stronger posture" on the Soviet Union, U.S.-China relations should not be built merely on a mutual distrust of the Soviets.

"I am a strong supporter of a friendly relationship between China and the United States based on its own merits and not based on any antagonism to any other country," he said. (p. 17)

For numerous reasons, I like Woodcock's statement. First, it is an honest appraisal of the present situation. Second, it is optimistic concerning the future of Sino-American relations. And third, Woodcock's assessment agrees with mine. Time will be required for the United States and China to embrace each other. But the time will come when the two countries show mutual respect for each other and are willing to cooperate because such a relationship is necessary to maintaining peace in the world.

Sunday, February 22

Because Wanda was fighting a cold we did not attempt to go to church. Instead, we slept late and hoped that she would recuperate enough to work on Monday. Staying home from church also gave me an opportunity to catch up on my correspondence. I wrote a long letter to Qi Wenqin, which she will take to the school's officials, as she did with the one I wrote in December. In my letter I included an evaluation of Leonard Woodcock's statement as reported in the bulletin *News from Foreign Agencies and Press.* I included some observations about the institute and about education as related to modernization. I also explained that American universities can do little to help until the Ministry of Education publishes clear-cut policies concerning study abroad. My letter is deliberately pointed because the risk for me is minor; the returns could be great.

In China to check on progress concerning birth control efforts, a delegation from the United Nations has recently found that some babies in the southern provinces are being allowed to die at birth. In other cases the babies are being put to sleep. Presumably these are cases not caught early enough to carry out an abortion, but one can conjecture two things from such a report. First, one can conjecture that the babies are largely, if not entirely, girls. Second, one can conjecture that the same women will be pregnant again. Discrimination against girls is still strong in the countryside, as it has been for hundreds of years. Many of China's peasants will not accept a girl knowing that they are allowed to have only one child per family. As for the future of the government's effort to bring the population under control, I will not be surprised if in the next five years having children becomes illegal altogether. The Chinese people love children and they find being limited to one child oppressive. They will have a difficult time accepting zero childbirth.

Monday, February 23

The day was dreary and cold. As I had done during the semester before, I caught a car for the institute at 6:50 a.m. Because the streets were slick, we were almost an hour reaching the institute. The old woman who brings my hot water had come and gone, but Shao Jingfeng was waiting for me with a host of questions about the literature she was preparing to teach. Some of my students stopped by the office to chat, but in spite of the interruptions I was ready when my first seminar began at 10:00. I soon found that my students were not ready. They had not been informed concerning when the seminar was to meet, and they had not been told concerning how or where to purchase books for the seminar.

When I went into the classroom, I took considerable time to explain how the seminar was to function. I knew that my students had never experienced a seminar, and I knew that they would be anxious about doing something alien to them. I took much time to reassure them, knowing that they will do well after a few days of adjusting. In a Chinese classroom the teacher teaches, and the students keep quiet. Making an oral presentation to one's classmates is simply not acceptable policy. As I outlined objectives for the seminar, I could tell that my students were becoming convinced. Although they will need to be reassured for some time, they will learn quickly because they are eager and cooperative.

Tuesday, February 24

I went to my office and waited for the old woman who brings the hot water. When she came, I poured myself a cup of tea and began working on my lecture for the next day. A number of students stopped by to talk about their seminar reports, and at mid-morning I took a brisk walk. I met Lu Zhibao's wife in the hall, and she told me I would be receiving a letter from her husband soon. She informed me that she and her son live with her mother now that Lu is gone, but she assured me they are both doing well.

After my walk Su Guifen stopped by for a short visit. She did not appear to be well. When I inquired concerning her health, she told me she was suffering from a kidney infection and was to visit the clinic the next morning. I wished her well and told her to let me know if I could be of help during her illness. She will not, because she is too proud. But I wanted her to know that I was concerned.

In the afternoon I went home and continued working on a lecture I had been working on for several days. I entitled my lecture "American Literary Naturalism and Theodore Dreiser," and by 6:00 p.m., about the time Wanda came home from work, I felt that I was ready to deliver a lecture my students would remember for a long time.

Wednesday, February 25

The lecture hall was filled, and students who had transferred into teacher training programs were also present. At the outset I explained that I would meet with students the next morning to answer questions. Then I began my lecture. I lectured for fifty minutes, took a short break, and then lectured for another fifty minutes.

After my lecture, Dean He came to see me. He asked if I might meet with a representative of the Australian government. When I met the representative I found that he was at the institute to determine whether the Australian government should send more teachers. We talked for about an hour, and I answered many questions concerning the quality of present foreign experts, concerning the advisability of bringing children to Beijing, and concerning what the Australian government might do to help the institute in addition to sending teachers. I suggested, for example, that books and teaching materials are desperately needed. I also suggested that the Chinese teachers at the institute need training, and that such training might best be accomplished by sending them to Australia to go to school. When our talk ended, I was pleased that we seemed to be in agreement on the issues I had raised. I hope my suggestions will work toward bettering the quality of education at Second Foreign Language Institute.

Thursday, February 26

For most of the morning I met with students and talked about the lecture I had given during the previous morning. My students had fine questions as well as perceptive observations. Tan Luying also stopped by to inform me that her mother was improving, having suffered for several weeks from a mineral deficiency for which Tan Luying could not remember the name. I had been concerned about Tan Luying, for I had seen little of her since the beginning of the second semester. I had begun to suspect that something besides her mother's illness was wrong.

When I arrived home, awaiting me was a letter from Ralph Wang. Wang's letter contained news that the Bureau of Foreign Experts had approved Victor and Ann Strite, from Baylor University, to teach in Beijing starting in August. I immediately wrote to the Strites to tell them the good news. When the telephone rang at around 3:00 p.m., I received more good news. I answered the phone to hear none other than our only son, Lon. It was indeed a pleasant surprise, for we had not heard from him in several weeks. The only bad news for the day was that I had met a new foreign expert at the institute in the morning. My impressions were not good. He will be a detriment to the school. I fail to see the rationale for employing such people, and I will inform the school officials that as far as I am concerned they have made a grave mistake.

Friday, February 27

As usual, on the way to the institute we were subjected to our normal routine of dodging bicycles and pedestrians. When I arrived at my office, I found that Patrick Cassidy had not yet returned from the United States, and that Diane Stark had not shown up to teach her classes. I had the office all to myself, and I talked with students who came to see me. Included among those students was Su Guifen, who is interested in attending a university in the United States. As we talked, I found that she has been suffering a dilemma. She wants to go to school in the United States, but she is also afraid. As a child she was brought up on horror stories about foreigners.

I met with three of the officials at the institute to discuss Victor and Ann Strite. I suggested that they contact the Bureau of Foreign Experts immediately and request that the Strites be assigned to the Second Foreign Language Institute. I also suggested that they write the Strites and issue an invitation. While we were in session I took advantage of having the officials as a captive audience to complain about the sorry lot of foreign experts being brought to China to teach, including the one employed only a few days earlier. I do not think they were pleased with what I had to say, but I made my point.

Saturday, February 28

It was the last day of the month, and therefore time to place another big "X" on the calendar. Wanda and I were counting the days until we could go home to Waco. We arose early because I had to go to town. I decided that I would ride a bus to town and visit the Bank of China. I had not been to town since before Christmas, and I had not ridden on a bus with the masses. I had not been in touch with the masses, and I was feeling at a loss concerning that. I left the bus when it arrived at the Beijing Hotel and walked from there to the Bank of China, which is located near the Chairman Mao Memorial. Because the bank was busy, I had to wait for almost half an hour to have a check cashed, and then I walked back toward Wangfujing Street. The weather was brisk, and I felt good about being among the Chinese masses.

In the evening Wanda and I went to the Minzu Restaurant to have dinner with Qi Wenqin and Zhu Zheng. We had a delightful evening. Prior to the dinner Wanda had worried that we might not find anything in common about which we could talk, but as it turned out we talked for two hours and could have continued for many more. I was surprised that they talked freely about their misgivings concerning China's political and economic system. They talked about their limitations as teachers in the Chinese school system. They are both very intelligent as well as realistic about the conditions under which they must live and work. Before the evening had ended, Wanda and I felt a genuine bond of friendship with Qi Wenqin and Zhu Zheng.

March

Sunday, March 1

We went to church in Xidan Street, and on the way we observed something I had not seen before. Hundreds of Chinese children were marching down the street carrying banners. They obviously belonged to the Chinese youth movement called the Young Pioneers. Mary Fisher, who was visiting from Tianjin, explained that what we were witnessing had at one time been a common sight.

She attributed the activity among the Young Pioneers to a general tightening up which has been taking place since Deng Xiaoping addressed a meeting of party officials a few days ago. Deng's speech, as well as the fact that the Young Pioneers are back in the streets, was related to the attempt to oust Hua Guofeng. Hua has decided that he will not step down until certain conditions are met, conditions which appear designed to slow down modernization as well as cool off relations between China and the West, particularly between China and the United States.

As for church, it would have been routine except that a young man sitting two rows in front of us suffered an epileptic seizure. Although someone was near him who knew what to do, his contorting and thrashing about was a gruesome sight. Wanda had never seen anyone suffer such a seizure; the experience was sobering for her. When the young man had finally ceased convulsing and was resting on the floor, I looked about to see that the heads of Chinese and foreigners alike were bowed in prayer, and I felt good. I interpreted what I saw as a symbol of hope for all of us.

When Mao Zhiren came to visit, he brought with him a letter of acceptance from Baylor University. However, he was worried because he had heard that the Chinese government had issued an order prohibiting the issuing of passports to intellectuals. Mao was afraid that the order might be intended for postgraduate students. He had heard that the ban was caused by a massive exodus of intellectuals from China over the last few months. According to the conditions set down by the government, only four categories of people are being issued passports. Those include students (what we would call undergraduate students in the United States), educated youth working in the country (meaning that they have completed middle school), educated but unemployed youth in the cities, and the uneducated. The four categories obviously do not include the most desirable people.

Monday, March 2

I went to the embassy to talk with John Thomson, counselor for cultural affairs, about Mao Zhiren. He confirmed that a mass exit of intellectuals has taken place, and that as a result the government has stopped issuing passports to professors and other intellectuals. But the flow of intellectuals to the West, he said, had not changed drastically in the last six months. I discussed Mao with John Thomson, and he anticipated that Mao would encounter no difficulty because the Chinese government would be asked to expend no money. Thomson explained that Mao should go directly to the Security Bureau rather than the Ministry of Education for his passport. Otherwise, Thomson added, the entire procedure is likely to be delayed because of bureaucratic red tape.

Tuesday, March 3

I arrived at the institute at 7:30 a.m. and left at noon. In that time half a dozen students came to my office to talk about their seminar reports, and I completed my reading for the next day's lecture. Because Patrick Cassidy, having recently returned from the United States, was in conference with a Chinese teacher most of the morning, I experienced few interruptions. At midmorning I found Qi Wenqin in the hall not far from my office, and that proved to be fortuitous. She went to the payroll office to pick up my pay, and when she returned she informed me that the school officials wanted a conference with me the next morning to discuss a letter of mine in which I proposed that we explore the possibility of an exchange program between Second Foreign Language Institute and Baylor University. Such exchange programs as I have proposed could eventually make a difference in the quality of Chinese education. China must educate the masses, but in the meantime the quality of what exists as education must be improved.

That March has come to Beijing was evident. Strong winds stirred up dust everywhere, and Beijing lacks vegetation to hold the soil in place. Being outside was unpleasant, even though the sun was shining. Throughout the afternoon I stayed inside and admired the sunshine through a closed window.

Wednesday, March 4

The lecture I had given a week earlier on literary naturalism had proved too difficult for my students. Since that time I had reworked it and had added simplified explanations. I was eager to try the revised lecture, and at 8:00 a.m. I did just that. All during the two hours in which I lectured I could tell that my students were understanding. I could tell from their facial expressions and the quiet, easy atmosphere throughout the auditorium that they were understanding and appreciating my lecture. I succeeded, and I was pleased.

After class I was taken across campus to meet with Vice President Lei Wen. He had read my letter proposing an exchange program between Second Foreign Language Institute and Baylor University. I direct the American Studies program at Baylor, and I have believed for some time that the future of American Studies lies in the kind of exchange that I would like to see take place between Baylor and Second Foreign Language Institute. That is, I believe the future of American Studies lies in training teachers to teach American Studies in foreign cultures. Both Americans and foreigners must be trained to teach about American culture and institutions in places other than America.

Lei Wen and I exchanged ideas for an hour or more, and he assured me that he was interested in my proposal. He said he would do anything he could to implement such an exchange program. A final plan, we agreed, would have to be examined and approved by the Chinese Ministry of Education as well as by the administration at Baylor University. If it were implemented, an exchange program would have mutual benefits. For example, Baylor students would have an opportunity to study Chinese language, literature, and history. On the other hand, Chinese teachers could receive much-needed training in pedagogy. They could also study American culture and language. Such a relationship would be beneficial to both schools.

Thursday, March 5

A senior partner in the firm building the Great Wall Hotel, Richard Young, explained to me the political motivation behind the government's freeze on passports for Chinese intellectuals. The action, according to Young, was triggered by the Reagan inauguration. As the story goes, representatives from both Taiwan and Beijing were invited to attend the inauguration, but when the government in Beijing found out that representatives from Taiwan would attend, officials in Beijing were upset. The government in Beijing sent word to Washington that representatives from the People's Republic of China would not attend if representatives from Taiwan were present. As it turned out, according to Young, representatives from Taiwan did not attend, but representatives from the People's Republic of China did. The government in Beijing interpreted the incident to mean that President Reagan had not made up his mind concerning relations with China.

The Chinese government is concerned that it might be forced to break diplomatic relations with the United States, as it threatened to do over the inauguration incident. In such an event, officials in the government fear that the United States government would grant asylum to Chinese intellectuals in the United States at the time and China would be robbed of brain power that the country desperately needs. The freeze on passports is a political ploy and a precautionary measure. But it creates great obstacles for people like Mao Zhiren who are trying to secure passports in order to study in the United States.

Friday, March 6

Friday was rather uneventful. I arrived at the institute at around 7:30 a.m. as usual. I graded papers and met with some of my students to discuss seminar reports. Then I met classes three and four and listened to seminar reports, after which I returned to the Friendship Hotel for lunch. In the afternoon, I sat in the apartment and graded papers amidst many disrupting noises. First, noises from hammers and saws constantly disrupted me. Electricians were installing air conditioners at the Friendship Hotel, and workmen were drilling holes in the walls to accommodate the units. Second, March is the time of dust storms, and the wind blew viciously. Outside the apartment window the wind sounded like a lost dog on a dreary night. Although the sun often shines brightly in March, the wind made me feel that the outside must be cold and uninviting. Perhaps such a delusion was necessary for me to continue writing and grading papers inside.

Saturday, March 7

It was Saturday, and Wanda had been invited to a celebration for Chinese women in the Great Hall of the People. In the morning we visited the market across the street and the shops in building number one. After lunch, while Wanda participated in the celebration, I stayed home and graded papers. I even managed to take a short nap. I am becoming a believer in the custom of taking a nap after lunch.

Wanda and I each wrote letters to Lon, our son. We had received a letter from him the day before, a letter full of difficult questions which I took to indicate a bit of despondency on his part. Our letters were attempts to answer his questions while bolstering his morale. How does one answer such questions as these: "What drives you to work hard every day?" "When you were my age, how did you handle peer pressure?" "Did you also need to be assured that you were loved?" Our son is obviously missing his parents, and we will be glad when we can return home to be with him. Writing the letters to our son was the most important event of the day.

Sunday, March 8

On our way to church, the taxi driver asked numerous questions of Wen Yee Chin concerning Christianity and the Bible. A young man who had never attended church, he was obviously curious. Once we arrived at church and left the car, I thought no more about the driver's curiosity. Carried away by the Chinese Women's Day celebration, the minister held the congregation longer than usual, and I became worried that our driver might leave us. I left before the service ended and went into the street to detain our driver. But as it turned out my going to retain the driver was not necessary. I found the taxi, but it was empty. Our driver had taken it upon himself to attend the worship service. I stayed with the car, and in ten or fifteen minutes I saw him coming across the street with a big smile on his face. He was accompanied by Wanda and Wen Yee.

After lunch Wanda and I took a car to the institute. We went to have dinner in the home of Qi Wenqin and Zhu Zheng. On the way we stopped at the Friendship Store and purchased a set of dishes to take home to Texas with us in July. We enjoyed a delicious dinner with our Chinese friends, including L. T. Lin, who is vice dean of the English department as well as party secretary. We ate too much, but the food was some of the best we had eaten since coming to China.

Wanda and I both enjoyed talking with L. T. Lin. We learned that he had been transferred to Second Foreign Language Institute from a People's Liberation Army headquarters over a year ago. We also learned that he came from a family of Christians. His father once studied at Iowa State College, now Iowa State University, and his brother studied at the University of Michigan. Another brother once studied at a college in Georgia. Because of these connections, L. T. Lin seemed very interested in both Christianity and America. All in all, it was a good evening, one of genuine warmth and friendship. I hardly knew how to react when we were preparing for bed later in the evening and without provocation on my part Wanda asked, "Is Qi Wenqin a member of the Communist Party?"

Monday, March 9

I met my seminars, and the presentations made by my students exceeded my expectations. My students, I discovered, are capable of more profound insight into literature than I anticipated. I commended those who made presentations; they had worked hard.

Gail Grejda returned from five days in Hong Kong and told us that the newspapers there carry daily reports about the growing unrest which appears to be sweeping across the mainland of China. One does not read such reports in newspapers in China, but the unrest is obvious. Thus far the only solution to the unrest offered by the government is to increase the time every Chinese person is required to spend at political meetings. A recently launched "learn-from-Lei Feng" campaign appears to be directly related to the unrest. Lei Feng pictures appear in many public places, including schools. Slogans about learning from Lei Feng are numerous. Newspapers are carrying articles glorifying the deeds of Lei Feng, once popularized by Mao Zedong to promote loyalty to the government. The present "learn-from-Lei Feng" campaign appears to be predicated on the premise that such a campaign should work because a similar one once worked for Mao Zedong.

The March 7, 1981, issue of *Xinhua News Agency News Bulletin* carried the following:

A nationwide campaign to learn from Lei Feng is taking shape in

China as young people throughout the country volunteer service to people in need in the spirit of the selfless army man.

In China's biggest city, Shanghai, 300,000 youth yesterday swept streets, cleaned public squares and helped direct traffic.

A "learn-from-Lei Feng week" has been launched in south China's Guangzhou, northwest China's Xian, southwest China's Chengdu and many other cities. Groups of young people and children are planting trees and flowers in parks, helping elderly people cross streets and doing odd jobs for local residents.

Lei Feng, a squad leader in an army engineering corps, died on duty in 1962 at the age of 22. He had dedicated his life to serving people and many times risked death to aid those in distress. He spent his spare time working in people's communes, at construction sites, and for his army comrades and others.

Yesterday morning 2,500 people in Lei Feng's hometown in Wangcheng County, Hunan Province, gathered to mark the 18th anniversary of the call issued by the Central Committee of the Chinese Communist Party and Chairman Mao to learn from this Communist hero. In Beijing, thousands of soldiers, workers, peasants and students visited an exhibition on Lei Feng's deeds at the military museum of the Chinese People's Revolution.

The campaign to learn from Lei Feng is also underway in the People's Liberation Army. Forums, meetings, and discussions are being held in units to discuss the Communist spirit Lei Feng embodied and to explore ways of emulating him. Many matched deeds to words by working in nearby villages, factories, wharves, stores and markets. (pp. 24-25)

One can make a number of conjectures about the article. For example, it seems directly related to a general tightening up which has been taking place. Also, it seems to indicate that the Hua Guofeng contingent in the government is gaining power over Deng Xiaoping and his followers. If the present trend continues, Deng may be headed for trouble; his name has been in the news very little over the last few weeks.

Tuesday, March 10

I held conferences with my students and met with Qi Wenqin. I presented Qi Wenqin with a copy of *Jesse Stuart: Essays on His Work*, which Mary Washington Clarke and I edited a few years back for the University Press of Kentucky. I checked my mail at the institute, and as usual found that I had none. I drank several cups of tea and in general found being confined to my desk strangely satisfying. In the middle of the afternoon Jessie McGaw, a friend of Genevieve and Wallace Strevell, called from the Beijing Hotel. Genevieve and Wallace are friends of ours in Waco, Texas. Jessie, who is in town on business, said she wanted to meet and talk with us before leaving Beijing. We agreed that Wanda and I would come to the Beijing Hotel and meet her in her room on Thursday evening. For the remainder of the afternoon nothing else interfered with my work. By five o'clock I had completed preparations for the next day of classes. I decided to rest before Wanda came home and we rushed off to dinner. I knew she would have much to talk about because during the day she was to attend groundbreaking ceremonies for the Great Wall Hotel, a joint project by China International Travel Service and the firm for which Wanda works.

Wednesday, March 11

For two hours I lectured on the topic "Skills of the Poet." My students showed great interest in the topic, and I was pleased. At break time, Dean He came into the auditorium with an assistant to take attendance. I was surprised because he had never done such a thing before. The head count was probably part of the tightening up taking place and was probably brought on by complaints from teachers that too many students have been missing class. My students have attended class regularly and have maintained a high level of interest.

I was reminded that in some respects Chinese students still do not trust teachers, Chinese or otherwise. Qi Wenqin came to see me, and in the process of our discussion told me that some of my students had complained to Dean He that I was about to give them an examination. Because their lives depend heavily upon the grades they receive, my students remain frightened of examinations. I have tried to explain to them the value of examinations, but explanations afford little consolation. For several days prior to an exam my students become nervous and anxious; some become physically ill. They are especially frightened of an exam on which they cannot collaborate with others. They are frightened of both immediate and long-term effects of personal failure. Perhaps living in a Communist state has not prepared them for success or failure in a personal sense; nor has it prepared them to be individuals as opposed to being mass-persons.

Before she left teacher Qi presented me with two terra cotta figures, replicas of soldiers in miniature from the Qin Dynasty. They looked like the life-sized terra cotta figures we had seen at the excavation in Xian. I was pleased at such a token of friendship, and I knew Wanda would be pleased. The figures had cost Wenqin and her husband much, and I thought of their meager salaries as I rode home at noon.

I called John Thomson at the embassy only to find out that he had no further information concerning Mao Zhiren's going to study at Baylor University. Mao, it appears, cannot leave the country until he completes the program in which he is presently enrolled. There is a "Catch-22," however, because once he completes the program his going will be prohibited by a document recently published by the Ministry of Education.

Thursday, March 12

It was a day during which two things happened, and both were disappointing. The first concerned a visit to the embassy on my way to pick up IRS publication number fifty-four, to pick up two copies of *Highlights of American Literature*, and to talk with John Thomson in regard to Mao's effort to go to America. I found the IRS publication, but the books were out of stock. Concerning Mao, John Thomson explained that the government had adopted a new policy. The Ministry of Education had issued a document stating that postgraduate students were not to be issued passports. In short, the statement said that such students must complete the programs in which they are enrolled before passports for foreign study will be considered by the government. The decision means that Mao will likely not go to study at Baylor for another year; it will take him about that long to complete his master's degree in economics at Beijing University.

Thomson and I talked about a number of other things. We talked about the fact that intellectuals have been leaving China in great numbers, about the fact that some leave and refuse to come back (as is the case with a number of musicians in Hong Kong), about a rumor that the government is about to shut off all passports for study abroad except for scientists, about the fact that the present split in the government is quite dangerous and could conceivably lead to a revolution of some sort, and about the fact that the United States government is changing its educational objectives as well as expenditures for education in China. According to Thomson, the United States government will abandon its effort to train Chinese teachers to teach English. In the future the United States government will concentrate on building American Studies programs in China. The basic premise behind such a move is that knowledge of American culture, including American thought, will prove valuable to the future of Sino-American relations.

The second thing that happened during the day concerned a visit by Jessie McGaw. When she called three or four days earlier, we had agreed on a meeting time and place. In short, we had agreed that Wanda and I would meet her at 7:00 p.m. in her room in the Beijing Hotel. Knowing that we would not have time for dinner at the Friendship Hotel after Wanda came home from work, I arranged to meet Wanda at the Beijing Hotel at 5:30. We had dinner in the restaurant at the Beijing Hotel and then went to Jessie McGaw's room. We knocked on the door, but no one answered. We then went to the information desk only to be told that the room was not occupied by Jessie McGaw, but by a man named Campbell. We decided that the man at the information desk could be wrong, so we waited for a while and then tried to call the room from the lobby. No one answered. We finally gave up and returned to the Friendship Hotel to find that our evening had been a comedy of errors. When we arrived on the fifth floor of building four, which is where we live, we found Jessie McGaw patiently waiting for us. She had been waiting for almost two hours, but I never did find out why she had come to the Friendship Hotel knowing that we were to meet her in her room at the Beijing Hotel. I dismissed the entire matter as a case of what traveling in China will do to an older person. Jessie McGaw must be about seventy years old.

Friday, March 13

We continue to hear reliable news from outside China concerning conditions within China. Because the Chinese press is owned and operated by the government, hearing anything from within that might throw an unfavorable light upon the government is impossible. But an example of an informative report is to be found in *Newsweek* (March 16, 1981). By James LeMoyne and Melinda Liu, a brief article entitled "Warning Signals on the Labor Front" discusses labor unrest and efforts to form labor unions in China. Like their Western counterparts, Chinese workers are trying to cope with inflation, the official rate of which is 5.8 percent. However, unofficially the rate is closer to 20 percent. In its determination to modernize China, the government has overspent. The government has recently reneged on construction contracts with foreign countries, slashing capital construction by 40 percent. According to the *Newsweek* article, between seventeen and twenty-six million are unemployed, and because of cancelled construction projects that number will grow rapidly. China's problems will increase, although handling unrest has already become a nearly full-time preoccupation of the government.

In the future there will be more reports like the one in *Newsweek*, which also relates an incident that took place last November:

> Deng is a lot tougher than Poland's shaky leadership, as he showed when Chinese troops killed scores of protesting workers last November on state farms in the western province of Xinjiang. A government memo sent to senior cadres after those shootings said such incidents were "warnings of the severity of measures we must take." (p. 23)

When I read something like this, I wonder whether the effort toward achieving modernization is a big mistake. China suffers a strange paradox: Joining the modern world is vital to the future of the country but doing so is rendered impossible by present conditions.

Saturday, March 14

All night the wind blew viciously, and all day Wanda and I stayed inside. We watched as a layer of dust coated everything in our apartment. Dust came in around windows, around doors, and even through exhaust vents. Outside, dust swirled and eddied around the corners of buildings and often formed large clouds over open spaces. When we left our apartment to go to lunch, we faced a swirling cloud of dust; and when we thought it had found its direction, thus allowing us to pass, it reversed directions and came directly toward us as though it were an animated thing with a will of its own. Except for walking to the dining hall for lunch and dinner, we spent the day inside. The March dust storms for which Beijing is famous are real. They are not merely exaggerations by tourists who come to Beijing and then dash off books and articles to entertain and intrigue those who do not come. On the other hand, the dust storms appear to be especially bad this year. Northeast China, particularly Hebei Province, has been undergoing a severe drought. Water supplies are low, and the growing season is near. Throughout the winter northeast China has suffered from a shortage of vegetables, and if the drought continues food supplies for next winter may be many times shorter than they are now. Already great unrest exists in the countryside. One cannot help but be impressed that China is a time bomb.

Sunday, March 15

The curiosity concerning religion seems to be genuine, and I have been told by many people that such curiosity extends throughout China. Today, as was the case last Sunday, a young Chinese driver drove us to the church in Xidan Street. As with the other driver, the driver this Sunday asked Wen Yee Chin questions about religion. All the way to church and all the way back he asked questions about the Bible and Christianity. Furthermore, as was the case last Sunday, the driver left his car when we arrived in Xidan Street and attended the church service.

When the service ended, Wanda and I struck up a conversation with a Chinese man who appeared to be in his thirties. He spoke English well. He was perplexed concerning the relationship between science and religion in America; he could not understand how religion and science could coexist. I explained that I would pursue the topic with him at a later date, at which point he changed to the topic of politics, both American and Chinese. He said he was concerned about the instability of the government in Beijing, and that he was concerned over the possible consequences of the power struggle in the government. He described the present state of government in Beijing as "a mess" and confided in me that he thought the power struggle would lead to serious problems in the near future. The young man did not want to stop talking, but after about an hour we had no recourse but leave him. Our taxi driver would wait no longer.

His parting words were that he would look for us the next Sunday.

On the way back to the Friendship Hotel I thought about the young man's difficulty in reconciling science and religion. I also thought of an article I had recently read in *Newsweek* (March 16, 1981, p. 67). Entitled "Scopes II in California," the article was about teaching evolution in Sacramento, California. It records a classic confrontation between a family of Christian fundamentalists and a school system, but implications for America at large far transcend the case. Nor is the essence of the case to be found in a struggle between creationists and evolutionists. Clearly, the implications are that America may be in the process of coming of age intellectually. The implications are that Americans are no longer willing to accept theories postulated by scientists as indisputable facts; as for the matter of origins, although one theory may be preferable to another, they both nevertheless remain theories, and theories are neither final nor complete. If it became widespread, such thinking could go a long way toward destroying scientific positivism, which has haunted Americans throughout most of this century.

Monday, March 16

More than ever I observed that fear and anxiety have been building up in my students since winter vacation. They are handling their fear and anxiety over what has been happening in the government and the institute, in various ways. For the most part, I have observed three patterns. The quiet and timid ones are withdrawing; they are afraid of being hurt. A second group has developed a nonchalant attitude toward learning, as if falling into a role they have played successfully on previous occasions. Still another group, the third, has become daring and reckless, as if they were refusing to be intimidated regardless of the cost. If trouble comes to the institute, they will be the ones to watch. They are obviously tired of being intimidated and tired of living in fear. When I attempted to joke about their being oppressed to one of my students, suggesting that they might be overreacting, she quickly replied, "You don't know China!" I was not startled by what she said but by the trembling voice in which she said it. I was even more startled that my effort to jest had made her double over in a convulsion of fear, as if the nerves in her body were pulling her toward a fetal position.

When I looked at my student, bent almost double and with tears in her eyes, I knew that she had cause to be afraid. I was both angry and sorry. I was angry at a system that operates by fear and sorry for the victims of that system. I wanted to cry with her, but I knew that my crying would not help. In spite of their fear and anxiety, my students gave impressive seminar presentations. They were reluctant to discuss, to talk. In that respect they reminded me of the condition in which I had found them when I first arrived at the institute almost seven months earlier. I hope the manual labor they perform on Thursday and Friday, in keeping with the national Lei Feng emphasis, will be therapeutic.

Tuesday, March 17

All morning I sat in my office brooding and marking seminar papers. Two of my students came to see me, but their questions were few and short. I sent for Qi Wenqin in order to discuss with her the possibility of arranging a time to make up the classes my students were missing because of having to perform manual labor. I also reminded her that I had not signed a contract, although one should have been signed shortly after my arrival in China. She tried to humor me by commenting about the inefficiency of the system, about which only Westerners seem greatly bothered. The Chinese expect inefficiency, and they have learned to tolerate it. But I knew that my anxiety was pointless. I knew that when the right whim struck the right officials the contracts would be signed. I also knew that until that time nothing would make a difference.

L. T. Lin presented me with a five-volume set of *Selected Works of Mao Zedong* and a copy of *Selected Military Writings of Mao Zedong*. The writings of Mao have been hauled into the institute by the truckload over the last several days. What it all means is very clear. The government has decided that resurrecting Mao is necessary to handling unrest; hence indoctrination is being intensified. To see whether the effort to crowd out radical thinking will result in crowding out all thinking will be interesting. The possibility that such will happen is rapidly increasing.

Wednesday, March 18

When I arose in the morning, I faced two questions. First, how would my students react to a long lecture on poetic meter or measure? Whether they would find the topic sufficiently interesting not to become restless bothered me. Considering the level of anxiety among my students, I was even more bothered by the fact that I would lecture in a large auditorium where the individual could remain anonymous and indifferent. As it turned out, I had nothing about which to worry. My students were fascinated by the idea of meter. Approximately two-thirds of the way through the lecture, I gave them an exercise in scansion, and they were fascinated by that. When the lecture ended, I reminded myself that I could not have been as successful in an American university, given the same topic. I felt better about my students because I realized they had made up their minds not to allow politics to interfere with learning.

The second question was this: What reaction will I receive when I assign study questions for an examination? Horrified by the idea of taking exams, some of my students have prevailed upon Qi Wenqin and the dean of the department to have me dismiss any idea of giving an exam. Such a tactic would work if I were a Chinese teacher. A Chinese teacher will yield to such a demand rather than face criticism. Because Qi Wenqin and Dean He both respect my judgment, they have advised my students to prepare for an examination. Because of their cooperation, when I assigned the study questions my students reacted with acceptance.

That Chinese students are petrified by exams is understandable. They want to exercise as much control over the future as they can. Surely in the backs of their minds exist reservations about the extent to which they can afford to entrust their future to a foreigner, especially one from a country they have been taught to label as Imperialist. That my students protested to Qi Wenqin and Dean He was not an effort on their part to register dislike for me. On the contrary, their daily performance indicates that they like me. For them the protest was a strategy for survival, and survival is utmost in their minds in this time of political crisis. The exam, I assured my students, will be given on schedule. I hope it proves to be a giant stride toward genuine interest in evaluation as an essential part of the educational process at Second Foreign Language Institute.

Wanda and I had dinner with about seventy-five Texans. David Meier had called two days earlier to say that he was bringing us greetings from President and Mrs. McCall as well as from Lois Strain, all from Baylor University in Waco, Texas. The Meiers invited Wanda and me to have dinner with them and their travel group; the Meiers own and operate a travel service located in Hurst, Texas. We met them at the Yanxiang Hotel, near the Beijing airport, and had an enjoyable evening. They asked many questions about China, as all wide-eyed tourists are prone to do. Our responses to their questions were not filled with optimism about the future of China, but they seemed to understand.

Thursday, March 19

Since my students had been assigned to do manual labor, I stayed home. I caught up on some reading and writing. I also performed a number of chores such as having my hair cut and purchasing various things at the store. I did considerable thinking. When Rita Clarke visited us the night before, I realized during our conversation that she was suffering from an acute case of "Chinamania." She has become obsessed by the idea of doing something for the Chinese people, and particularly for her students. She has become personally involved with a number of her students, and because she cares for them and loves them she also feels sorry for them. Because she has chosen not to remain detached, she is hurting inside.

What I realized during the day is that what happened to Rita has also happened to me. Feeling sorry leads to feeling desperate to help in some way. In turn, feeling desperate leads to feeling guilty about what one possesses and enjoys compared to the little the Chinese have. For one who becomes desperate enough, personal survival becomes the chief issue. I have concluded that a foreign teacher in China had better develop a sense of detachment. One had better possess a cold heart and a determination to keep a distance from the Chinese as individuals. He or she had better be capable of backing off at any time and viewing relationships philosophically. Only then will he or she be fit to help the Chinese.

Friday, March 20

While listening to Radio Moscow, I realized that the Soviets are intensifying their anti-American rhetoric. In a short newscast, the "Imperialistic Americans" were attacked on three counts: First, the newscast denounced the Reagan administration for backing the "rebel murderers of women and children" in El Salvador. Second, the United

States government was denounced for testing, in preparation for using, germ warfare on a massive scale. Third, the United States government was denounced for converting the space shuttle *Columbia* from a surveillance shuttle to one for military purposes, that is, one designed to launch nuclear warheads.

In all three cases, of course, the charges are those of the Soviets. They must intensify their rhetoric of fear to gain citizen support for handling the Reagan administration in the future. President Reagan's hard-line approach concerning the Soviets appears to have them worried over how to carry out their objectives for maintaining and enlarging the Soviet bloc.

Saturday, March 21

Wanda and I were preparing to leave our apartment for a walk when the phone rang. David Meier was passing through Beijing on the return trip with his tour group, and he wanted us to meet him at Sun Altar Restaurant for lunch. We agreed to meet with David and his group—partially because they had thirty-five New Testaments for us to distribute among the Chinese and partially because I wanted to make some contacts that might result in sponsoring some of my Chinese students in American universities. Also, we knew it would do us much good to talk with people from home. As it turned out, we were pleased with our visit. We enjoyed visiting with the Meiers. We did not stay long because we had to meet David Hendon, a Baylor University history professor on leave to teach in Japan, for a trip to the Temple of Heaven.

Our trip to the Temple of Heaven was rushed but pleasant. Although David was scheduled to leave Beijing on a late afternoon train headed for Siberia, he was able to see the major sights at the Temple of Heaven before we rushed him into a taxi and sent him on his way. On our way back to the Friendship Hotel, Wanda and I discussed our schedule for the remainder of the day. We had planned to have dinner at the Minzu Restaurant, but we decided to cancel our evening out in order that she might do some of the work she had brought home the evening before.

Sunday, March 22

It was a beautiful Sunday morning, and the church in Xidan Street was filled. Because Wen Yee Chin had overslept, we arrived late, but the service was rewarding enough to overcome any obstacles. It was after church that I began to wonder about the young man with whom Wanda and I had talked the Sunday before.

I did not want to become suspicious of him, but as had been the case previously he asked too many pointed questions about the government and the church in China. The more I talked with him, the more I realized that he might be a party member or an agent of the secret police. We knew that party members attended the church frequently to check up on who attended and what happened. To check on foreigners was also one of their tasks. We knew that Bibles must be registered so that the government knows who has them and where they are. Anyway, when the young man opened our conversation by saying, "I think the church will soon be suppressed by the government again," I felt that he was anticipating my committing myself concerning the issue. Suspicious of his motives, I responded by saying, "It all depends." The young man may not be a party informer at all, or an agent of the police, but I am convinced that he is not merely another church member.

Mao Zhiren came to visit us in the evening. Although disappointed, he seemed to have resigned himself to the fact that he will not be going to America for at least another year. He recognized that other postgraduate students have the same problem. He also talked about a student demonstration at Beijing University in which students broke thermos bottles, burned their bed clothes, and generally released their anxieties. As usual, we talked about the Chinese economy, the sad state of which Mao blames on Deng Xiaoping. As for Chairman Hua, Mao thinks he is a fine man. As for recent oppressive measures initiated by the government, Mao thinks they are essential in handling unrest.

Given the level of education among the Chinese people, I concede that Mao may be right, particularly when one considers the density of China's population. However, my concession does not make me appreciate oppression or Hua Guofeng, and I told Mao as much before he left to go home.

Monday, March 23

My day progressed well until it was time to leave the institute and go home. My students had been writing an exam, and as usual they did not want to stop. When I went to catch a car, I found that I had been left behind. All of the cars had gone, and I wondered what to do. I sent one of my students to the Office of Foreign Experts to inquire about transportation, and when he returned he told me that a car would come to pick me up in about two hours. We walked across campus to the dining hall only to find that it had closed. After arguing with a cook, I finally sat down to some dry and tasteless rice and some dry and tasteless scrambled eggs mixed with bean curd and chopped onion. I returned to my office and had a cup of tea while talking with a student. Eventually the car came.

While waiting in my office, I had read that President Reagan met with China's ambassador to the United States to assure him that the Reagan administration honored the official recognition of China which began under the Carter administration. An article I read in the *Xinhua News Agency News Bulletin* was full of optimism about future Sino-American relations. At the same time, an article in *News from Foreign Agencies and Press* highlighted United States' trade with China. According to the article, the National Council for U.S.-China trade is holding a meeting to consider ways of expanding trade between the two countries.

Tuesday, March 24

According to the front page of the *International Herald Tribune* (March 23, 1981), Gerald Ford was in Beijing over the weekend to reassure the Chinese government concerning President Reagan's intentions pertaining to normalization of relations between China and the United States. Considering Ford's part in the Reagan campaign, and considering the fact that Leonard Woodcock has not been replaced as ambassador, I would not be surprised if Ford were being considered for the post of ambassador. I think the Chinese would get along with Ford because of his "down-on-the-farm" personality. The Chinese liked Leonard Woodcock immensely, and largely because he combined a rustic style with a labor background. One thing is for certain: A political prima donna will never be accepted as ambassador by the Chinese.

On page two of the same issue of the *International Herald Tribune* appears an article by James P. Sterba entitled "As Seen from Peking, Links with U.S. Have Waned Since Reagan Was Elected." The article is accurate in stating that relations between the United States and China have cooled pending an official announcement on the president's position concerning Taiwan. Interest in China by American business firms has also waned, and mostly for the same reason. The American embassy, reports Sterba, is preoccupied with infighting and has become both ineffective and inefficient since the departure of Leonard Woodcock. According to Sterba, the embassy no longer serves American business interests or the interests of Americans in Beijing in general. To a great extent Sterba's allegations are true. The causes are threefold. First, without a clear signal from Washington concerning President Reagan's intentions, the Chinese government has behaved coolly toward the American embassy. Second, too much time has elapsed since Woodcock's departure, and the embassy still does not have a leader. And third, the current power struggle in the Beijing government, coupled with problems in the economy, has produced a "wait-and-see" attitude among American diplomats in Beijing as well as among American investors. Surely, President Reagan will not hesitate much longer in naming an ambassador. The American community in China needs a leader. Recently I read an article in *China Reconstructs* (30, No. 4 [April 1981], 54-56). Entitled "What Is China's Policy Towards Religion?" the article claims that religion cannot be stamped out by force. According to Lei Zhenchang, only when the Chinese people are enlightened by Marxism will the ignorance and superstition which accompany religion disappear. One short paragraph is typical of the article:

The Party and government have stood for a policy of freedom of religious belief. This fundamental, long-term policy accords to Chinese citizens the right to believe or not to believe in religion, or any sect thereof. Nonbelievers are free to become believers, and vice versa. All citizens, religious or not, are politically equal. All faiths, large or small, are on an equal footing. (p. 54)

Mr. Liu does not explain why the government forbids foreign missionaries or the accepting of Bibles from abroad. He does not explain that many work units prohibit their workers from attending church. In the United States citizens register handguns, but in China they register Bibles. By requiring that all Bibles be purchased through a church, the government has a record of how many are in circulation as well as the name and address of each person who owns one. As it looks now, the

New Testaments left with Wanda and me by the Meiers will have to be distributed through the underground church. We are breaking the law by having them in our possession, and distributing them through the underground church will be dangerous. Yes, the article in *China Reconstructs* does a fine job of explaining the government's position. But it ignores the facts about religion in China as they bear directly upon the lives of the Chinese people.

Wednesday, March 25

I lectured to my students on the nature of contemporary American poetry. Coming from a culture bound by rules, restrictions, and formulas, they find contemporary American poetry a bit inconsequential but difficult. I am not surprised; many American students feel the same way. On the other hand, my lecture was well received. My students seemed particularly to enjoy my efforts at illustrating. To them, seeing makes a big difference in understanding.

The most exciting event of the day was a visit to my office by Qi Wenqin. She came to give me answers to a number of questions I had asked her. For example, I had asked whether I might teach my last class on June 26 and leave shortly after that for America. She informed me that my request had been granted, and that even though I was leaving early the school would pay me for the month of July. I had asked her to check on arrangements for shipping a crate around the first of May as well as on travel arrangements for Wanda and me. Again the answers were satisfactory. Furthermore, she informed me that the annual contract would be signed the next morning at 10:00. I was pleased because I expected the signing of the contract to result in increasing my salary, and that would result in retroactive pay. It was a good morning, and by noon I was ready to retire to the Friendship Hotel and grade papers.

I finally succeeded in having a mysterious Chinese tract translated. The tract was the third of its kind that had been inserted into letters coming from friends and relatives in the United States. While the letters were en route to Beijing, someone opened them for the purpose of inserting antigovernment propaganda.

The recent tract argues that Marxism is not true socialism, that Mao Zedong was not a true socialist, that Deng Xiaoping follows Mao and is therefore not a true socialist, and that Hua Guofeng lacks a power base of his own but is not a true socialist either because he supports Deng Xiaoping. What China has in the form of government, argues the writer of the tract, is a dictatorship of the proletariat. He contends that Deng Xiaoping's real purpose behind modernization is to realize modernization in politics. He attacks the basic principles of the Communist Party and argues that these principles are not consistent with socialism. Published by the Shanghai Branch of China's Social Revolution Party on May 16, 1980, the tract calls for the young people of China to rise up and over-throw the present government because it is not the real democracy that the people of China want.

Thursday, March 26

Early in the morning Wanda and I listened to a radio program from Taiwan called "The Voice of Free China." The program consisted of a direct appeal to the mainland Chinese to rise up and overthrow the gov-ernment in Beijing. Broadcast three days before an important meeting in Taiwan of the Kuomintang, the message was remarkably like that of the tract we had received in our mail a few days earlier. It cited an oppressive government, the state of the economy, foreign investment, instability of the government, and other such things as reasons for inciting a revolu-tion to overthrow the government in Beijing in order to replace it with a democratic one. Such broadcasts, I suspect, have Deng Xiaoping and others in the Beijing government a bit worried.

News from Foreign Agencies and Press reprinted an article from *the New York Times* (March 22, 1981) entitled "President Reassures China on Ties as Signs of Strain Begin to Emerge." Recognizing that Sino-American relations have cooled, the writer of the article, Bernard Gwertzman, dis-cusses the importance of President Reagan's meeting with Ambassador Chai Zemin. He also discusses the president's campaign rhetoric concern-ing Taiwan and the People's Republic of China. Because of his campaign speeches, the Beijing government will be cautious in accepting Reagan.

Friday, March 27

I administered exams to classes three and four. In class four I found a blatant case of cheating and informed the guilty student that I would talk with him after the weekend. I thought I had better give my anger time to subside before confronting him. Fortunately, in the afternoon I turned my attention toward electrical work in an effort to subdue my anger. About three weeks earlier I had ordered a transformer for the typewriter, after burning out the old transformer. The new transformer had arrived from Hong Kong, but it would not work without an adapter plug. I took an extension cord to the electrical shop in the compound and had the work done in a short time. When I plugged the typewriter into the transformer, it worked well. I felt good about being able to use the typewriter again.

News from Foreign Agencies and Press contained the following item on March 24, 1981:

> Visiting former U.S. President Gerald Ford said his talks with China's paramount leader Deng Xiaoping here today had been "very, very enlightening, interesting, and instructive."
>
> Mr. Ford, who arrived in the Chinese capital yesterday [March 27] for a six-day visit, also told newsmen he had handed Mr. Deng a "message (from U.S. President Ronald Reagan) of very best wishes, and one of reassurance of a continuing relationship between the United States and the People's Republic of China."
>
> Mr. Ford met Mr. Deng, a party vice chairman, this morning at the Great Hall of the People in central Peking and the two men extended their talks during a luncheon given by the Chinese strongman.
>
> In the afternoon, the former U.S. President conferred with Chinese Premier Zhao Ziyang at the latter's residence.
>
> Early in the talks, Mr. Deng deplored that the 1979 Sino-American normalization had not come about when Mr. Ford was president, a wish expressed by Mr. Ford during his official 1975 visit to China.
>
> China expects concrete measures from the Reagan administration to carry on the Sino-American ties established under the Carter administration.
>
> Mr. Ford, who is here supposedly on a business trip but in fact at the invitation of the Chinese government, is due to leave here tomorrow for a swing across the country. He will host a farewell dinner for his Chinese hosts this evening at the U.S. embassy. (pp. 1-2)

Saturday, March 28

On Friday night we had gone to see a Chinese movie in the compound. It was typically warm and sentimental, and as usual for Chinese movies it brought Wanda many tears. It was the kind of human interest story that would have to be "hardened" to be accepted for showing in an American theater. But in China sentimentality is much in vogue.

On Saturday morning we walked. We walked in the direction of Beijing University for two or three miles and then stopped to visit in a basket shop. We also stopped at a market and purchased some dates. We ambled through free markets observing curious displays of merchandise as well as curious people, after which we returned to the compound hungry and tired.

For some time I had looked forward to returning to the Minzu Restaurant for dinner. Once again we went with the Grejdas, and we had an enjoyable evening. We enjoyed a dinner of pork chops, fried eggplant, potato cakes, and wine. When we returned to the compound at 9:00, the four of us played bridge. When Wanda and I retired for the night, which was around midnight, I reminded myself that the day had been peaceful. Mostly isolated, I had heard no bad news about China. I had simply not heard any news, and that had made my day an enjoyable one.

Sunday, March 29

On Sunday I became forty-seven years old. We did not go to church because Wen Yee Chin had laryngitis and could not interpret for us. In lieu of going to church, we had planned to go on a tour of Yong He Gong (Temple of Harmony and Peace) sponsored by the Bureau of Foreign Experts. Located in northeast Beijing, Yong He Gong, a famous lama temple, has recently opened. When time came to go, I begged off, for I was far behind in my paper grading.

On my birthday I graded exams for about eight hours, and again I was isolated from the news of the world. In the evening I was pleasantly surprised. Wanda had arranged for the bakers at the dining hall to bake a large chocolate cake. She had also invited a number of our friends. At around 8:00 p.m., we had a birthday party. It was an enjoyable time, but I was already feeling fine before the party began. In the afternoon I had written Sun Travel Agency in Hong Kong requesting reservations for our trip home to Texas. We will leave at the end of June or the beginning of July, making stops in Shanghai, Honolulu, San Diego, and Phoenix. I was excited about the prospects of going home, about seeing our friends and colleagues at Baylor University.

Monday, March 30

I listened to seminar reports in classes one and two. I passed exam papers back to my students and talked about them. Prior to the first class I had graded exams. I also expected a visit from Su Gufen, but she did not come. I wanted to talk to her because she is still fluctuating from day to day over whether to go to school in America. She is afraid of "that mysterious land" which was closed off from the Chinese for thirty years. Su Gufen did not come, but Wang Yanmin did. We talked about her performance as a student and about a series of lectures I have been giving entitled "Skills of the Poet." Wang Yanmin told me she was considering doing her senior paper on some aspect of poetry.

I also had a conference with the young man I had caught cheating during his examination on Friday of the previous week. From his haggard appearance, I could tell that he had done more worrying than I expected. We discussed his having cheated, and I agreed that I would not inform the school officials. I also told him that I would lower the grade, and that if he ever cheated again I would take the matter to the dean of the department. He was ashamed of what he had done and apologized; he knew that it reflected upon the honor of his family. When we ended our conversation, I was convinced that he had received a lesson in honesty that he will never forget.

Tuesday, March 31

While I was in the process of taking my morning bath, Wanda opened the bathroom door and announced, "President Reagan has been shot." We listened to the news and quickly heard that the president had in fact been shot while coming from delivering a speech to AFL-CIO members at the Hilton Hotel in Washington, D.C.

We heard that his press secretary, James Brady, had also been shot and was in critical condition. We heard that the assassination attempt had been carried out by a young Colorado man by the name of John

Hinckley, Jr., who has a record of mental disorders. A policeman and a secret service agent were also wounded, we were told. In the meantime, the murdering of black children in Atlanta continues. In 1980 crime in America rose more than it had in any other year in the previous twelve. When I called Tony Trimarchi to tell him about the attempt to assassinate the president, his remark summarized my feelings: "My country, oh my country!"

News of the attempt on the president's life made the day's activity seem beside the point. Nothing mattered except the condition of the president. Not until evening, when we received an update on the president's condition, were we able to relax. We were greatly relieved when we heard that the president had survived an operation and was on his way to recovery.

April

Wednesday, April 1

Again I lectured for two hours on "Skills of the Poet," and again my students followed the lecture with great enthusiasm. Perhaps it was partially due to my relief over the condition of the president that I became so carried away that in one case I illustrated a point I was trying to make by singing a few bars from an old negro spiritual.

In the evening Wanda and I had as guests from the institute Vice President Li, Vice Dean Lin, and Shao Jingfeng. After a delicious dinner at the compound dining hall, we returned to our apartment and talked. We talked about the institute, about the foreign teachers, and about the need of Chinese teachers for teacher training. We talked about weaknesses in the program at the institute and what to do about those weaknesses. We talked about the students at the institute, about the courses they are taking as well as about their learning habits.

Vice President Li and I agreed that his teachers need more education, but we disagreed concerning which of his teachers he should send abroad for further education. I argued that he should send his young teachers because they are more flexible, more teachable, more energetic, and will have the longest impact on education in China. But he argued that he should send his older teachers to reward them for their years of faithful service. I achieved nothing in maintaining that rewarding poor teaching would not necessarily lead to good teaching. Only the day before, I had talked with Qi Wenqin about the same issue. She had informed me that the Ministry of Education will not let students go abroad unless they have relatives in the country to which they are going or unless they are sponsored by their school in China. What such restrictions mean is that the capable students will not be allowed to study abroad. Rather, the loyal party members, those who replace good teaching with party loyalty, will be the ones to go, and the result will be that educational reform in China will be a long time in coming.

Thursday, April 2

I completed grading exams on which I had been working for two weeks. My students had done well. In the afternoon I treated myself to a long walk. Because I had not been exercising sufficiently while grading exams, I walked for two hours. I enjoyed walking in the sunshine. I enjoyed the bright colors appearing in the clothing of the young people. I enjoyed the green leaves coming to the trees in Beijing. I enjoyed the colors of various bushes in bloom. I enjoyed the steady flow of bicycle traffic and in general the hustle and bustle of life in the streets. It was one of those warm, wasted, but rewarding days.

Ralph Wang called to tell me that he was in town and wanted to talk. He called at 5:00 p.m., and Wanda and I were supposed to leave the compound to see a ballet at 7:00. I invited him to come to our apartment at 7:00, and when Wanda came home from work I convinced her that she should attend the ballet without me. I had a good visit with Ralph Wang. We talked about Mao Zhiren, his son-in-law. We also talked about the possibility of my traveling to Changchun in June to lecture at Jilin University and spend some time with the foreign teachers there. We talked about the attempt on the president's life, about the Chinese economy, about the Chinese government, and bureaucratic inefficiency in China as it affects every level of society. We talked about restrictions on studying abroad and about the sending of older teachers abroad as political favors. We talked for two hours, and when Wang had gone I realized how good it was to talk with my Chinese friend again.

Friday, April 3

News reports concerning President Reagan's condition continued to be good, and we were happy. On the other hand, news about Poland was not good. The Russians have been conducting military maneuvers along the Polish border. It looks as though Russia will invade Poland to restore confidence in the Communist government there. The Soviets have about given up on the idea of bringing striking workers under control without using military force. The pretense for a Soviet invasion of Poland will be that right-wing union members were plotting to overthrow the Communist government. The consequence of an invasion could be very bloody, and the blood could flow beyond the borders of Poland. At any rate, the next few days will be tense ones for that part of Europe.

We received radio news of a renewed drive for gun control in the United States. Gun control may be a good idea, but the issue will likely remain unresolved for many years yet. The idea of gun control contains within it numerous problems. For example, the constitutional right to bear arms has psychological reasons which are as strong as they were when the constitution was written. Chiefly, American life has always been given an element (and perhaps a delusion) of security based on the ideas of self-support and self-preservation. On the American frontier, a man protected himself with his gun. With his gun and his dog, he confronted the enemy with confidence that he could protect himself.

Such a mentality still characterizes the American people. Particularly because the crime rate is high, Americans feel they need their guns to protect themselves, their families, and their property. Only a few years after the uprisings of the sixties, Americans view their guns as a means of protecting themselves and what is theirs in times of civil disobedience. Finally, Americans still feel they can protect themselves against foreign invaders, even after the military has failed. The red scare of the fifties has begun to resurface in the form of another cold war with the Soviets, and the result will be an even greater increase in gun sales. Americans collect guns. They purchase guns for hobbies and sports. But behind the American need for owning guns is a strong belief in a tradition of self-preservation.

Gun control would be useless unless it was enforced, and on both national and state levels enforcement of gun laws would be a mammoth task. As for controlling the shipment of guns through the mail, China has what appears to be the solution. In China one cannot wrap a parcel and take it to the post office to be mailed. One must take one's goods and wrapping material to the post office for inspection. Once they have been examined, a postal clerk watches while the wrapping is performed. The parcel is then turned over to the clerk. Supplying postal clerks to inspect every parcel shipped is obviously expensive, but in America supplying the postal clerks would be only a small fraction of the total cost of gun control. The matter will not be settled easily.

Saturday, April 4

We met Qi Wenqin in Dongdan Street. Wanda wanted to do some shopping for which she felt she needed an interpreter. Qi Wenqin brought with her a month's salary from the institute; she also brought seven hundred *yuan* in retroactive pay as a consequence of my finally signing a contract with the institute. With money and an interpreter at her disposal,

Wanda was eager to shop, and we spent the entire morning purchasing such things as crystal, a tea set, and rubbings to take back to America with us. The Bureau of Foreign Experts sponsored a trip to Ming Tombs, and we very much wanted to go, but we knew we could not return in time for an evening outing we had planned. The outing consisted of dinner at the International Club with Ed and Gail Grejda, followed by a movie entitled *Kramer vs. Kramer*. The showing of the movie was for foreigners only; a committee of Chinese had previewed the movie and ordered that it not be shown to citizens of the People's Republic of China. Wanda and I had seen the film once before, and had not been able to justify the nude scene in it. The second time around we still failed to see any value to the nude scene. The strong impact of the film on its audience of Americans in China occurred because the film presents a stereotype of breaking up and divorcing. The film is obviously timely because the stereotype it presents is one with which millions of Americans can identify. We talked about the film on our way back to the Friendship Hotel, and we agreed that we had enjoyed the evening.

Sunday, April 5

Sunday was a beautiful day. As we rode to church, I observed flowering trees and bushes. Bibles that had been on order for several weeks had finally arrived. Those members of the church who had waited patiently for their Bibles were elated, and the sermon was on the appropriate way to use the Bible. More than anything else, the sermon was a commemoration and celebration on having received the Bibles.

After church Wanda and I met a young man from Arizona. As we discovered during a conversation with him, he is an uncle of our son's roommate at Baylor University. He told us he was in Beijing for two weeks to administer tests, and that he hopes to return in September with five or six other young missionaries disguised as teachers. He is a missionary, and his goal is to evangelize rather than to educate. His church, he told us, had decided to slip missionaries into China disguised as teachers. His missionary zeal will likely get him into trouble. Because it is much too crude and naive, such an approach to spreading Christianity will bring a strong protest from school officials as well as from students.

After our visit, Wanda and I went shopping and purchased a beautiful camphor chest to take back to America with us. In the evening Ralph Wang came to visit. We had a good time reminiscing about Wang's visit in our home in Waco. We also discussed the possibility that Wanda and I might visit him in his home in Changchun sometime in June. Because he would like me to lecture at Jilin University, in Changchun, he has agreed to accompany me to Second Foreign Language Institute to work out the details of such a visit with school officials. If all goes well, we will visit Ralph Wang in Changchun before we leave China.

Monday, April 6

After class one of my former students dropped by to see me. Now attending a teacher-training program, as well as attending my Wednesday morning lectures, she came by to tell me that she was applying for admission to Baylor University. For her sake, I hope she is admitted, but I doubt that it will happen. As is the case with all Chinese students, she has no money. Furthermore, my recent evening with Vice President Li Yueran convinces me that the institute will not release her to study abroad. For years she has dreamed of going to America, but that dream will not be realized unless Second Foreign Language Institute and the Ministry of Education change policies.

Ralph Wang returned in the evening, and we took him to dinner. After dinner we returned to our apartment with Wang and continued talking well into the evening. Before the evening ended it became obvious to Wanda and me that Wang was homesick for America. We felt good about his thinking so highly of our country, but we were sorry he was homesick. We were also homesick, but our homesickness would soon end.

Tuesday, April 7

At the usual time, about 6:45 a.m., I took Ralph Wang with me and left for the institute. Shortly after we arrived we met Qi Wenqin, who took us to meet with Vice President Li Yueran and Vice Dean L. T. Lin. Wang proposed to Li and Lin that the institute send Wanda and me to Changchun so that I might lecture at Jilin University on contemporary American poetry. He also proposed that Qi Wenqin go along as guide and interpreter. Vice President Li was pleased with the proposal, and

Qi Wenqin was ecstatic over the possibility of traveling to Changchun. After our conference, Lin took Wang for a tour of the English department. When the tour ended, at about 11:00 a.m., we returned to the Friendship Hotel.

It was an exciting afternoon. Once Wang had left, I succeeded in securing the first of a series of telephone numbers necessary to make contact with the underground church. It was the beginning of my effort to distribute the thirty-five or so New Testaments David Meier and his touring group had left with us. The underground church is likely the safest avenue through which to distribute the New Testaments, and I hope to have my mission accomplished in another week or two.

While listening to the Voice of America in the evening, I heard that the Russians are urging negotiations of arms control with the United States, and that they are insisting on including space platforms in the proposed negotiations. Nuclear attack can be launched from space platforms, and space platforms can be used for storing nuclear weapons. The use of such platforms for storing nuclear armaments could make on-site inspection of such armaments a delicate matter. At any rate, the Russians are worried about the United States space shuttle about to be launched. They are apparently convinced that the shuttle is designed for military use. This fact, combined with the present position in Washington concerning negotiations, continues to increase suspicion in the Soviet Union that Russia and the United States are moving closer to a confrontation.

Wednesday, April 8

Because my lecture for the morning had to do with contemporary American literature as a mirror of the anxieties and concerns of the American people, I began by talking about some important news items, including a recent article in *Time* concerning the teaching of evolution in California. Actually, the article was about a recent court case similar to the one in Dayton, Tennessee, in 1925—the much-publicized Scopes Trial. To begin the class I requested that my students write a brief essay in which they attempted to answer this question: "How did the universe begin?" Sixty-two of my students (about two-thirds of them) turned in answers.

When I tabulated their answers, I found that their responses to the question fell into seven categories, and that members of the class held a considerable difference of opinion concerning the issue. For example, twenty-two of the sixty-two wrote that they thought the universe came about through natural change or evolution. The next largest group, consisting of thirteen, wrote that they thought the universe came about through some form of molecular cohesion. The third group, the surprising one, wrote that they thought the universe was created by God or some supernatural being. Of the eleven students who gave this answer, at least six were quite specific in saying that the universe was created by God. Five students held the idea that the universe was created by an explosion of some kind, and five indicated that they simply did not know. Five stated that they thought the universe had always existed—that it had no beginning and will have no end, as they put it. One accounted for the beginning of the universe by calling it a "happy coincidence."

I was surprised at the answers; I was surprised that more of my students did not embrace the idea of evolution. I was even more surprised that so great a number believed in creation. I was surprised that anyone, given the conditions under which my students must live, would say that he or she believed in God. Furthermore, my guess is that those who chose not to answer the question chose to be silent rather than expose their interest in religion. My students cannot talk about religion openly; the fear of being criticized remains strong.

My students wrote thoughtful answers. For example, one student wrote, "I believe in Darwin's theory of evolution and the scientific explanation of the beginning of the universe and the origin of life. I just blindly believe it because I don't have the slightest idea about it." Another student wrote, "We have been taught or 'brainwashed' to believe that man and present animals are the results of the evolution of something primitive. That's the scientific explanation of man, Darwinism. It's true of the origin of the earth and the universe as well." Another student wrote, "It [the universe] is eternal. Religion tells us it was created by God, but who can prove it? Science teaches us a theory of evolution. Yet, it is not so convincing either because nobody so far can justify the theory. I think if there was a beginning of the universe, there must be something which existed before the universe became the universe because it must have been created out of something. Unfortunately, we have not got a word to call the something. We created the word 'universe' to represent the eternal and boundless universe, so it must be eternal."

What I like about my students' answers is that they show a healthy skepticism. I like the fact that I received sixty-two answers instead of one answer sixty-two times. I like it because it shows that my students have done some thinking—that they have been questioning what they have been taught.

Thursday, April 9

All morning students came to my office for conferences, and two Chinese teachers came for help on lessons they were preparing to teach. Qi Wenqin and Shao Jingfeng both had numerous questions concerning literature they were preparing to teach. As for visits by my students, the most interesting was that of a young woman named Liu Huiping. Miss Liu had numerous questions about poetry, but she also wanted to show me a poem she had written. She was excited about poetry.

During the afternoon, I tried to make contact with the underground church. Following instructions I had been given, I called one party and supplied information appropriate to identifying my query as legitimate. Having supplied that information, I requested the phone number of the second party I was to call. When I was given the second number, I hung up and called the second party. Again I went through the routine of identifying myself and of supplying necessary code information for receiving the next phone number. The third call was supposed to allow me direct contact with the underground church, but the result was not what I had expected. On the third call I was given information about a contact man, including his telephone number, but as it turned out he was in the Philippines. I was told that he lived in the Philippines and came to China only two or three times a year. I was disappointed because such information meant that I would not be able to distribute the copies of the New Testament in my possession through the underground church. I abandoned all hope of making contact with the underground church and began looking about for another means of distributing the copies.

Friday, April 10

"You don't know China!" Those words come back to me often. They haunt me because I can still see the young woman who spoke them bent almost double with fear that she might say or do the wrong thing and thereby destroy her chances of surviving in a system that controls the individual through fear. Individually, my students have expressed this fear many times, and every time I meet them as a class they express it collectively. They refuse to talk about anything controversial, about anything for which they might be criticized. They prefer not to talk in class at all, but I force them to talk in hopes that they will become bold enough to control their fear. Admittedly, I often wonder whether forcing them to talk is the right thing to do because they have learned to survive by keeping quiet, or by maintaining what in America would be called "a low profile." Perhaps what I am teaching them is subversion, and I often wonder what trouble it will cause them in the future. I also wonder how long they can continue to survive by keeping quiet, by expressing their opinions on nothing. To alter the conditions under which my students live, someone must take a chance, and my students are as qualified as anyone else I know for doing that.

On Friday afternoon I took the Friendship Bus to town. I went to the Friendship Store and purchased a lock for our new camphor chest. I then went to the Wangfujing Department Store and purchased a pipe. Once I had completed my shopping, I stopped at the Beijing Hotel to relax and enjoy a bottle of beer. Mostly, I took the trip to town because I needed to get out and walk. I needed to think about my Chinese students, and about my own stay in China, which will last for about two and a half more months. I needed to think about whether trying to find a way around existing restrictions concerning studying abroad might be worth the effort, or if it would only generate more problems for my students.

In the evening Ralph Wang came to dinner, and I discussed the issue of studying abroad with him. He expressed his disapproval of the system, but he also cautioned that there is no way around it. Ralph Wang is in his sixties, and I wonder if he will see any significant changes in the system during his lifetime.

Saturday, April 11

Saturday was not particularly eventful, but it was a day of thinking. Mostly, I thought about a matter which had been explained to me two days earlier by teacher Qi. She explained that the fifteen students who were pulled out of my American literature course would have to have credit though they were attending a teacher-training program instead of my course. My response to teacher Qi was that I would not participate in such a fraud, that I would not assign grades to students who were elsewhere while my classes were meeting. They had done no work related to the course; they did not even possess textbooks.

The course in American literature is only one instance in which students who were not in attendance will be issued grades by someone in the school. Furthermore, in most cases those grades will be an A. In other cases, students who have served as tour guides will be assigned grades even though they may not have attended any of their classes for more than a few days. The practice is common. For the remainder of the year entire classes of students will serve as tour guides, but they will be given credit just as though they had attended their classes. Such cases of academic fraud are numerous, but at the same time school officials express concern over the quality of education in China.

Sunday, April 12

At 8:00 a.m. we left "The Golden Ghetto" (a term the Chinese facetiously apply to the Friendship Hotel) on a trip to Nankou Pass and the Great Wall. When we began our journey the wind was blowing dust about furiously, but by the time we arrived at the Great Wall it had subsided.

It was Sunday morning, and the Great Wall was crowded. The narrow entranceway leading up to the wall was jammed. The entranceway was also a place of much scuffling, pushing, and general temper-flaring. Occasionally someone was knocked to the ground, but always someone else picked that person up and kept going. Because passing through the entranceway was dangerous, we waited until the crowd had thinned a bit before trying to climb the steps to the wall. When we were finally on the wall we found that being there was also dangerous. We did not go very far.

Instead, we retreated to the safety of the tourist shops, to which the Chinese are forbidden entrance. We examined many souvenirs, and then we returned to our bus for a lunch of cheese, crackers, wine, and fruit.

During the trip home, we stopped on a narrow, winding mountain road in order for the camera bugs in our group to take pictures of an old garrison that once housed troops to defend the entrance to Nankou Pass. While climbing the steps to the garrison, Wanda fell and broke the camera. She also injured her leg. While parked on the narrow, winding road, our bus almost caused two collisions, but the remainder of the journey home was quiet and peaceful. We were all glad to return to our sanctuary, the Friendship Hotel.

Monday, April 13

I went to the institute early in the morning and walked around the track for about an hour. I walked and thought. I thought about the space shuttle *Columbia*, which had been launched into orbit the day before. I thought about what that launching means to American technology. I thought about the wealth that most Americans possess in relationship to their spiritual poverty and emotional bankruptcy. In America, I thought, our knowledge has surpassed our emotional capacity for adjusting to the conditions our knowledge has produced. I also thought about my students across the campus in building number one. I thought of their material poverty as well as the emphasis they place on spiritual well-being. Again I thought of the fact that China has never been a religious country, and most of all not a Christian one. Yet my students often talk about their spiritual existence. I wonder what they mean. I thought about all of these things, and then I went to my office to prepare for my morning classes.

In the afternoon I walked for another three hours. I needed the exercise, but I also needed to think. I realized that my grieving for my students was all in vain. I realized that in some ways they live rich lives, that their material poverty is perhaps preferable to spiritual poverty. I do not find my students crying over what they do not possess. On the contrary, I find many of them eager to learn, eager to serve, and more often than not I find a cheerful disposition when I talk to one of them. I had a profitable walk in that I realized that I had learned much since coming to China.

Tuesday, April 14

According to the news on Voice of America, Joe Louis, the Brown Bomber, died on April 12, and General Omar Bradley, America's last five-star general, died on April 14. Announcements of these deaths would have caught my attention under any circumstances, but when they came they affected me even more because I had been teaching the intellectual and cultural conditions of the twenties in America. Before the announcements came, I had spent considerable time talking about what happened to the idea of hero worship in America during the twenties. While talking about hero worship, I had been reminded that as a boy in the forties I too had worshiped idols, not the least of whom was Joe Louis. I had idolized him because he had risen from depths of poverty to great heights of glory by his own initiative. He was a great credit to his race, and during his fighting days gave the black people of America one of their few heroes.

On the other hand, General Omar Bradley was never a great idol of mine. But he was a contemporary of General Douglas MacArthur and General Dwight D. Eisenhower, both of whom were idols of mine. Nothing looked more impressive and stunning to me as a boy than did General MacArthur in his uniform. He looked every inch a man and every inch a leader of men. As for Eisenhower, I remember when he came to Defiance College, Defiance, Ohio, in the fifties. Kevin McCann, formerly speech writer for Eisenhower as well as special aid, was president of Defiance College at the time. I remember that we had a tea for Eisenhower, and that I, a junior faculty member, shook hands with President Dwight D. Eisenhower. I met one of my idols face to face, and I was impressed that as a boy I had chosen a man worthy of my admiration. No, Omar Bradley was never one of my heroes, but his death brought memories of former days when two of his fellow military leaders did much to shape my dreams. Kevin McCann has also died; my heroes are all gone.

Wednesday, April 15

I found a note on my desk from L. T. Lin. The note indicated that I was to meet with members of the Ministry of Education on Friday, April 17, at 2:30 p.m. The meeting, according to the note, was to take place in the office of the Bureau of Foreign Experts, which is located at the Friendship Hotel. On a number of occasions, I had told school officials that I would like an audience with members of the Ministry of

Education, but what will I tell them now that I have my chance? What could I possibly tell them about education in China? I have been in China eight months; they have been in China all their lives.

Thursday, April 16

I left the institute and returned to the compound by way of the Bank of China. In the afternoon I walked and thought about my upcoming meeting with representatives from the Ministry of Education. In the evening Wanda and I joined Morag Stauffer and went to the Maundy Thursday service in Xidan Street church where we enjoyed taking communion. On the way home, Morag told us there had been an attempt on Deng Xiaoping's life two weeks earlier in Tianjin, and that an anti-government demonstration had taken place in Tiananmen Square only a week earlier. I was not surprised. In such cases the Chinese people act from frustration and fear. Their meager salaries are purchasing less and less. Droughts, floods, and storms have threatened food supplies, and the people in Beijing are afraid they will go hungry, as is already the case in some parts of China. The concern of the government, in the meantime, is to maintain order, and the techniques for doing that are fear and intimidation. Sooner or later increasing oppression on the part of the government will become intolerable. The Chinese people will have to be appeased.

Friday, April 17

I went to the office of the Bureau of Foreign Experts. The time for my meeting with representatives of the Ministry of Education had come. When I arrived I found that six foreign experts had been invited. As for the Ministry of Education, the most important representatives appeared to be a Comrade Hua, first minister of learning, and a Comrade Wu, first minister in charge of the Bureau of Foreign Experts.

In his opening remarks, Comrade Hua explained that the purpose of the meeting was to listen to the suggestions of foreign experts. David Crook, a foreign expert from First Foreign Language Institute, was the first to speak. David had been teaching in China for thirty-five years, and by virtue of his seniority was expected to begin. David spoke for about ten minutes, after which I began to set before the gathering of educators suggestions and criticisms I had compiled two days earlier, and which I had discussed with Jeanne Lonnoy. Jeanne's suggestions had proven helpful, and I was ready to make my presentation.

Before I had talked more than ten minutes I could see that Comrade Hua was in pain. He was obviously disappointed that I had not come to participate in another of those back-slapping sessions in which both parties, American and Chinese, engage in the greatest deceptions and telling of lies in the name of friendship. On the contrary, I had come to tell the truth as I knew it. Comrade Hua was not prepared to hear the truth, but the other foreign experts were prepared. They applauded what I set before them. Furthermore, they began discussing the most critical of the issues. They beleaguered Comrade Hua with questions for more than two hours.

When our meeting broke up, I was impressed that Comrade Hua had heard the same criticisms and suggestions on previous occasions, but I was also impressed that he likely had never seen such a demonstration of consensus concerning them. Whether what was said to the representatives of the Ministry of Education on Friday afternoon, April 17, 1981, will make a difference in Chinese education remains to be seen. In any case, it turned out to be an informative session that Comrade Hua will likely not forget.

Saturday, April 18

We awakened to strong winds, and the sky was filled with dust. Dust came in around every door and window in our apartment, coating everything that was not covered. At midmorning Wanda and I ventured out to purchase soap, skin cream, and other supplies from a store in building one. It was only a five-minute walk from where we lived in building four, but the trip was difficult. While going to and from the store, we walked through sheets of dust. We walked through so much dust that we were coated by the time we got home.

At mid-afternoon, we decided we would venture forth again. Wanda wanted to visit shops in the Summer Palace. She had been looking for a special decorative piece in the form of a horse with one foot on a bird. Although she had looked in many shops, she had not found such a piece to her liking. We were gone from home for more than two hours, and all during that time we were fighting our way through the dust. The shops at the Summer Palace proved disappointing. Not only did they not have the horse, but as far as I could see they had little else except what I would call five-and-ten-cent-store junk. Disappointed, we returned to the compound determined not to go out again until the dust subsided.

Sunday, April 19

It was Easter Sunday, and we went to church in Xidan Street. The service was well attended; even the aisles were filled. More than five hundred Chinese people had come to church to celebrate Easter. Pastor Qi preached a superb Easter sermon, but the best was yet to come. After the sermon, forty new converts were baptized by immersion, and the baptisms were the first in the Xidan Street church since before the Cultural Revolution.

The baptismal service was an emotional experience. The forty new converts were baptized one at a time, and then they stood in the front of the church to be introduced to the congregation at large. To me they were symbols of the boldness I have found in Chinese Christians. They knew they were putting themselves in a precarious position by declaring publicly that they were Christians. They knew that party members were likely present to take note of them. They knew the government could outlaw church services at any time. They knew they were opposing all they had been taught by the schools, the government, and the party concerning religion. In short, they knew that what they were doing was extremely dangerous, but they did it anyway. They took a stand, knowing full well that it could cost them their lives in the future, and I stood there with a camera in my hand wondering what I would do if I were called on to be as bold as they were. Many things in China do not command or deserve admiration, but one must admire the Chinese Christian. For him a commitment to Christ is truly a matter of life and death.

Monday, April 20

I conferred with Zhu Zheng about a problem concerning foreign currency, and I talked with L. T. Lin about the fact that Victor Strite had not been informed concerning his appointment to teach in China. I also met with students, answering questions and evaluating seminar papers. I met two classes and listened to oral presentations. The morning was very routine, and when noon came I was ready to retreat to the privacy of our apartment in the compound.

On Thursday, April 16, 1981, *News from Foreign Agencies and Press* had carried an article which had been picked up from the UPI wire service on April 15. In part, the article read as follows:

> Defense Secretary Casper Weinberger, Wednesday, rejected Soviet charges that the space shuttle's main mission is military, saying such uses are "really secondary" to civilian and scientific applications. . . .
>
> The official Tass News Agency said Tuesday the U.S. defense establishment is thinking of taking over the shuttle program. There have been suggestions the shuttle could be used to put weapons systems into place, and also could be effective in tampering with other nations' satellites.
>
> "The shuttle has such significant military aspects the pentagon is seriously thinking of taking it fully into its own hands," Tass said. It also quoted reports that the United States is developing plans for a military space station. (pp. 16-17)

For several days news in Beijing has indicated that the Soviets have become paranoid over the United States' space shuttle. As the information quoted above indicates, they see it as a great threat to their military superiority.

Tuesday, April 21

I spent much of the morning grading papers. I also met with students to talk with them about their seminar papers. I met and talked with Qi Wenqin about details pertaining to going home at the end of June or the first part of July. I spent much of the afternoon preparing my Wednesday morning lecture. The lecture was to be on intellectual currents in the twenties, with specific emphasis on Sigmund Freud. I was particularly concerned about how my students might react to what I had to say about Freud, especially since one does not talk about sex in mixed company in China. In the process of preparing my lecture, I took time out for two short walks, but mostly I stayed at my desk and planned what I had to say about Freud and psychoanalysis. It was nine o'clock in the evening before I could put my notes aside with confidence that I could lecture for two hours on Freud. I was a bit troubled by the subject matter, and remained so until I gave my lecture the next day.

Wednesday, April 22

My lecture on Freud went well. My students understood in spite of my fear that the lecture would prove too abstract for them. I could tell from their faces that they appreciated what I was saying. They had never heard a lecture on Freud and psychoanalysis, and they recognized in the lecture many things that were contrary to what they had been taught. In that sense, the lecture was shocking, but my students maintained a high level of interest for the two hours. During the remainder of the morning, I accomplished little. Tired from lecturing, I met with three or four of my students for a brief time and then took a car for home.

After lunch I called our son, Lon, in Texas. Then I took the Friendship Bus and went to the American embassy. I stopped by the Friendship Store on the way and made arrangements for having a crate of household goods shipped home to Texas. The school year is rapidly drawing to a close, and in another thirty days many foreign experts will be making such arrangements. Wanda and I had decided to ship our things early in order to beat the rush. I was pleased to read the following in *Xinhua News Agency News Bulletin* (April 20, 1981):

> Over 7,000 Chinese and foreign Catholics attended Easter Sunday high Mass here today in the church of the Immaculate Conception and the church of St. Joseph. Celebrants were Bishop Fu Tieshan and Bishop Tu Shihua.
>
> Zong Huaide, Chairman of the Chinese Patriotic Catholic Association, and Yang Gaojian, Vice Chairman of the National Administrative Commission of the Chinese Catholic Church, assisted in the masses.
>
> The church held Holy Week ceremonies, such as receiving palms, holding a procession of the blessed sacrament, kissing the crucifix, following the stations of the cross and blessing the new fire and font.
>
> A church official said that this was the first time Easter Sunday had been celebrated simultaneously at two churches since the beginning of the Cultural Revolution in 1966. The church of St. Joseph opened last year after being closed for fourteen years.

Bishop Fu Tieshan told Xinhua: "Our clergymen and congregation are happy that our freedom of religious belief is guaranteed according to the party's and government's religious policies; we will continue our efforts to contribute to the country's modernization program and its stability and unity."

Among the over 300 foreign Catholics and compatriots from Hong Kong and Macao attending Easter Sunday mass were diplomatic envoys, experts, students and visiting delegations.

Easter Sunday services were also held at two Protestant churches here. (p. 12)

Considering how Christianity has fared in China for the past twenty years, that 7,000 people attended the two Catholic churches in Beijing, and probably another thousand at the two Protestant churches, is some kind of miracle. On the other hand, Bishop Fu Tieshan's statement to Xinhua tells much about the precarious position of the church in China. The bishop knows that freedom of worship can be taken away just as surely and quickly as it was granted. His statement was designed to appease the party and the government. His statement was an appeal for consideration. Yes, Bishop Fu Tieshan fully recognizes that the few churches which have opened were allowed to do so on a trial basis, and he knows that they have no alternative but to please the government and the party if they are to remain open.

Thursday, April 23

Two young Chinese writers were arrested over the weekend for promoting ideas contrary to the policies and positions of the government. According to a Chinese-American representative from Indiana University Press to the Foreign Languages Press in Beijing, the writers were simply espousing democracy Western style. The two are not well-known writers, but they could become well-known in the way the Russian Alexandr Solzhenitsyn did—by becoming outspoken critics of their country's government. This could prove true if the government does not succeed in what the Chinese call "re-education." In severe cases, however, "re-education" can amount to an intellectual lobotomy, and the government will likely resort to whatever means it deems necessary to make sure the two writers are rendered harmless.

At night we went to Capital Theater to see a production of Shakespeare's *Measure for Measure*. The lines were all in Chinese, and the acting was performed by Chinese actors. But the performance was superb. Why the Chinese are attracted to Shakespeare escapes me, for there is little in Shakespeare that would support communism. On the other hand, while watching *Measure for Measure*, I may have discovered why the Chinese are attracted to that particular play. First, it is about a corrupt official, and the Chinese people are fed up with corrupt officials. Second, the play contains a short passage which asks what can be expected of the common people if the officials are corrupt. When the lines of that passage were spoken, the audience applauded loudly. It was the only applause during the performance. The question is one of how long the performances of *Measure for Measure* will be allowed to continue. The arrests last weekend did not stop with two writers. About forty people were arrested.

Friday, April 24

I evaluated and marked a long paper on post-Civil War reconstruction in America, a paper which had been given to me about a month earlier by the young Chinese teacher named Spring. In the usual Chinese manner, the paper had been largely copied from a book. Because of that, the most helpful thing I could do was to make suggestions about taking notes and crediting sources in the process of writing one's own paper. I marked the paper closely and wrote a note suggesting that Spring might want to take advantage of my markings to work on his writing.

Later I went to the Forbidden City. Two of my students, both girls, accompanied me to serve as guides. I enjoyed seeing the Forbidden City again, but I was more impressed by what I saw as a transformation in the girls. At school they had both been quiet and reserved, but when we were alone and away from the institute they came out of their protective cocoons. They were talkative and outgoing. I found that they could laugh and have fun, and I was surprised.

I also found that they could be inquisitive and profound. They wanted to talk about religion, and in a short time I became convinced that their interest in talking about religion had been their motive for volunteering to serve as my guides. They asked me very bluntly if I believed in religion, as they put it, and I told them that I did. I gathered that they were grappling with the idea of religion in the context of their atheistic upbringing, and that they were encountering many frustrations. We talked throughout the afternoon, and when I went home in the evening I could not help but believe that I had talked with two very fine young women.

Saturday, April 25

While listening to the Voice of America on Saturday I heard that 130,000,000 Chinese are suffering from food shortages. The hunger is confined mostly to nine provinces, and as of yet no deaths from starvation have been reported. I also read that Hong Kong harbor has been invaded by hundreds of Chinese in fishing boats; they have been fleeing southern China in fear of a devastating earthquake. Hong Kong has had problems in keeping Chinese aliens out since 1978. Thousands of them have escaped to Hong Kong, placing a great burden upon the Hong Kong economy. But the problem will increase, for the Chinese will escape to freedom whenever they can.

In China one looks for fellowship and entertainment, and in our case Wanda and I find both in playing bridge. Thus it was that we played bridge after dinner. We played until almost two o'clock in the morning. I am not a good bridge player, but I enjoy playing because bridge serves as a connection of sorts with the past as well as with my own culture. In China, playing bridge, like reading one's hometown newspaper, has its psychological compensations.

Sunday, April 26

The sun was shining, and I could see the Western Hills from my window. It was a pleasant day, and attending church was reassuring. Church lasted longer than we expected because the regular worship service was followed by a communion service at which approximately two hundred people took communion. After church, Wanda and I visited with some people from Norway; we then made our way back to the Friendship Hotel for lunch.

Once we had eaten lunch we began collecting our purchases, purchases made over a period of eight months, in order to arrange them in a pile. Packers will inspect them and wrap them. They will build a crate of the appropriate size for shipping our purchases to our home in Waco, Texas.

Four or five days earlier I had gone to the transportation department of the Friendship Store to make arrangements for packing and shipping. At that time, I was told that someone would come to our apartment on Monday or Tuesday to begin the process of packing and shipping. The first step consists of taking inventory, which will be followed by the building of a shipping crate.

At dinner Wanda and I visited with Diether and Margot Raff; the Raffs arrived from Germany only a week or ten days ago. We enjoyed talking with the Raffs so much that after dinner we retired to our apartment and talked for another hour or so.

Monday, April 27

I had my students write an evaluation of the American literature course they have been taking. I asked them to evaluate and make suggestions about improving the course for the remainder of the year. Later in the day, when I read their suggestions, I was pleased to find that they were happy about the course. Their evaluations corresponded to the enthusiasm for learning they have exhibited since last fall.

I met with students and marked seminar papers, but my attention was mostly directed toward news in and about China. For example, I had learned that the people arrested a few days earlier had gathered to draft a petition to present to the government concerning freedom of speech. Also, I read in *Xinhua News Agency News Bulletin* (April 21, 1981 pp. 22-23) that a large rally was being planned to celebrate the hundredth anniversary of the Chinese writer Lu Xun. The celebration will be held on September 24 and will involve five thousand people, according to the article. The aim of the celebration is to promote Lu Xun's works, but it is also politically motivated.

As a writer, my response to the proposed celebration is one of mixed emotions. I think writers should have a more prominent place in Western civilization. On the other hand, I deplore the idea that a writer must be a tool of the state and a puppet of the government. The Chinese celebrate their writers. They build temples and memorials in their honor. But almost always such things are done for political reasons. Either what the writer has written is useful as propaganda, or his philosophy is beneficial to the government in some way. Ultimately, all hinges on the issue of freedom to tell the truth as one sees it without fear of reprisal from the government or any other group. As for me, I prefer freedom to government-sponsored celebrations and the erecting of statues and temples. Admittedly, such freedom carries with it a grave responsibility for the betterment of mankind that contemporary writers in the West have frequently ignored. For the serious writer, there can be no freedom without responsibility.

Tuesday, April 28

In China the truth remains a mystery; the hard facts of daily existence are the only realities. The commune leader or work unit leader holds the power of life and death over his charges as though he were a feudal lord in the Middle Ages. He bestows favors as he wishes. He exacts penalties and metes out punishment, and no one had better attempt to interfere. Over the entire feudal maze of communes and work units hovers the spirit of Mao Zedong, and China does not know what to do with Mao. He is dead, but he is also very much alive. He is a great detriment to modernization, but the Chinese people cannot accept him for what he was and let it go at that. The government is still polarized, with the balance of power shifting back and forth between the pro-Mao forces, headed by Hua Guofeng, and the anti-Mao forces, headed by Deng Xiaoping.

A recent article in *Time* (April 27, 1981, p. 45) analyzes the situation, but it reaches the wrong conclusions. What the Communist Party in China has needed, the article contends, is "a definitive perspective on Mao." That perspective, continues the article, was handed down last November in a speech by Huang Kecheng, head of the party's Central Discipline Inspection Committee. However, the article ignores what was happening in the government at the time Huang gave his speech, and it ignores what has happened since. It ignores the effort to oust Hua Guofeng, and it ignores the fact that the attempt to oust Hua Guofeng failed because Hua appealed to the sentiments of pro-Maoists. It ignores what has happened recently to promote Mao's teachings throughout the country and to enforce Mao's ideas and policies. The article ignores the facts so completely that whoever wrote it must have been suffering from tunnel vision. The last paragraph of the article reads as follows:

When Deng, in a 1978 interview, discussed Mao's inadequacies, he suggested that the old man had been 70% right and 30% wrong. Huang's assessment, though lacking in specifics, follows that ratio, and Western diplomats in Peking last week interpreted the speech as a trial balloon. If those masses who visit the Tiananmen tomb do not accept the critique, the leadership will probably go a step further and reveal specific errors. If they do, the way should be clear for a sixth party plenum next summer at which Mao's place in history will be more clearly defined, and out-of-favor Mao followers like Party Chairman Hua Guofeng may face a purge.

The paragraph ignores that many of the "specifics" have recently been published. It ignores that new copies of *Selected Works of Mao Zedong* have recently appeared on students' desks throughout China. It ignores the recent Lei Feng emphasis. It ignores new and intense activity among the Young Pioneers. It ignores the fact that the power of the military is squarely behind Hua Guofeng and the pro-Maoists. It ignores that the Chinese people blame Deng Xiaoping and his anti-Maoist followers for the present economic woes of China. I suggest that Hua Guofeng and the pro-Maoists are not on trial; Deng Xiaoping and the anti-Maoists are on trial. Furthermore, any effort to oust Hua next summer will back-fire unless conditions change drastically.

Wednesday, April 29

Every day in China brings new experiences, but three things happened on Wednesday that stand out in my mind. First, I showed my students two reels of the film documentary entitled *America*, narrated by Alistair Cooke. When time came to see the two reels of film, the projectionist had not shown up and the doors to the auditorium where the two reels of film were to be shown were locked. I sent a messenger to the home of the projectionist, and about an hour later he started the first reel of film. My frustrations did not end, for fifteen minutes after the first reel started the electricity went off. When that happened, students and teachers alike left the auditorium. Five minutes later the electricity came back on and they flooded into the auditorium again.

Once we had settled in to view the two reels of film, I had hoped that all would be calm for the remainder of the showing, but such was not the case. Throughout the two-hour showing students came and left at will while slamming the door and generally disrupting those who wanted to watch the documentary. The students were not mine, but had drifted in from all over the institute when word circulated that a film would be shown. The incident reminded me of how the Chinese people behave in crowds and on city buses. They are the most sheep-like people I have ever known. They do not think; they merely follow. I was convinced that had someone picked up his chair and jumped out the window, even though we were on the fourth floor, at least a hundred others would have followed him or her.

The second thing that stands out in my mind is that Su Guifen came to see me. Although Miss Su, Miss Chen, and Mr. Feng were transferred from my class to a teacher training program before the first semester ended, the three of them have attended my lectures voluntarily. Contending that they would have attended my seminars had their schedules allowed, they requested that I give them credit for the course in American literature. After discussing the matter with them, I agreed to give them credit provided they write a series of papers based on the readings required of all students in the course. Miss Su also warned me that other students would ask for credit, even though they had not attended the lectures. I informed her that I would not engage in such falsifying of student records. I realized that the students involved would not appreciate or understand my position, for they are accustomed to such practices. They see nothing wrong with a teacher's giving students credit for courses they have not taken because the practice is widespread. The question of honesty has never occurred to them.

The third thing that stands out in my mind involved a student named Liu Huiping. A week earlier she had attended my lecture on Sigmund Freud, and what she heard apparently bothered her. When she came to see me, she brought me a letter, which read as follows:

April 28, 1981

My dearest LeMaster, would you please help me solve my problems? You may think my questions seem ridiculous and like a baby's, but please don't laugh at me since I am so troubled by them. (1) Why must one transfer his love to others? Can't he remain at the stage of self-love? (2) What is love? How can one know when he begins to love another? (3) Don't you think suppressing love is hard to do? If so, why do people dare not show their true feelings? (4) How does love come into being? What kind of person is worthy of love?

(5) Can respect and love be interchanged or exchanged with each other? (6) Is it reasonable to say that marriage is the tomb for love? How long can a couple love each other? (7) Why can consciousness be controlled by subconsciousness? Where does consciousness come from? (8) A Russian writer once said that there is no friendship between male and female, only love. Do you think this is right? Why?

I hope you will give me some answers.

Very respectfully yours, Liu

Liu Huiping's letter, or one similar to it, could have been written by any of my students. Having looked up the word "Freudianism" in her dictionary, Miss Liu told me that she found as an entry the word "ridiculous." Whether Freud's ideas are ridiculous or not, a number of my students have told me they will never marry, and Liu Huiping is one of those. They will not marry, they contend, because Chinese marriages have nothing to do with love. But the Chinese government has different ideas. To survive economically, and in order to have a place in Chinese society, sooner or later my students will surrender their notions about love in exchange for the traditional Chinese marriage of convenience.

Thursday, April 30

I did not go to the institute because packers were coming from the transportation department of the Friendship Store to pack our household effects for shipment home. They were scheduled to arrive at 9:30 a.m., and they came on time. It took six men about an hour to wrap all we possessed carefully. All breakables such as glass and crystal had to be padded and then packed in cardboard boxes.

After the packers left, I wrote a long letter to our son, Lon. Rather, I completed a long letter which I had started earlier. Then I went to lunch and listened to rumors that foreign teachers would soon be phased out. According to the rumors, Chinese students have been exposed to too many foreign ideas and as a result have become difficult to manage.

Such rumors circulate frequently, and I have learned to put little stock in them. On the other hand, Chinese students are being exposed to foreign ideologies. They are being taught to think. I do not doubt that they are increasingly difficult to manage.

After lunch I went to the Friendship Store and looked up Mr. He, the manager of the transportation department. I discussed with him details about the building and shipping of our crate. I was concerned that shipping might take months, for I had seen packed crates sit around at the compound for two and three months before they were picked up for shipping. Mr. He assured me that shipping would be no problem since four or five United States cargo ships leave Hong Kong for the United States every month. The crate will be built and shipped, he told me, after the May 1 weekend.

May

Friday, May 1

At 8:30 p.m. on April 30, we had left the Friendship Hotel and were on our way to the train station. We were going to Taiyuan in Shanxi Province for a couple of days of sightseeing. When our bus passed Tiananmen Square, I noticed that four large portraits had been erected on the front of the square for the May 1 celebration. Approximately twenty feet high and ten feet wide, the portraits were along the street, facing the Forbidden City. On the west side of the square we passed portraits of Stalin and Lenin. On the east side the portraits were of Marx and Engels. Directly across the street, and in its position above the gate to the Forbidden City, a portrait of Mao Zedong smiled down at the others. The portraits made me wonder about the hard line the Chinese have supposedly adopted in their opposition to Russia. I have been impressed all along that the hard-line opposition is a rhetorical one calculated to entice Western countries into supplying China with economic, technological, and military aid. Only time will reveal the significance of the four portraits raised on the front of Tiananmen Square for the May 1 celebration.

We arrived in Taiyuan, a city of two million people, at 7:30 a.m. Taiyuan is the provincial, political, economic, and cultural center of Shanxi Province. As for Shanxi Province, 80 percent of its population lives in the countryside. In that sense, Shanxi Province is typical.

From our hotel window I could look down on a large section of hovels which were doubtlessly dreadful places in which to live. The hovels reminded me of what I had seen two days earlier when I accidentally took a wrong turn while walking from the Friendship Hotel to Haidian. I had seen row after row of mud huts, and I had tried to tell myself that no one could possibly live in such conditions. I tried to tell myself that no one could live in such conditions, knowing that much of the population of China will continue to live in such conditions for a long time to come. On our trip to Taiyuan, I had looked out the train window to see an area in which people were living in caves carved into the side of a mountain, and I reasoned that the caves were comfortable compared to much of the housing I had seen. In Taiyuan the hovels looked desolate and cold.

Saturday, May 2

On the evening before, we had attended a reception with officials from the governments of the city and of the province. Wanda and I shared a table with the vice governor of Shanxi Province. Named Bai, he spoke no English, but we managed to communicate through an interpreter. He seemed remarkably encouraged about Sino-American relations, and we asked him numerous questions about Shanxi Province. Comrade Bai was an interesting man.

Taiyuan does not hold much of interest for the average tourist. Mostly, one views the usual temples and monasteries. For example, we saw the Memorial Temple of Jin, which was first built for Tang Shuyu, founder of a small state called Jin during the Shang Dynasty in the eleventh century B.C. We also visited Chongshan Si (The Temple Where Goodness Is Worshipped), which has a large bell over the gate as well as a large collection of sutras dating from the Song, the Yuan, and the Ming dynasties.

Of the monasteries we visited, the first was called Xuanchengchi, or the Stone-Screen Monastery. It was built in 472 by a monk named Tanluan, and Buddhist rites were performed there during the Sui and Tang dynasties. We visited the Double-Tower Monastery, located south of the village of Haozhuangou. Famous for its two pagodas, and built under the Ming during the Wanli period (1573-1620), the Double-Tower Monastery is made attractive by its gardens. The twin pagodas, which are thirteen stories high, were impressive, but not nearly as much so as was the dust storm which came upon us while we were viewing the pagodas.

The sky turned yellow and strong winds blew dust everywhere. The dust was so thick that it finally blotted out the sun. We knew we were in the kind of dust storm about which we had heard, but which we had never experienced. The winds blew all night, and even with the drapes pulled in our hotel room Wanda and I found breathing difficult. Furthermore, when the winds came to Taiyuan the weather turned cold and remained that way. It was still cold when we returned to Beijing on the morning of May 3.

Sunday, May 3

An article in *Time* (May 4, 1981, p. 43) comments on the Chinese government's most recent effort to curtail dissent:

> The latest dip in the ebb and flow of China's uncertain liberalization came in a sudden midnight raid by Public Security Bureau

agents. Their targets: Xu Wenli, 37, and Yang Jing, about 30, the editors of a hand-mimeographed dissident newsletter, April Fifth Forum, named for a 1976 anti-government demonstration. Though Chief Editor Xu scrupulously avoided outright criticism of China's leaders and shunned the label of dissident he has been outspoken in demanding more freedom of expression. Last year he noted that "if only views that echo the leadership are allowed, there is no way to speak of real freedom of speech." Though April Fifth Forum had a circulation of only 1,000 before publication was suspended early last year, it was, according to one Western diplomat, "a twinkle in a vast void." Thus the arrests of Xu and Yang further weakened an already anemic democratic movement.

What the article fails to point out is that the Security Bureau had a busy weekend, making between forty and forty-five arrests. The arrests should have made clear for everyone in China that the government is not willing to tolerate dissent. Xu Wenli is right. Because only the views of the government are allowed, "there is no way to speak of real freedom of speech."

Monday, May 4

I met with my seminars and listened as papers were presented. I also learned that on April 30 two buses had collided near the gate to Second Foreign Language Institute killing twenty people. It was not the kind of tragedy one reads about in the newspapers because it was not good news. I had seen buses collide on that road about a month earlier, and I have often wondered about how pedestrians escape being killed. It is a heavily traveled road on which drivers become impatient and reckless.

I took the Friendship Bus to town hoping to complete a number of chores. Once I was in town the first thing I did was go to the Bank of China and cash a check. On the form I was required to fill out, I signed my wife's signature; the check I was cashing was hers. Because Wanda had endorsed the check, when the teller compared the two signatures he stared at them for a long time and then shrugged his shoulders. He said nothing. Upon leaving the bank I went to Wangfujing Department Store and purchased pipe tobacco. Then I caught a bus to the Friendship Store to check on progress concerning the shipping of our crate of household effects. After that, I went to the office of Philippine Airlines to check on the possibility of returning home via Manila. At that point, I ran out of time. I needed to visit the American embassy, but I had to catch the Friendship Bus and return to the Friendship Hotel instead.

Tuesday, May 5

I met with several of my students. Then I went to see Zhang Chincai, director of the office responsible for matters pertaining to foreign experts at the institute. I carried with me a form to be stamped by Zhang authorizing the transportation department of the Friendship Store to ship our crate home to Waco. While on the way home later, I delivered the form, which Zhang had stamped, to the transportation department of the Friendship Store. While I was there, I was given a statement of charges to deliver to the institute, but little did I know that Zhang would reject the charges on the basis that the institute was being overcharged. When I went to see Zhang for the second time, he told me the matter of the charges would be settled the next day.

Books for the institute finally arrived. Contributed and mailed by members of the English department at Baylor University, the books had been in the mail for almost three months. At one time they had been neatly wrapped in approximately thirty small packages, but when they arrived the packages were badly tattered. They had been opened for postal inspection and tied back together with string. But the books arrived and sometime soon I will present them to officials at the institute.

I spent a large part of the afternoon evaluating the English language proficiency of a young Chinese woman named Joan Huang. Twenty years old, Joan had come from Zanzhou in Gansu Province to have me examine her ability to speak, read, and write in English so that I might write a letter on her behalf. Joan's uncle, Walter Huang, lives in Waco, Texas, and he has been trying to have Joan admitted to an American university. Since the TOEFL (Test of English as a Foreign Language) exam is not given in China, the next best thing for a student to do is have a foreign expert perform an evaluation and write a letter of recommendation. In this case, when I completed the report I mailed it to Joan's uncle in Waco. Because her father is in the provincial government, and because she has a relative in the United States, the chances of Joan's being permitted to study in the United States are good. If she were the daughter of a factory worker and had no relatives in the United States, her chances would be slim. Such things make a great difference in China.

Wednesday, May 6

I showed two more reels of Alistair Cooke's documentary *America*. When I showed two reels a few days earlier, students wandered in and out all during the two-hour showing. This time I was determined that my class would not be interrupted. I posted myself at the entrance to the auditorium and stopped anyone who tried to enter. On several occasions I asked students whether they were members of grade 77. When a student lied to me, I told him I knew better and sent him on his way. Some appeared to be offended, even though they had lied. They were accustomed to wandering in and out of film showings at will, as though constantly slamming a door was supposed to make no difference. I had served notice that I would not tolerate such behavior.

After eight months in Beijing, I have lost much of my naivete concerning the Chinese people. I have learned that all that glitters in China is not honesty. Only yesterday I learned that one woman has been taking the English proficiency for numerous wives of government officials; the exam is required as part of the process of securing a visa. Although it is a minimal exam, interviewers at the American embassy have been mystified by Chinese women who supposedly passed the exam but could not so much as recognize when they were being asked their names in English. Nor have they been able to answer such questions as "Who is your husband?" or "Where do you live?"

The woman who has been taking the exam for the wives of Chinese officials wants to go to America, and the Chinese government will not let her go. As a result, she has vowed to quit taking the exam; she refuses to do for others what she cannot do for herself. The incident is only one of many such cases of fraud and dishonesty. In China, what one sees is not the reality, although I say this with some reservation because a moral code to which the great masses of Chinese subscribe appears to exist. As of yet I have not been able to determine the relationship between the morality of the individual and the extent to which the individual is motivated by fear.

Thursday, May 7

If I were to write an open letter to the universities of America about enrolling Chinese students, I would include the following. First, do not expect Chinese students to be as emotionally mature as are American students. In most cases a Chinese student of twenty-five will fit in well with a class of eighteen-year-olds in an American university. Second, do not expect a Chinese student to know how to handle his freedom or his money. In China he is accustomed to little of either. He is accustomed to being told what he needs to know as well as having his decisions made for him. Third, do not expect a Chinese student to understand American study habits or classroom procedures. He is accustomed to studying in a group. He is accustomed to sharing what he knows, even while taking exams. What Americans consider to be plagiarism, a Chinese student calls sharing. A Chinese student borrows the information he needs in writing a paper and presents it for the most part as he borrows it. He believes it must be good if it comes from an authority, that it must be better than anything he is capable of writing. Fourth, do not expect a Chinese student to be adept at critical thinking. He has not been taught to think; he has been taught to memorize.

Fifth, do not expect a Chinese student to perform well on comprehensive examinations. He is accustomed to limited bits of information which he is either given by his teachers or acquires through intensive reading. He has no knowledge about or experience in reading extensively. Sixth, do not expect a Chinese student to understand or appreciate the idea of "flunking," or even of receiving low grades. In China giving a low grade is a disgrace to the school. Chinese teachers give A's and B's, with a preponderance of A's. They dare not do anything else for fear of being criticized. Seventh, do not expect a Chinese student's transcript of credits to be an accurate reflection of the student's performance. When a student is accepted by a school in China, the school is committed to seeing him through whether he does anything or not. As for sending a transcript abroad, more often than not a student jots down his grades on a piece of paper and someone in one office or another stamps it with the school seal. All of this, of course, may be done without checking any records.

Friday, May 8

When I arrived at the institute, I took a walk. Reflecting on a number of things, I walked around the campus. I thought about the books which had arrived from Baylor University only a few days before, and I wondered whether they might make a difference in the quality of education at the institute. I wondered about those of my students who want to study in the United States. I weighed the chances of their ever having such an opportunity. I reflected on the disheveled and chaotic appearance of the campus, and for a moment it stood for all of China, causing me to feel sorry for my students as well as for the teachers and school officials I have come to know. I reflected on the fact that Vice President Li wants to have Wanda and me to his house for dinner, but that he is too ashamed of the flat he lives in to invite us. As Shao Jingfeng told me, Vice President Li describes his flat as "shabby." I reflected on these and many other things, and my reflections made me sad.

After lunch I went to the American embassy to return films I had borrowed. I also went to the office of Philippine Airlines to check on flights to the Philippines. I went to the Friendship Store to check on shipping our crate.

I learned that passports are finally being processed for a backlog of Chinese students who are waiting to go to America to study. Some restrictions have been lifted, and the result is that some of my students, such as Wang Yanmin, who has been accepted by Harvard University, will likely be allowed to go. I also learned that procedural policies concerning financing for students going abroad have been changed by the Ministry of Education because of protests by foreign universities. Chinese students will no longer be required to surrender part of their living allowance to the government in Beijing. The news was good, and I went to bed in the evening very happy as a result of having heard it.

Saturday, May 9

The wind blew fiercely, and we stayed inside most of the day. Another shipment of books arrived from Baylor University; we stacked the books in the corner of the living room. We received a long letter from Victor Strite informing us that official authorization for his teaching at Second Foreign Language Institute next year had finally reached him. Because

Victor had many questions, I spent more than an hour typing a letter in response to his questions. I composed two or three other letters, but they were short compared to my letter to Victor.

We went to the Minzu Restaurant for dinner with Diether and Margot Raff. We enjoyed a delicious meal, but the best part of the evening was the conversation. Diether related to us stories told by his Chinese students, who are really Chinese teachers studying the German language. One of the stories told to Diether by a woman in his class I found extremely interesting.

According to Diether, one of the women in his class has a brother who worked as an ambulance driver during the Cultural Revolution. Such a job sounds routine, but one must remember that the incident took place during the Cultural Revolution. One must also bear in mind that the Cultural Revolution was marked by much senseless bloodshed and that the Red Guards frequently annihilated groups as well as individuals. During the Cultural Revolution, the chief business of an ambulance driver was to haul the corpses of those who had been annihilated to the crematorium.

As the story goes, the woman's brother detested the job, but he had no choice about whether he would do it. He could have tolerated his job more readily, the woman told Diether, had he been hauling only corpses to the crematorium, but such was not the case. He often hauled people who were still alive to be placed in the crematorium. According to his sister, this caused the ambulance driver much pain, but he dared not complain to the authorities.

One day he was hauling a load of bodies to the crematorium and noticed that many of them were still alive. He was very disturbed, but he said nothing when he arrived at the crematorium. As he usually did, he helped throw the bodies into the pit. Body after body he helped throw in, trying to remain calm in light of the fact that many of them were alive and moving. When the last of the bodies was being thrown in, one of them reached out its hand toward him as it went over the side and into the pit. It was his favorite aunt, he realized, his mother's sister, but he quickly tried to convince himself that such simply could not be the case. Nevertheless, before the door closed he looked into the pit and realized that he was not suffering from a delusion. It was his favorite aunt, and she was alive.

The young man wanted to help his aunt, but he could neither move nor speak. He knew that any effort on his part would be futile, and he knew that his aunt was there in the pit because she had been declared an enemy of the Cultural Revolution. He realized that any effort on his part to save her would result in his being condemned by association as an enemy of the Cultural Revolution, in which case he would surely join the endless stream of bodies he had been helping feed into the crematorium. He did what was expedient, and he lived to tell the story of his favorite aunt. He is not a young man anymore, but he has a family and has managed to live a reasonably happy life. At least his life has been as happy as could be expected considering that his mind is a storehouse of scenes of horror from the Cultural Revolution.

Sunday, May 10

All day and all night Saturday the wind had blown dust and sand into Beijing. Wanda and I had stayed inside to avoid as much of it as we possibly could, but staying inside was only to escape the worst of it. A thick layer of dust collected on everything in the apartment, including us, and we could not help but choke on the dust-filled air. After lunch we tried to escape by going to bed and covering ourselves with sheets, but that afforded only temporary relief. In the evening we had ventured out to the Minzu Restaurant with our friends to distract our attention from the dust.

On Sunday the dust storm continued, but it worsened. Wanda and I decided that we would go to church in Xidan Street in spite of the dust, and I was glad we did. Since we had missed church the Sunday before to take the Taiyuan trip, it was good to be in church again. Being in church was almost too good because the service was unusually long. We listened to a guest speaker who had not preached since before the Cultural Revolution, and having his first audience in twenty years he did not want to stop. He droned on and on, and I became bored, but his Chinese audience remained attentive.

In the afternoon the dust continued to color the sky and everything under it. Once again Wanda and I decided that we would escape the effects of the dust by sleeping. Going to bed was not merely an escape; I knew Wanda needed the rest. In the evening, we invited friends to play bridge, and while the wind blew fiercely we played until 11:00 p.m. By the time we went to bed, the intensity of the wind seemed to have increased. All night long the wind howled, and dust continued to coat everything in our apartment. I lay awake and listened, knowing that I would be tired when I taught my classes the next morning.

Monday, May 11

As far as the dust storm is concerned, Monday proved to be no different from Saturday and Sunday. The wind was more vicious. I arrived at the institute around 7:30 a.m. and graded some papers. Then I took a walk. I tried to follow the natural windbreakers, staying on the leeward side of the buildings and rows of spruce trees. That did not help. Dust was flying all about me, and escaping it was impossible. The consequences of my walk were unpleasant, for my sinuses plugged and I was miserable for the remainder of the day.

At about ten o'clock L. T. Lin came to inform me that a crew from the Friendship Store would arrive at our apartment at one o'clock that afternoon to pack our crate for shipping. When my last class ended at noon I immediately caught a car for home. When I arrived at the Friendship Hotel, I knew that I would not have time to go to the dining hall for lunch; the crew from the Friendship Store would arrive in fifteen minutes. I stopped long enough to purchase a small piece of meat, a loaf of bread, and a bottle of beer. I reasoned that I could eat in my room.

The crew from the Friendship Store was early. They were waiting for me when I reached the apartment. To my surprise, the crew consisted of eight men, and even more to my surprise they had the crate packed in about fifteen minutes. I still had time to go to the dining hall for lunch before it closed, but I had my meat, bread, and beer. When I had finished eating, the wind was still blowing fiercely. It made good sense, I thought, to spend at least part of the afternoon in bed.

Tuesday, May 12

Classes had been called off for a track meet, but I went to the campus anyway. I needed to see Qi Wenqin about having a projectionist show a film the next morning as well as talk with her about the possibility of my drawing an advance on my salary. I wanted the advance because I will have to dispose of all my Chinese *yuan* before leaving the country. Outside China, *yuan* cannot be exchanged for other currency, and therefore has no value except in China. I thought I would try to draw my July salary and a departure settlement of half a month's salary the first part of June. That way I could dispose of my Chinese money before leaving the country.

When I went to the car stand, I told the dispatcher that I wanted to go to building four to pick up books that had been shipped by Baylor University. Next, I told him I wanted to go to the American embassy to pick up films. Finally, as I explained, we would go to the institute from the embassy. While taking down my instructions, the dispatcher failed to enter the stop at the embassy on the dispatch, but as soon as we passed the embassy area I knew something was wrong. Although I tried to explain to the driver that I needed to go to the embassy, he could not understand me. Using many gestures and the little Chinese I knew, I managed to have the driver turn around and head in the direction of the embassy. From that point, I navigated by pointing a finger in the direction I wanted the driver to turn. As we approached the embassy, he told me how to say "American embassy" in Chinese, but after repeating it several times I promptly forgot it.

When I arrived at the institute I went to Qi Wenqin's flat. She was not at home. I walked along the track and then went to my office to work. I worked for an hour or more before returning to Wenqin's flat. She was at home, and we talked for half an hour or more, after which I visited the track to watch two or three events before returning to the compound. I needed to walk, and I needed to think. I took the afternoon off and walked to a famous bell tower not far from the Friendship Hotel. I saw one of the largest bells in the world.

Wednesday, May 13

It was a perplexing day, but at least one thing turned out well. Zhu Zheng brought my July salary and my departure settlement, which I had not expected before the first part of June. Once he had gone, I went to the auditorium to begin showing films. The projectionist was nowhere to be found. I sent a student to his home to remind him that he was scheduled to show films, and at about 8:20 he had the first reel under way. Because we were late in starting, we ran beyond the allotted class time, and as a result the next class was also late in starting.

I had announced that I would lecture following the films, and teacher Qi had assured me that the lecture would not conflict with any other classes. Before the end of the last reel of film, however, I was told by three or four students that they had class the next period. With that in mind, I announced at the end of the last reel that all students who did not have class should report to classroom three for a lecture. As I had found out when the films ended, half of my students were scheduled for a class in interpretation, and I was sure the remainder would fit into classroom three.

When the classroom had filled, I began my lecture, but I was not prepared for what followed. After about five minutes the door opened, and a group of students entered. They continued to come until a hundred students had crowded into a room built to accommodate twenty-four or twenty-five. I stopped lecturing until they were all situated; then I lectured for another forty minutes. Those students who were scheduled for a class in oral interpretation had convinced their teacher that they should attend my lecture. I was embarrassed.

When Wanda came home from work, she informed me that she had enjoyed lunch with a friend from the agricultural section of the embassy. I knew that she was to have lunch with her friend, but I was not prepared for what she had to tell me. According to Wanda's friend, two days earlier the embassy staff had received orders to destroy all secret documents in the embassy. No reason was given for the order, but the order was urgent and clear, according to the friend. One never knows what might surface in China, and one never understands what is happening at any one time because of government control over the news.

Thursday, May 14

Early in the morning we awakened to hear on Voice of America that Pope John Paul II had been shot by a radical Turk, and that the pope was in critical condition. It was hardly the way to begin a day—in shock and mourning with all of Christendom. On the other hand, one must begin every day with hope, even in the face of disaster. We also heard that the senate had approved President Reagan's budget, and that Alexander

Haig would soon visit Beijing. I hope Haig will bring news concerning a new ambassador to China. Leadership is still missing from the American embassy.

Good news came from John Thomson, counselor for cultural affairs at the embassy. I had taken Thomson a query concerning Ralph Wang, a query about the feasibility of Wang's receiving a Fulbright award that would enable him to spend a year at Baylor University teaching and ordering books on Chinese culture. The answer came by telephone that the chances of Wang's receiving such an award are good. Wang's presence at Baylor could add a much-needed impetus to Baylor's fledgling program in Asian Studies. Thomson informed me that he would mail the information I needed to pursue the matter of Wang's spending a year at Baylor under Fulbright auspices.

On the way to work early in the morning, Jeanne Lonnoy supplied me with another bit of news. From the time we started to the institute, I could tell she was upset, and when she explained her problem I could see why. She had argued with President Tang Kai concerning her students. An announcement had come from the Ministry of Tourism that no jobs existed for those students who would be graduating in French, and Jeanne was furious because her students had studied French for four years only to be told that they were unemployable. When she had pressed the matter with Tang Kai, she was told that the Chinese government had accepted the fact that English is the international language. The explanation makes no sense unless the government plans to close the country to French tourists, for the students Jeanne has taught have trained to become tour guides. The government's decision could be a signal concerning the future of relations between France and China, but that is not likely. That the government in Beijing recently sent congratulations to President Elect François Mitterrand would indicate that the government expects a positive relationship with France in the future, and this is particularly so because of Mitterrand's position on the Soviet Union. Such decisions as that pertaining to teaching French are typical of Chinese policy making; those who make policy frequently seem to ignore the facts.

Friday, May 15

I met with class three to listen to seminar reports, and I witnessed an interesting change in behavior on the part of my students. For the first time since February my students began asking questions as though they were no longer afraid. The first young woman to make a presentation was named Shao, and she prefaced her presentation by saying that she would gladly answer any questions once her report had been given. She gave a superb report, and her classmates took her at her word. Since the tightening up began around the beginning of the year, my students had refused to ask questions in class. On this occasion they "let go," and they had questions after the second seminar report as well. It was a breakthrough that made me happy, and I think my students could sense that I was pleased.

Another thing took place during the day that pleased me. I saw an American teacher at the institute meet her match. Ever since school started in the fall, she had bullied the Chinese teachers into giving her whatever she wanted. But on this occasion she was not dealing with the Chinese teachers.

It was 11:00 a.m., and I was in a car waiting to go home. A teacher from England came to the car next, and then a large German man who was visiting the institute to deliver a guest lecture. When we were all three in the car, the teacher from London requested that the driver take us to the Friendship Hotel only to be told that we would have to wait for an American teacher. We waited, and in about ten or fifteen minutes the American teacher came escorted by two Chinese teachers. When she saw three teachers and the driver in the car, she was perturbed. She wanted to go shopping and had decided to take the Chinese teachers with her, but the three of us already in the car refused to be ejected.

For about ten minutes the American teacher stood in front of the car with the two Chinese teachers and argued with the driver as well as with the man responsible for dispatching cars from the institute. The visiting German became increasingly agitated as the argument progressed; he finally reached the breaking point. He got out of the car, raved in German at the American woman, and then pulled the driver into the car and ordered him to start the motor. The driver started the car and revved the engine, at which time the American woman moved from in front of the car and we were on our way. I was told later that the American woman tried for two hours before she was successful in finding a driver who would haul her and the two Chinese teachers. The American teacher had met her match, and after that even the Chinese teachers have refused to be intimidated by her. Because of her obnoxious behavior in the past, I considered the incident a victory for Chinese civilization.

Saturday, May 16

Wanda had become anxious that she might not see everything there is to see in Beijing before we leave for the United States. Because of her anxiety we spent the day as tourists visiting Beijing University, using as our guides Mao Zhiren and a friend of his named Hu Jingning. When we returned to the Friendship Hotel, we agreed that there was not much to see that we had not already seen. We went to lunch, after which we visited Yonghe Gong, a well-known lama temple in the northeastern part of the city. Yonghe Gong was different from the Buddhist temples we had visited. One hall contained figures illustrating ancient fertility rites, some of which consisted of animals and human beings mating. If I had known the stories or myths that go with the figures, they probably would have seemed appropriately and plausibly placed. But as it was the figures appeared pornographic. I was later told that they appear that way to the Chinese.

After our visit to Yonghe Gong, we had one more stop to make. Wanda had not seen the Bell Tower, even though I had visited it only a few days earlier. When we tried to explain to our driver where we wanted to go, he misunderstood and took us to Beihai Park. Realizing we would never be able to communicate with our driver, we had him return us to the Friendship Hotel, from which we walked to the Bell Tower. We walked for twenty minutes along a dusty and heavily traveled road which had been under repair for some time. Once we arrived, we viewed bells from all over China, some of which were more than six feet tall. In the Bell Tower we saw the largest bell in China, which weighs 46.5 tons. It is also one of the largest bells in the world; the largest is in the Soviet Union. After we had seen the bells, we walked back to the Friendship Hotel very tired.

Sunday, May 17

It rained all night Saturday, and it was still raining when we went to church in Xidan Street on Sunday morning. Four bus loads of foreign experts and their families had signed up to visit a newly opened temple. As the rain continued to come down Wanda and I were glad that we had not signed up for the trip. We listened to a fine sermon by Pastor Qi as rain continued to fall on Beijing. After the church service we met a group of American tourists and a group of Canadian tourists; both were attending the church service. The group of American tourists contained two brothers from California who had lived in China during their childhood years. Their father had been a missionary in China, and the brothers were happy to be reliving their childhood.

I found the brothers' excitement over China to be filled with nostalgia and curiosity. I suppose they know more about the expulsion of missionaries from China than I will ever know. On the other hand, a young Chinese Christian recently told me that the cause for expelling the missionaries is clear. Said he, "The government expelled missionaries because U.S. spies were coming to China disguised as missionaries." The young Chinese Christian was explaining the reason given by the government for expelling the missionaries; he was not stating his own belief regarding the matter.

Monday, May 18

When Patrick Cassidy came to my office early on Monday morning, one of my students was there asking questions about literature I had assigned to be read. Patrick commented that she had been coming too frequently, and his remark started me to thinking. I had not been aware of the frequency with which she had been coming to ask questions, and I had almost forgotten the danger involved. She enjoyed talking, and I was convinced she had also forgotten about the danger. But Patrick's gentle reminder was well intended and well taken. I am a foreigner. I must not become overly familiar with the Chinese, and that includes my students.

Madame Sun Yatsen (Soong Ching-ling) is ill. She developed lymphatic leukemia several months ago, and since May 14 her condition has grown worse. Recently she has been visited by such party and state leaders as Hua Guofeng, Ni Zhifu, Peng Chong, Hu Qiaomu, Xu Deheng, Kang Keqing, Hu Yuzhi, and Deng Xiaoping. Denied membership in the Communist Party until last week, she has aspired to such membership for many years. Now that she is on her deathbed, Ching-ling is being fully recognized. For example, the Standing Committee of the National People's Congress met last Saturday and named her Honorary Chairman of the People's Republic of China

Tuesday, May 19

I graded papers and met with Qi Wenqin. It would have been a pleasant day except that one of the American teachers was sulking. She has done a poor job of teaching, and her students have finally told her as much. They have protested to school officials. They have missed classes and refused to do assignments. They have done about everything students can do to protest being cheated. As for the teacher, she told me that she had decided to reorganize her classes and start over, and although I listened I said nothing. The school year is almost over, and she lost the confidence of her students long ago. It is too late to start over, and even if it were not, her negligence and lack of concern can never be rectified. I wanted to tell her these things, but I did not. She is not one to accept advice or friendly suggestions. After lunch I took a walk and spent the remainder of the day writing. The writing I found to be relaxing, comforting; an old feeling of satisfaction which comes only from writing crept back into my soul. In the evening Wanda went to see a Beijing Opera, but I stayed home and read. I retired early, feeling that the day had been one of my best in a long time.

Wednesday, May 20

My students and I viewed two more episodes from the *America* film series. Episode number eight, "Money on the Land," focuses on the building of industry and the railroads in the era of the great Robber Barons. "The Huddled Masses," episode nine, focuses on the great waves of immigrants coming into the United States, especially during the nineteenth century. My students enjoyed both episodes, but one young man was perplexed by a statement in "The Huddled Masses" to the effect that members of the Communist Party are denied citizenship in the United States.

Later in the day I went to town on the Friendship Bus. I had two chores to perform. First, I needed to visit the embassy. I needed to return the two reels of film I had shown and to check on the whereabouts of episode ten. I had heard through another foreign teacher that episode ten was missing. I also needed to visit the Friendship Store in order to look for a gift for Wanda. The next day would be our fifteenth wedding anniversary. When I went to the Friendship Store, little did I expect to run into Wanda. Fortunately, I had purchased her present before we happened upon each other. The electricity had been turned off at the construction site of the Great Wall Hotel, and Wanda had decided to take advantage of that to do some shopping.

Thursday, May 21

It was the day of our fifteenth wedding anniversary, and I decided that I should honor that fact by altering my daily routine. For the first time since September of 1980, I did not leave before seven o'clock to go to the institute. I arrived at the institute after eight, and I immediately set out for a walk. I walked for about twenty minutes before deciding to return to my office to grade papers and meet with students.

About nine o'clock I decided I would take another walk, a longer walk. I left campus and wandered down a back road that I had not previously traveled. Lined on each side by high walls, the road reminded me of a tunnel, but when I had gone a mile or so I crossed a bisecting road and the walls ended. Once again I could observe the huts and lean-tos inhabited by thousands of Chinese people. They were a gruesome and sordid sight.

After my walk I returned to the institute and graded more papers. I also met with Qi Wenqin to discuss a letter of recommendation I had composed. The letter had been requested indirectly by the dean of the English department. The letter was one in which the dean was supposed to recommend a foreign teacher at the institute for employment in the United States, but the dean did not know enough English to write the letter. Nor did he know how to write it. In turn, the dean had assigned the task to Wenqin, and she had come to me to write the letter for her. When I showed her the letter, she was pleased. She told me that she would use it as a model for writing such letters in the future.

Friday, May 22

I had decided that I would start eating breakfast in the dining hall before going to the institute. Always before, Wanda and I had enjoyed a piece of dry toast and a cup of coffee in our apartment, but I recently reasoned that I needed breakfast to prevent becoming overly tired. I also rationalized that I no longer needed to arrive at the institute by 7:30 a.m. As a result of all this reasoning, I was on my way to the dining hall for the second morning in succession when I came upon Jeanne Lonnoy. Jeanne had always been able to count on my being at the car stand at 6:45 a.m., and I in turn could count on her being there. We had ridden to the institute together every morning since last September. That is, we had until the day before when I stayed behind and enjoyed my first breakfast in the dining hall.

When I met Jeanne and asked her how everything had gone, she explained that she had experienced difficulty in getting to the institute because the driver would not go with only one passenger in the car. I must have been looking for an excuse to discontinue having breakfast and to return to my old routine, for I immediately volunteered to accompany her, thus assuring that she would not be late in arriving at the institute. Jeanne protested, but I accompanied her anyway. I felt good about returning to my old habit, and I do not believe I will be an eater of breakfast until after I have left China. All day long I felt good about having arrived at the institute at my usual time. I had no classes to meet and no pressing appointments, but I was on the job, and that was what counted.

Saturday, May 23

Having given up our idea of an outing to Ming Tombs, Wanda and I decided that we would visit Fragrant Hill Park. We took a car and arrived early in order to escape the great mob we knew would arrive later. We entered the gate and immediately turned the wrong way. When we could not find the Temple of 508 Buddhas, we knew we were lost. We stopped a young Chinese couple and asked concerning directions. Since they spoke a few words of English, we thought they understood, but they did not. After wandering among the hills with them for almost an hour, we realized that. It was then that Wanda resorted to gestures, and almost immediately the Chinese couple understood that we wanted to go to the Temple of 508 Buddhas.

The Chinese couple had a little boy of two or three years with them.

He was their son, and they were obviously proud of him. We managed to communicate well enough with them to find out that they comprised one of those divided Chinese families. We learned that the husband lived in Hong Kong with his family, and that the wife lived in Shanghai with her family and her son. We could not communicate well enough to learn details, but we did learn that the Chinese couple was on their annual vacation with their son. Many Chinese families live in a similar predicament. They are often separated, and it seems that little or no concern is given to the idea of keeping them together when work assignments are made.

In the afternoon we stayed at home and rested. The pace at which one lives in China is much slower than the pace at which he lives in the United States. Rest is essential to compensate for the poor diet as well as to allow a way of handling daily frustrations. It is much less painful to bang one's head against a brick wall softly and slowly than it is to bang one's head against the same wall hard and rapidly. In any event, the day was a special one because I reasoned that we would be leaving China in five weeks. I thought about that, and I thought about possible adjustment problems we will encounter when we go home. How will we ever fit into the society that we left such a short time ago?

Sunday, May 24

Because Wen Yee Chin was out of town, Wanda and I decided to attend the church service at the American embassy. Peter Johnson, from the British embassy, delivered the meditation, and I thought he did a fine job. Nina Taylor led the congregation during the remainder of the service. The crowd was small, consisting of twenty-five to thirty people, but the service was enjoyable.

We spent the afternoon at Beihai Park, and while we walked in the park I thought about my students. The education they receive is very poor. They are in school for about forty-four weeks during each academic year, but they are frequently away from the classroom serving as tour guides or in some other capacity. The education my students receive is sporadic. It consists of bits and pieces they receive when they are actually in the classroom. Run by people who for the most part are not well educated, the educational system is designed to defeat and frustrate serious students.

They are being sold short, and some of them are beginning to realize it.

Wanda and I heard an interesting story about a young Chinese man who recently charged into the French consulate waving a large saber and threatening to commit suicide if he was not given political asylum. From Shanxi Province, the young man thought he was in the American embassy. When the French discovered this, they happily put him in a car and took him to the American embassy. As far as they were concerned, they were tactfully avoiding what could have turned into an international incident. The American embassy had been forewarned, and when the young man was making his way from the car to the door of the embassy he was wrestled to the ground and relieved of his saber. Once that had been accomplished, he was promptly turned over to the Chinese police. Thus an incident which could have proved embarrassing to the American embassy turned out well. I have wondered about the desperate young man; he is not alone. The People's Republic of China contains many such desperate young people.

Monday, May 25

News has been circulating that Secretary of State Alexander Haig is coming, but no one seems to know the reason for his coming. He may be coming to discuss possible nominees to fill the post of ambassador. Leonard Woodcock has been gone for a long time, and a replacement has not been named. Even rumors about who might become the next American ambassador to China have ceased. The post remains empty, and the American community in China needs leadership more than ever.

In one respect the day was a strange one. I was approached by a friend and colleague for my advice concerning which of three Chinese women he should marry and take back to the United States with him. After we talked about the idea of taking a Chinese wife, I realized that he had made up his mind. My friend is thirty-nine and has never been married, so I tried to impress upon him that it would be a mistake to marry a Chinese woman for no other reason than to save her from the evils of communism. I suspected such to be his motive.

Twenty-one, twenty-five, and twenty-nine years old, the women are all attractive. We talked about some of the problems that might result from a difference in age between husband and wife. We particularly talked about possible problems in one's social life caused by that difference. When we had completed our discussion, I thought he had decided to marry the twenty-five-year-old, who happens to be a teacher as well as one of his students. I was amazed that he registered no particular emotion over making such a decision. It was as though he were choosing a new suit.

I wondered about my friend's motives. I thought he had become too attached to his students, too involved in their personal lives. I tried to make him understand that personal involvement in China will not necessarily produce a sound and enduring marriage in the United States. At the same time, I can appreciate his high regard for Chinese women. They are very unlike American women in that having had so little in life they are extremely appreciative. They are family oriented. They want children and a home.

Tuesday, May 26

When I arrived at the institute, I took a walk. The weather was sticky, even at 7:30 a.m., and I had to cut my walk short. Instead of walking longer, I went to my office and planned for the next day's classes.

Later I visited the embassy and the Friendship Store. I went to the Friendship Store to check on progress concerning the shipping of our crate, and found that no progress had been made. The shipping company had not confirmed that space was available. Realizing that I could do nothing about shipping the crate, I went to Wangfujing Street where I wandered in and out of shops. I also visited the National Art Gallery to view an exhibit of paintings by Dong Kingman, a Chinese-American. When I left the art gallery, I went to the Beijing Hotel. Ed and I shared a taxi to the compound, and when I arrived at our apartment a message was waiting for me that a man named Vernon McClelland had called from the Beijing Hotel.

I returned Vernon McClelland's call to find that he was in Beijing with a Meier International tour group, and that he wanted to have dinner with Wanda and me the next evening. I agreed that we would have dinner with him at 7:30. He did not indicate what it was he wanted to talk about, and I had no idea what it might be, but he obviously wanted to talk. I knew I would find out the next evening.

Wednesday, May 27

When one has a month before leaving China, one develops certain anxieties. One also views each day in terms of events that make a difference. On this day, May 27, two things happened that seemed to make a difference. One of the attendants on the floor on which we live at the Friendship Hotel came to our apartment and knocked. When I answered the door, she began jabbering excitedly in Chinese. I had no idea about what might have excited her, and she could not tell me. Finally, she gestured for me to follow her. When we arrived at the lobby near the entrance, I found a short, stocky Chinese man waiting for me. Holding a paper in his hand, he also began jabbering in Chinese. Because I could not make out what he wanted, the attendant from our floor took me by the hand and led me outside. Then I understood what was happening. Not far from the entrance to the building a huge crane was being used in loading our crate onto a truck for transporting to the coast. From there it would go to America. Once I realized what was taking place, I knew the paper in the man's hand was a release form, and that he wanted me to sign it. I was right. He handed me a pen and pointed to the line on which he wanted me to sign.

The second significant thing that happened involved Vernon McClelland and his wife. Wanda and I took a taxi to the Beijing Hotel, arriving at about 7:15 p.m. We went to the McClellands' room, where we found Vernon shooting pictures of a beautiful sunset from the balcony. After talking for half an hour, we went to dinner and talked more. As it turned out, the McClellands had two things about which they wanted to talk. First, they had smuggled in a cache of Bibles that they wanted to unload. And second, they wanted to know about our experience in China. They realized that as tourists they were sheltered from the "real China," and we were posed the inevitable question: "What is the real China like?" We spent a pleasant evening with the McClellands, but we were tired by the time we returned to the Friendship Hotel.

Thursday, May 28

I spent much time walking and meditating. I thought about welfare-state education. My students at the institute are paid about thirty-five *yuan* per month to go to school, and the effect is that receiving an education is turned into a low-paying job. I wonder whether such an arrangement can ever be productive, for just as Chinese students all receive high grades regardless of the work they do, they also receive the same pay. No reward for having done a good job comes at graduation; the government assigns them the same jobs.

The more I thought about such things as they apply to Chinese students, the more I thought about the American welfare state and the American university. With the growth of the student financial aid industry, grade inflation has soared in American universities. American universities are beset by numerous other problems, many of which can be related directly to "easy money." Perhaps we Americans can learn something from the Chinese: The best way to kill education in America is to give it away. As for me, I often think about Arthur Miller's play *The Price*, and not because I think it is a particularly good play. On the other hand, I agree with the sentiments expressed in the play. We must pay a price; otherwise there is no value. Yes, I think the surest way to make education valueless is to give it away.

Friday, May 29

In the United States, to read in the news that China has no crime is still common. The Chinese people read the same thing in their newspapers. But those who are the least bit perceptive know better. Many stores in Beijing have bars across the doors and windows. In that respect they resemble stores in Detroit or Chicago. Last winter a student from First Foreign Language Institute robbed a shop in Wangfujing Street and killed the shopkeeper. With gangs of unemployed youth wandering the streets, crime in China is on the increase. Probably because the government wanted to make an example of the killer, one such incident was reported in the newspaper *China Daily* on Thursday (May 28, 1981). Entitled "Killer Punished," the article reads as follows:

> Monday afternoon, the city's Intermediate People's Court in a session passed sentence on Nie Fu Gang and ten other young criminals on charges of killing Wu Chun, a No. 354 bus conductor on February 12.
>
> Nie, who fatally plunged a knife into Wu's liver, was sentenced to

death with a reprieve of two years. The ten others were given sentences of imprisonment of from three to 16 years.

Wu Chun, seeing Nie and his followers smoking on the bus, told them to extinguish their cigarettes. Offended, they reacted by first insulting Wu and spitting at him. Then they all beat Wu with their fists, feet, and bike locks. Nie, who stabbed Wu in the right side of his back, killed him. (p. 3)

The story of Wu Chun is a gory one, but it is like any number of stories about crime committed by gangs in major American cities.

Saturday, May 30

On Saturday we slept late, having gone to see a movie called *The Last Remnant* the night before. When we finally arose, we had breakfast and went to Purple Bamboo Park. We spent the morning near a lake in the shade of large willow trees. A cool breeze was blowing across the water, and we enjoyed watching people in small boats. We tarried as long as we could, for the scene and the breeze were pleasant. Ching-ling died at 8:18 p.m. on May 29, 1981, at the age of ninety. The statement issued by the government following her death, and printed in its entirety in *China Daily* (May 30, 1981) reads as follows:

> The Central Committee of the Communist Party of China, the Standing Committee of the National People's Congress of the People's Republic of China and the State Council of the People's Republic of China, announce with the deepest grief: Comrade Soong Ching-ling, a great patriotic, democratic, internationalist and communist fighter, outstanding international political figure and prominent state leader of China, Honorary President of the People's Republic of China and Vice-Chairman of the Standing Committee of the National People's Congress of the People's Republic of China, died of chronic lymphocytic leukemia in Beijing at 20:18 hours on May 29, 1981, at the age of 90.

> Comrade Soong Ching-ling's death is a great loss to our country and the people of the whole country. We hereby declare that a state funeral be held for Comrade Soong Ching-ling to express the profound mourning of the people of all our nationalities.

A funeral committee for Comrade Soong Ching-ling has been formed.

Eternal glory to Comrade Soong Ching-ling, a great patriotic, democratic, internationalist and communist fighter and outstanding state leader of China! (p. 1)

Sunday, May 31

We arrived at the church in Xidan Street at 8:50, ten minutes before time to begin the Sunday morning service. It was communion Sunday, and Chinese Christians in the Xidan Street church regard the sacraments seriously. I knew that we were confronting two hours of church. Communion is dear to my Chinese Christian friends. They pray, they weep, they take communion, but it also appears to be a time of reliving the horrors many of them suffered during the Cultural Revolution. They are grateful to be alive, and I wish every Christian in America could attend church with them on a communion Sunday. They confess that Christ paid the price for their sins, but they too have paid a price, and the price they have paid seems to make Christ even more dear to them.

It proved to be a fine service. But a group of American tourists came in during the service and disrupted the congregation. Many of the Chinese worshipers relocated and made way for the American guests to sit together. After having been in church for fifteen minutes, however, the American tourists decided to leave. Once again they distracted the congregation, and I was glad when they left. My experience has been that American tourists in China are a rude, arrogant lot, and the American tourists who visited the Xidan Street church on Sunday, May 31, proved to be no different. They would have objected strongly had such an incident taken place in one of their churches in America, but Chinese Christians are tolerant and forgiving. They will not complain about such an intrusion.

June

Monday, June 1

When I went to visit Diane Johnston at the American embassy last week, I went to check on a letter she was to have mailed me concerning the possibility of a Fulbright award for Ralph Wang. While we were discussing Ralph Wang, she asked me to submit a list of names of my students whom I considered worthy and qualified to study in America. I told her that I would be glad to submit such a list, for I have a number of fine students whom I would like to see have the opportunity to study in America.

Monday proved to be a profitable day. Some weeks earlier I had promised Rita Clarke that I would lecture to her class of teachers on the topic of the poet in modern America. As it turned out, I lectured for about an hour. Then I read and analyzed poems for Rita's class to illustrate the contentions I had made in the lecture.

As for my own classes, the day proved rewarding but a bit strange. At 10:10, I met with class number one, and for the first time in several weeks I had a full classroom. By way of contrast, I met class number two at 11:10 and only three students were present. Although the experience was frustrating, what had happened was immediately obvious. Students from class one had returned from serving as tour guides; students from class two had left school to begin serving as tour guides. Although I had only three students in class two, we had an enjoyable time discussing Katherine Anne Porter's short story "Theft." Because they were only three in number, my students talked freely. They asked many questions. And they obviously enjoyed themselves.

Tuesday, June 2

The day was frustrating in a number of ways. I had with me a list of approximately a dozen things I needed to discuss with Qi Wenqin. For example, I needed to discuss numerous details concerning our return to the United States. I needed to discuss details pertaining to a proposed meeting between officials at the institute and Abner McCall, President of Baylor University, when he arrives in Beijing on June 29. I needed to discuss my proposed trip to Changchun on June 8, as well as what to do with my students during the week I will be gone. I needed to discuss plans for a dinner which Wanda and I plan to host for teachers and officials at the institute. I needed to discuss being issued another contract by the institute because I had shipped my copy home in the crate without realizing that I would need the contract to complete plans for going home. I needed Qi Wenqin to take me to the bureau of experts at the institute and serve as interpreter while I discussed money for our plane tickets with Mr. Zhang. Qi Wenqin proved very helpful. We discussed all of these things and more.

I devoted the afternoon to preparing a lecture for the next morning on patterns of Southern experience. Psychologically ready to leave China, I found preparing a two-hour lecture to be unusually difficult. I worried whether actually presenting the lecture might be more difficult than preparing it. Fortunately, after dinner Wanda and I had another couple in to play bridge, and that took my mind off the lecture. I got a good night's rest, for I knew that at eight o'clock the next morning I would find out whether I had put together a lecture worth the time my audience would spend in listening.

Wednesday, June 3

After my lecture on patterns of Southern experience I met with numerous students. They all had questions. Then I met with Qi Wenqin to work on details pertaining to our going home. I have been informed by a Mr. Chen at the Bureau of Foreign Experts that CAAC (Civil Aviation Administration of China) has no Wednesday flight to Shanghai. Wanda and I want to spend two days in Shanghai before leaving China, and because Pan American Airlines has only one flight from Shanghai to Los Angeles each week, the timing is crucial. Qi Wenqin and I discussed the possibility of a late evening flight on June 30. We also discussed the possibility of taking a train to Shanghai in order to make connections. Our discussion was all in vain; for such information one must go to China International Travel Service, and even then one cannot be sure the information received is accurate.

I visited the offices of Pan American Airlines in the afternoon. I found out that CAAC does not have a flight to Shanghai on July 1. I was impressed by the efficiency of personnel in the Pan American office. I was so impressed that I ordered tickets for our flight home. Not only will Pan American book space on CAAC for our flight to Shanghai, but on

Friday I will walk into the Pan American office and pick up the tickets for the portion of our journey from Shanghai to Dallas.

Thursday, June 4

On some days my patience wears thin, and Thursday was one of those days. Thursday was the day we were to be paid, and I had been assured that the money for our flight home would be ready. When Qi Wenqin went to the office to pick up the money, she was told that it was not ready. I sent her to see Mr. Zhang, who was supposed to have arranged for the payment. Mr. Zhang was busy hosting a Japanese delegation. Since Qi Wenqin had called him out of a meeting to inquire about the payment, he promised that he would have arrangements made for payment the next day and returned to his meeting.

The vultures are at it again. In the twenties, thirties, and forties various countries each had a large stake in China. When the Communists came to power they drove out the foreigners. That was more than thirty years ago. Now the vultures are back looking for ways to exploit China, and the Japanese are the most aggressive of the lot. Offering aid to higher education in China is one way of "getting a foot in the door." The French, the West Germans, the Canadians, the Australians, the Americans, and the Japanese are all vying for a stronger relationship with China in this way. Chinese officials are accustomed to such behavior, however, and they are making the foreigners pay dearly. The Chinese are on the receiving end, and they know it. They are beating the foreigners at an old game. When they have played the game to their advantage long enough they will expel the foreigners. It is a dangerous game, and the Chinese are playing to win.

According to the newspaper *China Daily* (June 3, 1981), Sino-American relations are not likely to improve rapidly until the United States changes its position concerning Taiwan. An article entitled "Beijing Blast at U.S. for Taiwan Meddling" explains the problem:

> Beijing's *Guangming Daily* has delivered a blistering attack on the U.S. Taiwan Relations Act, saying that it "violates the principles of the China-U.S. Joint Communique on the establishment of diplomatic relations and American pledges on a series of actions."
>
> In a lengthy commentary, the paper said the Act hampers and

undermines smooth development in Sino-American relations.

The commentary went on to say the Act openly interferes in China's internal affairs, and the future of Taiwan is solely a problem to be solved and decided by the Chinese themselves including the people of Taiwan.

A second point made in the commentary is continuing sales of arms to Taiwan. These, it noted, despite the fact that the U.S. government has acknowledged the People's Republic to be the sole government of China, are handled by the government and cannot be considered as unofficial relations. (p. 1)

The article goes on to claim that the United States is treating Taiwan as though it were a country, and is therefore maintaining a "two-China" policy. Finally, the article points out that damaging relations with China will make the United States' effort to counter Soviet challenges more difficult. As was the case with the article in *Guangming Daily*, the article in *China Daily* seems designed to issue a warning to those in the United States government who are urging an overall implementation of the Taiwan Relations Act.

Friday, June 5

For most of the day I was enraged over money. I had been promised money for plane fares for Wanda and me by the first of the month, but that had not materialized. After June 1 had come and gone, I was promised that the money would be ready on June 4. When June 4 came, I was told that the money was still not ready. On June 4 I was assured that the money would be ready on June 5. Consequently, when Zhu Zheng came to inform me that the money was still not ready, and that Mr. Zhang could not be found, I sent him to look for Mr. Zhang. Zhu Zheng returned in half an hour to inform me that Mr. Zhang was off campus with a Japanese delegation, and I told him to check every half-hour with Mr. Zhang's office until Mr. Zhang returned.

In about an hour Zhu Zheng came and called me out of class. Not only had Mr. Zhang returned to campus, but Zhu Zheng had brought me 2,500 *yuan*. He explained that he would have brought the entire amount (approximately U.S. $2,000) except that Mr. Zhang had been given two quotations on the fare from Los Angeles to Dallas and did not know which one to use. Zhu Zheng told me the matter would be resolved in a short time and I would receive the balance of my money.

I was pleased to have the 2,500 *yuan* because I will be out of town over the coming week, and when I return only two weeks will remain until our departure. I also know that I will experience several more encounters with Chinese bureaucracy before leaving the country, and I was pleased to have won a round in my ongoing struggle with the bureaucrats. In the afternoon I went to the offices of Pan American Airlines and picked up tickets for our flight from Shanghai to Dallas. We have yet to purchase tickets for our flight from Beijing to Shanghai. That will constitute another round with Chinese bureaucracy and I am not looking forward to it. Purchasing our tickets and reserving a room in Shanghai will both be frustrating.

Saturday, June 6

China has a new symbol of decadence. In spite of the fact that the country has a history of close family ties, and in spite of the fact that Chinese morality appears to be based on ancestor worship and the idea of the extended family, a recent newspaper article entitled "Happy Old Days at New Elderly Home Welcomed" causes me to wonder about the future of the family as a unit in China. Sounding like a commercial for old people's homes, the article in *China Daily* (June 3, 1981) reads as follows:

A "Home of Honour" elderly home, first of its kind in the Peking area, has been established in Ping Gu County, northeast of Peking. The home provides for elderly dependents of revolutionary martyrs and disabled or retired servicemen.

Occupying an area of 1800-square metres, the home has such facilities as a clinic, reading room, barber shop and a tailor shop as well as bathing rooms. A spacious bed-sitting room of 18 square metres is given to every two persons.

Leading comrades of the city's Municipal Government paid a special visit to the aged residents in the home last Friday.

Ma Yuchuan, one of the old folks, said: "The good days that we have never dared dream of in the past now have come to us. I enjoy my life here very much." (p. 3)

So much for the beginning of old people's homes in China. I have no doubt that there will be more of them when the country realizes a bit more of what is being referred to in China as "modernization." Wanda and I went to the institute, to the flat of Zhu Zheng and Qi Wenqin, for dinner. Zhu Zheng is an excellent cook, and this time he had outdone himself. We ate and talked for three hours, and all the time we enjoyed ourselves immensely. When our taxi arrived at eight, we had no choice but to leave, even though we wanted to stay and continue our conversation. During our ride home Wanda commented on how remarkable she found it that people from such drastically different cultures could find so much to talk about. The ride home took most of an hour, but we were contented over having had a good visit with Zhu Zheng and Qi Wenqin.

Sunday, June 7

We went to church, as was our Sunday morning habit. The Chinese Christians in the Xidan Street church were especially congenial and warm, as though they might have heard that we were about to leave them. After the church service a man I had never met before wanted to talk about the fact that he came from a Christian family and that he had a brother in New York. A woman wanted to tell me that she came from a Baptist background, and when I commented that the sermon we had just heard was very like those heard from Baptist pulpits all over America she replied that such was not the case in China. Because Christianity is gaining momentum in China, I encouraged her to be optimistic. Sooner or later the government will have to decide whether Christianity poses a threat to communism. I do not think government and party officials ever anticipated that Christianity would become so popular; otherwise freedom to practice religion might not have come at all.

Pastor Qi preached on the working of the Holy Spirit, and as a speaker Pastor Qi is impressive. He possesses a remarkable stage presence. He mesmerizes his audience with gestures, clear articulation, and a highly cadenced delivery. He speaks boldly, and he speaks with a great sense of conviction concerning his role as pastor. When one leaves after hearing a sermon by Pastor Qi, one feels doubly blessed. One feels blessed for having felt the presence of God and for having been in the presence of such a fine Christian man.

Monday, June 8

I did not go to the institute. Ralph Wang had visited on Sunday evening to explain that he would accompany me to Changchun, and that we would leave for the train station at 1:00 p.m. I stayed at home and packed for the trip. Once I had completed packing, I took a long walk. I knew I would be on the train for sixteen hours, and because of that I wanted to exercise.

While walking through a shopping area, I was approached by two young men. One of them took two large silver coins from his pocket and held them out for me to see. I had seen such coins before, and I knew that possessing them was illegal. When Mao Zedong confiscated all gold, silver, and everything else of value to wage his war of Liberation, many Chinese families had such coins. Most families surrendered their coins to the government, but some held out on the government and hid their gold, silver, and other valuables. Although illegal, the coins are beginning to appear, and that they are probably indicates two things: that times are hard for the Chinese people and that the liberal atmosphere of months past has made people less afraid.

The young men followed me down the street and approached me a second time. Although I was curious about the coins and wanted to ask many questions, I soon found that neither of the two young men could speak enough English to hold a conversation. Out of curiosity, I offered them two *yuan* for the coins, but they wanted four. When I responded with a firm *bu* (no), they went on their way and I never saw them again. Yes, I told myself, there is crime in China, and I remembered being cautioned by an old Chinese woman the day before about pickpockets who ride the buses. She saw my tobacco pouch sticking out of my hip pocket and mistook it for a wallet. She was concerned that I not lose my money.

At 1:00 Ralph Wang came. We went to the train station immediately, but once we were there we waited for two hours. Wang apologized profusely for being in error about the train schedule, and at 3:30 we boarded and headed north toward Changchun. We talked throughout the remainder of the afternoon. After dinner we talked more. I had been advised by Wang that the weather would be much cooler in Changchun than it was in Beijing.

Tuesday, June 9

We rode through the night, and at 6:30 a.m. we arrived in Changchun. I recalled another arrival, one which had taken place four years earlier, when we arrived in Waco, Texas. It had been four years to the day since we arrived in Waco, Texas, where I would teach at Baylor University. As I recall, when we arrived in Waco we stayed the first night at the Holiday Inn. On the next day the four of us—Lynn, our daughter, Lon, our son, Wanda, and I—moved into the house at 201 Harrington Avenue, where we still live. Four years have proven that move to be a good one; we have come to like Waco and Baylor University very much. For us Waco is home. We have fine friends and neighbors in Waco. I was thinking about Waco when we arrived in Changchun and were met at the train station by the director of the department of foreign affairs and the associate chairman of the department of foreign languages at Jilin University. I was immediately taken to a hotel and checked in, after squabbling over a room that was to have been reserved for me.

Because the train ride had been exhausting, once I had checked into the hotel I took a bath, had breakfast, and then went to bed for about two hours. Before lunch I sat at a desk and wrote. I enjoyed lunch with half a dozen foreign teachers at Jilin University, who also lived at the hotel, and then I was taken to the university for a briefing and a tour. After lunch I was taken for a tour of a film studio, the first one I had ever seen. I was still tired, and the schedule for the next few days would not be light. After dinner I went to bed determined that I would feel better the next day.

Wednesday, June 10

The day was a long one. I was up at 6:00 a.m., had breakfast at 7:00, and did some last minute preparing for a meeting with postgraduate students at 9:40. Since they were in the midst of writing theses, I knew they would expect me to say something that might help them. As it turned out, I lectured to them for more than an hour on research techniques, and I could see that what I was saying was totally new to them. After I lectured, we discussed what each student was doing in the way of a thesis, and they in turn asked numerous questions concerning the writing of a thesis.

After meeting with the postgraduate students, I went to lunch at the hotel and then returned to my room. I wanted to rest, and I wanted to think about the lecture I would give at 3:30 in the afternoon. I had planned to give a combination lecture and poetry reading, but I had begun to have some doubts about that. When coming to China, I had been told that Chinese students were not interested in poetry, and particularly in contemporary poetry, although I had proven this to be wrong at Second Foreign Language Institute. But in Changchun, which is "out in the provinces," I wondered whether what I had been told about poetry and Chinese students might be true. I worried that my combination lecture and poetry reading might prove to be a failure, but I decided that I would stick to my plan.

My judgment proved right; the students at Jilin University responded enthusiastically to my combination lecture and poetry reading. I read poems I had written about China, and that gave the students names and incidents with which they were familiar. They were also curious because the poems were about China. I talked and read for almost two hours, after which the students asked questions. Exhausted, I was happy when I could escape from the lecture hall and return to my hotel room.

Ralph Wang came to visit in the evening. We talked about his daughter, Wang Jingling, and about the fact that she would soon leave China to study at Lamar University in Beaumont, Texas. According to Wang, his daughter recently received word from the Ministry of Education in Beijing that in addition to the financial aid supplied by Lamar University she will also need an American sponsor. Wang was furious about such a requirement. He confided in me that he had recently visited the Ministry of Education to inquire about the purpose of the requirement only to be told that it exists for three reasons: because some students go abroad for a year and do not want to return to China, because some students go without adequate financial support, and because someone must be responsible for the student while he or she is abroad. The reasons amount to anxiety on the part of the government over the fact that when given a choice the Chinese people will choose freedom over oppression. Wang is concerned about final approval for his daughter to study in America because his son-in-law has recently been denied a similar opportunity.

Thursday, June 11

The streets of Changchun were lined with tall, stately cottonwood trees, but they were in the process of being cut down. As far as I could see, they were the only attractive thing about the city. I watched the tall cottonwoods as the driver made his way to the university where I would talk with postgraduate students. As we drove through the streets, I thought about the hotel where I had been staying, and I realized that except for about six foreign teachers I had seen only Japanese guests. Some were businessmen, but some were educators who had come to work out exchange agreements with Chinese school officials.

When I returned to the hotel from talking with the postgraduate students, I took a long walk in order to explore the hotel grounds. Located outside the city, the grounds were surrounded by a tall fence, and a guard was posted at the gate. The buildings were large, but many of them appeared run down from neglect. The hotel complex appeared to comprise a large estate of which approximately 25 percent seemed to be in use. I do not know the details behind the building of such a huge complex, but I presume that it was well utilized at one time. In addition to housing foreign teachers and guests, the complex also housed a detachment of the People's Liberation Army. Perhaps the hotel was headquarters for the Japanese during the ten years they occupied Changchun and the surrounding area. Whatever the case, it was an impressive hotel complex.

At 7:00 p.m. I lectured to a Chinese audience of approximately two hundred. Only one foreigner was present, a visiting American philosopher and teacher. I enjoyed giving the lecture, and the audience seemed to enjoy what I had to say, even though I realized that many would have to struggle to understand. Whether teaching or lecturing, I try to challenge the best minds, believing that they are the ones who will make a difference. As a result, those who are less capable must struggle. I lectured on the poet in modern America, on his or her preoccupations, and on the nature of his or her art. When two hours had passed, I was tired, but the students were full of provocative questions.

Friday, June 12

Friday was a chaotic day. I had been told that a car would pick me up at 8:10 a.m. to take me to see school officials. I waited for half an hour, but the car did not come. About 9:00 a.m., Ralph Wang came in a car and took me to visit school officials as well as a museum and the university library. The museum housed some old and fascinating mummies; the library housed old and rare books. After lunch, Ralph Wang called to tell me that a car would pick me up and take me to see school officials. I had been told earlier that I was to meet with the vice president of the university, but the vice president, Wang informed me, was busy hosting a Russian delegation. As for Wang himself, he would be busy reporting on a conference he had recently attended. Wang also told me that the lecture I was to give at 4:00 p.m. had been cancelled. The students, he explained, were expected to attend a track meet. I began to suspect that something was wrong, but I had no idea what it might be.

At 3:00 p.m., a car came and took me to the office of foreign affairs, where I found out what was wrong. I talked with a Comrade Wu, who was director of the office, and he explained that I had "created quite a stir," as he put it. A division had developed between Chinese students and teachers because my lectures had "gone beyond literature." Comrade Wu singled out one of my poems as the major cause of contention, saying that some Chinese teachers and students liked it very much while others objected on the grounds that they saw it as an indictment of the Chinese government. In short, for them the poem was both political and reactionary. Entitled "Christmas: 1980," the poem reads as follows:

> It was late last night
> in a park in Peking
> when a young man burned himself.
> "A modern Moses," I told my wife.
> "Truly a Chinese Moses
> about to cross over."
> He burned like a Christmas candle
> or the star that led the wise men,
> and I knew that all the water in the Yellow Sea
> could not put out that fire.
> "There will be a leader," I said.
> "He will come out of the desert
> and march through the streets of the city.
> The people will strew his path with lotus blossoms
> while singing, Hosanna to our leader!
> Hosanna to our Chinese King!"

I was surprised when Comrade Wu told me about the furor on campus, and I had a feeling that Ralph Wang was at the time somewhere in a meeting trying to defend me. I realized that the students were not at a track meet, but that the afternoon lecture had been cancelled because of the controversy I had generated. It had been cancelled to avoid promoting further controversy, and likely to assure my safety. I was scheduled to fly out of Changchun the next morning, and I was glad.

Saturday, June 13

By Saturday morning I was angry about the way I had been treated at Jilin University. On Friday evening I had gone to dinner with Wang, after which I visited in his home. He explained that Jilin University was suffering from political problems, and he apologized for the way I had been treated. I expressed concern that he might be in trouble for having brought me to Changchun, and he told me that I should not worry about him. He was angry over the way I had been treated, and he explained that my treatment was symptomatic of the problems at Jilin University.

I boarded the plane at 7:00 a.m. on Saturday. I knew the flight would take three hours, with a refueling stop in Shenyang included in the time. I was eager to return to Beijing because I had obviously angered the Communist Party in Changchun. I had made the mistake of talking about ideas, and the party functionaries at Jilin University were not prepared to handle or tolerate anything beyond their common stock of political slogans. I had suggested that scientific positivism might not be entirely good. I had suggested that a great price would be exacted when a society went so far as to make science into a religion. I had suggested that all of the so-called facts and laws promulgated by scientists are of tentative worth and are constantly in a state of change. I had talked about two sources of ideas located in the old Judeo-Christian tradition on the one hand and in the evolution of science on the other. And I had illustrated how through these traditions we have conflicting views concerning metaphysics, epistemology, and axiology.

I had talked about all of these things in order to explain what it is that concerns poets in America, what it is they are writing about, but I had gone too far. The functionaries of the Communist Party were offended; thus I boarded a plane for my flight back to Beijing on Saturday feeling that I might have done a great service to those who suffer oppression in

Changchun. I did not begin a revolution, but I fed a growing spirit of dissent. My trip to Changchun reinforced things I already felt and knew about communism.

Sunday, June 14

It was Sunday, and I was thankful to be in Beijing. Wanda had gone to Beidaihe, a seaside resort, for the weekend, and I was at home alone. I took a long walk, and then I settled in to catch up on a backlog of correspondence. I wrote to Jesse Stuart, for I had heard nothing from him since coming to China, and I knew that he was in poor health and would likely not live long. I wondered whether he might have died, but I wrote my letter anyway. I saw him a year ago last month, and even at that time I felt he did not have long to live. I wrote to Lon, our son, and I planned for the following week of classes. The day went by fast, but all in all it was a good day.

In Beijing the big event of the day was the arrival of Secretary of State Alexander Haig. He came at a critical time; the Beijing government is perturbed over recent comments coming from Washington pertaining to the Taiwan Relations Act. Unless something happens soon to indicate that the United States intends to honor its normalization agreement with the People's Republic of China, the government in Beijing will likely break diplomatic relations with the United States. As originally printed in *Guangming Daily* (May 31, 1981) and as quoted in *Xinhua News Agency News Bulletin* (June 3, 1981, pp. 1-5), objections to implementing the Taiwan Relations Act are clear: "Firstly, the 'Taiwan Relations Act' is an open interference in China's internal affairs. . . . Secondly, the U.S. 'Taiwan Relations Act' stipulates that the U.S. will continue to sell arms to Taiwan. . . . Thirdly, the U.S. 'Taiwan Relations Act' treats Taiwan as a 'country' with an attempt to create 'two Chinas' or 'one China one Taiwan' in a move to turn back the wheel of history." The government in Beijing expects to negotiate with Secretary of State Alexander Haig and the United States government from a position of strength, as the article indicates:

> The relationship between China and the United States is a matter which relates to an overall global strategy. Some American persons with vision have long pointed out that if relations with China are

damaged because of the Taiwan issue, it will be impossible for the United States to have a successful global strategy and it will be difficult for that country to counter the Soviet challenges.

What the article does not say is that because of its geographical location Russia is a greater threat to China than it is to the United States. A successful global strategy is as essential to China as it is to the United States, and hopefully the government in Beijing has not overlooked that.

Monday, June 15

It was my first day at the institute in more than a week. Some of my students came to the office to welcome me back, and I taught a selection from Saul Bellow's *The Adventures of Augie March* to class one at 10:00 a.m. Then I met with Qi Wenqin to work on details pertaining to going home to the United States. For example, Wanda and I need alien travelers' permits to visit Shanghai. We need letters of introduction from the institute that will allow us to utilize discount rates for foreign experts. We need exit visas. We need a bill of lading for the crate we shipped. We need the remainder of our travel money. We need to convert 1,510 *yuan* to U.S. dollars. We need to purchase our tickets for the CAAC flight to Shanghai. We need to make hotel reservations for two nights in Shanghai. We need these things and more, but the bureaucrats move slowly. "One must have patience," Qi Wenqin tells me. "One must have patience."

Later in the day I made reservations at the dining hall in the Friendship Hotel to host seven Chinese teachers and institute officials at a dinner on Wednesday evening. It should be a good occasion, and I am looking forward to it. Also, Qi Wenqin came to my office and said the dean of the department wanted to see me, but she did not say why. I was worried because the first thing that came to my mind was that news had traveled from Jilin University and that I was being called in to explain what had gone wrong. As it turned out, nothing of the kind happened. Instead, the dean and the vice dean presented me with a beautiful lace tablecloth for our home in Waco. I was both pleased and relieved.

Tuesday, June 16

Chinese Catholics are having problems. The Holy See has not

accepted that a Catholic church can exist outside the guidance and protection of the pontiff. But the government in Beijing insists that the pope has no jurisdiction in China, and any meddling on the part of the pope is resented. Entitled "Chinese Catholics Reject Pope's Appointment of Archbishop" (*Xinhua News Agency News Bulletin*, June 11, 1981), the following is illustrative of the relationship which exists between the Catholic church in China and the universal Catholic church:

> Bishop Michael Yang Gaojian, leading member of China's three Catholic organizations today rejected the Pope's appointment of Deng Yiming (Monsignor Dominic Deng) as Archbishop of Guangdong Province.
>
> In a statement, Yang Gaojian, on behalf of the Chinese Patriotic Catholic Association, the National Administrative Commission of the Chinese Catholic Church and the China Catholic Bishops College, said: "The Holy See's appointment of Deng Yiming as Archbishop of China's Guangdong Province is illegal. We firmly oppose it."
>
> The statement said: "The Holy See's move rudely interferes in the sovereign affairs of the Chinese church. This cannot be tolerated."
>
> Pope John Paul appointed Deng Yiming last Saturday (June 6).
>
> The Chinese statement said: "The Holy See has always adopted a hostile attitude towards the Chinese people. It has resorted to various kinds of means to subvert and sabotage new China.
>
> "To safeguard China's independence, integrity and sovereignty and the purity of the Chinese church, all our clergy and congregation have freed themselves from the control of the Holy See and now run their church independently.
>
> "This is in conformity with the traditional spirit of Jesus Christ establishing the church and the apostles propagating the gospels."
>
> The statement said: "Deng Yiming was released from jail on June 5 last year because he had shown repentance. The clergy and congregation in Guangzhou then restored him to his former post of Bishop of Guangzhou Diocese, with the consent of the National Administrative Commission of the Chinese Catholic Church and the China Catholic Bishops College.

"Later the Chinese government approved his application to go to Hong Kong for reasons of health and to visit his relatives. But, without any sense of dignity, he went to Rome to receive the post of so-called Archbishop.

"He also went to other places to engage in activities harmful to the dignity of Chinese clergy and the Chinese people, violating the independent principle of the Chinese church.

"His behavior cannot be tolerated by Chinese clergy and congregation."

The statement concludes: "Gone are the days when the Holy See controlled the Chinese church. Guided by the Holy Ghost, we will run the church better along the road of independence." (pp. 32-34)

Wednesday, June 17

I began administering final exams. Because of the difficulty of administering a written exam, I decided on an oral exam. Students came to my office one at a time and pulled a card at random from a pile of cards. Each student answered the question on the card he pulled from the pile. Given such a system, no way existed to collaborate in taking the exam. But administering the final exam in this way occupied me each morning for the next ten days. I hoped it would serve to keep my mind off leaving. According to Voice of America broadcasts and other news sources, the primary topic of discussion between Alexander Haig and the government officials in Beijing is Taiwan. The Beijing government will resort to blackmail or whatever is necessary to resolve the Taiwan issue. On the other hand, when one ponders the significance of Taiwan, one realizes that it is a nagging reminder to the People's Republic of China of the extent to which communism has failed. As for the land area which comprises Taiwan, China is a large country and does not need it. That Taiwan has been favored by the free world since the time of Liberation remains a source of envy and embarrassment for the government in Beijing.

President Reagan's reluctance to abandon Taiwan is likely wise strategy for a number of reasons, and one of those is that China has a way of turning its attention elsewhere when it accomplishes a task easily. Taiwan can be politically advantageous to the United States in dealing with the government in Beijing, but caution will have to be used in all cases.

Thursday, June 18

At a dedication ceremony attended by Chinese students, teachers, and officials from the institute, I formally presented books which had been shipped by the English department at Baylor University to the English department at the institute. I challenged each person attending the ceremony to make use of the books. I challenged each not to live in disgrace because of learning less than he or she is capable of learning or achieving less than he or she is capable of achieving. I stressed that one lives one's life for others, and that a life of service to one's fellow man is the only kind of life worth living. I told my audience something of my own struggle to find my place in the world. I told them that I was proud to be a teacher because as a teacher I am a molder of lives. I challenged them to examine worlds other than their own through the books given to them by members of the English department at Baylor, and I urged them to use the power they gain in the form of knowledge to make China into a great nation. My speech was very idealistic, but no one needs idealism more than youth, and no one needs a vision of hope more than the youth of China.

Wanda attended the ceremony of dedication, and my students were pleased that she was present. When I had completed my speech, a student by the name of Han, a young man, stood up to address the audience. Extremely shy, he talked for ten minutes with a dry mouth and a faltering manner because he was deeply gratified for my having been his teacher. He struggled to utter each word, but I was convinced that his speech was one of the great accomplishments of his life. At least for a short while, he was the master of his life; as for me, I was deeply moved. He had wanted to talk with me on numerous occasions but could never do it because of his shyness. He knew this was his last chance, and he was not about to let it pass him by, even with a sizeable audience present.

As my young student talked I surmised that his shyness was a psychological phenomenon related to his having been warned all of his life not to associate with foreigners. While he talked I was also aware that the very thing which had produced his shyness was being promoted in many ways. For example, the other evening a young British couple took a young Chinese man to the Saturday night disco dance at the Minzu Hotel. They had met the young Chinese man in Inner Mongolia, and because he was in Beijing on business, he looked up his British friends. When the three of them attempted to attend the dance, they were stopped at the door by security police. The Chinese youth argued with the police and was consequently beaten. The young British couple intervened and were also beaten.

The Chinese are being reprimanded for associating with foreigners. Young women are particularly reprimanded for visiting foreigners at the Friendship Hotel. One young American woman has recently been warned by the attendants in her building that they will have to report her. They have been ordered to report to the police all visits by a young Chinese man who has been coming to see her. The new effort to keep the Chinese away from foreigners seems to have intensified since Alexander Haig's visit and may be related to the fact that Haig's talks with the Chinese concerning Taiwan did not go well. The talks were sufficiently heated that they had to be called off periodically, and even though details pertaining to the talks have not been published in China the results are being "felt" in the streets of Beijing.

Friday, June 19

I administered oral exams until 10:00 a.m., and my students did remarkably well. Before the oral exams I had not heard many of my students talk. Surprisingly, I have discovered in the last few days that the quiet ones are often very knowledgeable concerning the literature we have studied. They converse well about what they have learned, and I find that gratifying.

Just as the oral exams supplied the joy of my day, a visit to the CAAC office supplied my frustration. When I went to the office, I took a student named Wei so that he might serve as interpreter during my effort to purchase tickets to Shanghai for Wanda and me. My student and I arrived at the CAAC office with what we thought to be all the paperwork necessary for purchasing the tickets, only to be told by the ticket agent that he could not issue tickets without seeing my worker's card. Through the interpreter I explained that the Security Bureau had kept Wanda's card and mine when we were issued our exit visas two days earlier. The explanation was not acceptable, and after arguing for an hour and a half we had made no progress toward purchasing the plane tickets to Shanghai.

The student who was serving as interpreter, Mr. Wei, had worked for CAAC in Shanghai before becoming a student at Second Foreign Language Institute, and he decided that we should use the "back door." He took the papers I had brought with me, went into one of the back offices, found a friend of his, and explained my problem. The friend assured him that she would "fix it," and she did. She came to the lobby and talked with me. Then she disappeared for a few minutes after which she returned with a letter written in Chinese characters. Mr. Wei in turn presented the letter to the ticket agent, and in a matter of a few minutes I had tickets for the flight to Shanghai. There is little wonder my students believe so strongly in using the back door to get anything done. They have learned that the front door leads to nowhere. I went home pleased that I had succeeded in purchasing our tickets to Shanghai, but I was also disgusted with the way I had to go about purchasing them.

Saturday, June 20

Wanda and I have seen many fascinating things since arriving in China on August 30, 1980, but on Saturday, June 20, 1981, we saw the thing that has impressed me most. Two of my students had made arrangements for us to visit the Underground City. Consisting of a series of tunnels and rooms under Beijing, the network we examined is 3,700 meters long. The first level of tunnels is 8 meters deep. The second level is 15 meters. Begun during the Sino-Soviet border clash in 1969, the Underground City was built as an air-raid shelter. It contains power generators, an underground water supply, an air filtering system, hospitals, dining halls, and other equipment necessary to making it self-sufficient and self-contained. The entire system of tunnels and rooms was excavated by hand, utilizing both conscripted and volunteer labor.

The amazing thing about the network of tunnels we saw is that it is only one of many in Beijing. Furthermore, the various networks of tunnels interlink and provide escape routes into the countryside. I doubt that the catacombs in Rome were ever as impressive. Work units such as factories and schools have their own networks, according to our government guide, and the combined networks make up an Underground City capable of housing the population of Beijing long enough to allow the population to escape into the countryside. We were told that all major cities in China have such underground networks, and some of them are constantly under construction to accommodate the growing urban population. Of relatively little use in the case of nuclear attack, the cities underground remain as remarkable engineering feats. In 1969 the Chinese government was tipped off by United States agents that the Soviets were preparing bombing raids on the major cities of China, and the maze of networks and tunnels resulted from Mao Zedong's fear of such bombing raids. Although such sights are off limits to the Chinese masses, they are truly an impressive feat of engineering.

Sunday, June 21

It rained all day on Saturday. Wanda and I had gone to the Minzu Restaurant with Ed and Gail on Saturday night, and we had played bridge until after midnight. On Sunday morning the rain stopped. When we went to church in Xidan Street, the sun was shining. Diether Raff, our friend from Heidelberg, Germany, accompanied us. The sermon was preached by one of the associate pastors in the absence of Pastor Qi, and he lacked the forcefulness of delivery that I have come to expect from Pastor Qi. His sermon was not as impressive as I had hoped it would be.

After church we had lunch, lay in the sun at the swimming pool, and took our usual Sunday afternoon nap. In the evening we visited with Mao Zhiren and prepared ourselves for our last work week in China. In nine days we would leave for Shanghai, and we were excited.

Monday, June 22

I listened to a story told by a Chinese woman of twenty-seven. A teacher from south of Beijing, she told me that her father was arrested and thrown into prison in the late fifties because he disagreed with tactics of oppression and punishment being used by the Communist Party in his province. He was himself a member of the party, and he held a high position, but that did not prevent his being purged. Although he never formally registered his complaints against the party, he made the mistake of recording them in a diary. The diary was used as evidence on which to condemn him as a traitor to the state. According to the teacher, her father remained in prison until he died of cancer about five years ago.

When her father was sent to prison, the woman telling the story was a girl of thirteen. Her brothers and sisters were banished to Inner Mongolia, but she was allowed to stay at home with her mother, who was ill. As it turned out, the thirteen-year-old may have fared worse than the others because of being left at home. She and her mother were ridiculed, scorned, and generally abandoned to a life of loneliness and isolation. Forced to live a solitary life, the girl had no friends. She was afraid to develop friendships because of what had happened to her father, and she knew that she could trust no one. The sad part of the story is that the psychological damage caused by the incident continues. The woman of twenty-seven still has no close friends. Tortured by memories of her father's imprisonment and death, as well as memories of her own isolation and loneliness, she remains afraid to become close friends with anyone. Afraid of being hurt again, she lives a life of self-imposed seclusion.

As I listened to the woman speak, I appreciated the fact that I was the first ever to hear her story. I also realized that the psychological damage inflicted upon a thirteen-year-old had caused her to remain a thirteen-year-old emotionally. The damage is obviously permanent. As in so many other cases, the "People's Party" has done a good job in destroying a human life in the name of the people. I wanted to fight. I wanted to cry. But I knew that nothing would undo the pain and sorrow my friend had suffered.

Tuesday, June 23

Throughout the morning I conducted oral exams, and throughout the morning I was amazed at how much my students knew about American culture and American literature. In addition to being impressed by their knowledge, I was also impressed by the confidence and poise they demonstrated while talking about the literature.

I have been an intrusion into the lives of my students. I have constantly challenged the way they think, the way they learn, and the way they live. I have constantly challenged their values. I have constantly exhorted them to question, to evaluate, and to accept nothing that insults their intelligence. Contrary to much they have been taught throughout their lives, all that I have said and done has been a source of frustration for them. I have tried to make my students into thinking human beings, and that runs counter to much of their previous experience. To say the least, I have been a foreign intruder.

As I administered the oral exam, student after student lingered after the exam to tell me how much he felt he or she had learned, how much he or she appreciated having me as his teacher, and how he or she hoped to continue studying American literature. On the way to the Friendship Hotel at lunch time, Patrick Cassidy commented on how much literature my students knew. Both Patrick and I agreed that for our Chinese students the year had been a good one.

Wednesday, June 24

I delivered my last lecture at the institute. In the first part of my lecture I talked about the American black, about civil rights legislation, about black literature, and about Ralph Ellison's novel *Invisible Man*. To talk about Ellison's *Invisible Man* in the context of Martin Luther King, Jr., and Selma, Alabama, makes good sense. *Invisible Man* is a call for civil rights, human rights, much in the way that the speeches of Martin Luther King, Jr., constituted such a call. Several years ago, when I first read *Invisible Man*, I thought it was a great masterpiece of fiction. But I no longer view it that way. In terms of invention, it is not a great masterpiece. In terms of language, it is not a great masterpiece. But as a statement on human rights, I find it convincing—even with the help it receives at the outset from Dostoevsky's *Underground Man*.

The second part of my lecture was a farewell address. I took advantage of the opportunity to thank my students for their hard work, and I expressed my gratitude for having been their teacher. I exhorted them to continue working hard, and at the end of my farewell address I told them about Larry Levy, who had once been a teacher of mine. I told them about how Larry Levy had influenced my life, and how I had been unaware that I had influenced his life until he died and I was called to New York to help conduct his funeral. I told them about the funeral and about how I participated in it. I wanted to impress upon my students that they influence the lives of others, that influencing the lives of others is not something which happens only to those who are over fifty. Behind my telling the story of Larry Levy was an effort on my part to impress upon my students that our relationship had not been one-sided. I had learned much from my students. They had affected my life profoundly, and I wanted them to realize that.

Thursday, June 25

Thursday was another day of oral exams, and my students continued to perform well. Knowing that presenting gifts to foreigners is illegal, they brought gifts of appreciation, gave them to me clandestinely, and asked that I tell no one. I assured each one that I would protect him in his expression of gratitude. Some of my students had written poems, and a young woman presented me with a poem entitled "To the Gardener," a poem which I like very much:

> Here on the barren land yesterday,
> There were young shoots planted in early May,
> Thirsty for water, yearning for care.
> In time, came you, the gardener,
> Bringing with you spring and water.
> Under the hot sun,
> You watered the seedlings, tireless and tender.
> And now as the trees are growing stronger,
> You leave with the confidence
> That your efforts are not to be wasted.
> Oh, farewell to you, my respected gardener!
> Tomorrow, delightfully in your dreams,
> You'll see fruits sweet and fragrant.

How can a teacher receive such a tribute without being touched deeply? My students have become very emotional over my leaving them, and I became emotional when I delivered my farewell address on Wednesday.

In the evening Wanda and I were visited by Tony Trimarchi, a friend from Syracuse, New York, and Meng Su, a young teacher from First Foreign Language Institute. Meng Su had come to the Friendship Hotel to see Tony throughout the winter, and Tony had succeeded in having Meng Su accepted into the graduate program at the University of Pittsburg with impressive financial support.

Although Meng Su had come to bid us farewell, I knew that her heart was heavy. I knew her unit had recently ruled that she could not go to the United States to study, and with that ruling a life-long dream of

Meng Su's had been shattered. She was on the verge of hysteria when she came to visit. She was thin and emaciated. She was broken in spirit, but she came to bid us farewell. Meng Su had been crushed by the "People's Party," and I knew that she would suffer terribly in the weeks to come.

Friday, June 26

I completed the oral exams on Friday, but even after the exams my students continued to bring me gifts and bid me farewell. In that respect the morning was a time of emotion. Late in the morning I sneaked away from my office to hold an interview with a young teacher named Li. Mr. Li is proficient in English, and he would like to do graduate work at Baylor University. Furthermore, of all the people I have interviewed since coming to China, I would say that he is most likely to succeed.

One of the reasons I came to China was to explore the student potential for graduate work in American Studies at Baylor, and for the most part I have been disillusioned. The Chinese students have no money, and their government does not support study abroad except in science and technology. The government does not support study in the humanities. A second reason for my disillusionment is that Chinese teachers and students have been poorly educated. A big difference exists between education in China and education in the United States. A third reason for my disillusionment is that although many Chinese students study the English language, they do not have the level of proficiency necessary to perform in an American university. At least they do not have the level of proficiency necessary to do graduate work.

After lunch I took the Friendship Bus to town. I wanted to get away from my room and away from the telephone. I walked in Wangfujing Street, and then I went to the Friendship Store. Although the humidity was high, the sun was bright and I enjoyed the walk. I knew that I would leave Beijing soon, so I wanted to walk among the masses and feel the heartbeat of the city. As I walked I thought of Carl Sandburg. There is something durable about the Chinese people. They have suffered much, but perhaps Sandburg had the right idea. Perhaps he was more than foolishly optimistic. Perhaps the people in China will learn from their suffering. Perhaps they will triumph and build a better life for themselves and their children.

Saturday, June 27

While rummaging through recent newspapers, I found two articles which impressed me. One of the articles, which appeared in *China Daily* (June 24, 1981, p. 4), was about Ma Yinchu. Entitled "Tribute to One Man and His Theories," the article tells how Ma Yinchu had the audacity to speak out against Mao Zedong when Mao was encouraging large families so that he might have sufficient cannon fodder for conducting extended warfare. Known as China's Malthus, Ma, who was educated in the United States, was stripped of his position and his prestige as a scholar. For twenty years he wandered in China's political wilderness, but on June 24, 1981, China paid tribute to Ma Yinchu. It was his hundredth birthday, and his predictions had come true. China suffers from far too great a population, and how to feed the Chinese people worries government officials daily. The other article that impressed me was reprinted in *China Daily* (June 24, 1981) from *Guangming Daily*. It was about crime in China. Entitled "Legal System Should Now Be Enforced More Strictly," the first part of the article reads as follows:

> Ever since the Party's Third Plenary session, public security all over the country has taken a turn for the better. But because class still exists to a certain extent and the pernicious influence of the Lin Biao and Jiang Qing counter revolutionary cliques has not been eradicated, crime still runs amuck in some areas.
>
> There are reasons for this, an important one being that legal measures have not been enforced strictly.
>
> People's complaints and criticisms of the legal authorities should receive the serious attention of all Party comrades, especially the legal officers. To crack down on all kinds of illegal activities will consolidate our system of people's democratic leadership.
>
> Our country's legal system is a powerful weapon to strike at the enemy, punish crimes and protect the people. Legal and security officers should be encouraged to take their work seriously. The most hated criminals are murderers, robbers, rapists, arsonists, terrorists, abettors and gang leaders. Although they are very few in number, they can do great damage.
>
> One major crime in a district or organization will disturb many people, affecting their work and study. Such criminals should be dealt

with quickly and strictly. Serious criminals and those who repeatedly commit offenses should be kept away from cities and towns permanently and taken to places where they will find it difficult to repeat their crimes.

Young people make up a very big proportion of the criminal offenders. They are victims of either the Lin Biao and Jiang Qing reactionary cliques or outside bourgeois decadent ideology and way of life. (p. 4)

Reports in the West to the effect that China has no crime are ludicrous, as such articles indicate. American tourists, who are often responsible for propagating such reports in the United States, had better look more closely at the facts.

Sunday, June 28

On Saturday night Wanda and I had attended a farewell dinner in her honor. The dinner was sponsored by the company building the Great Wall Hotel. After the dinner we went to the apartment of Joe and Ellen Irish to visit, but I was tired and ready for bed at eleven o'clock.

On Sunday morning we attended church in Xidan Street, knowing that it would be the last time. Pastor Chao delivered a sermon based on the thirteenth chapter of John, but Pastor Chao is not the dynamic speaker Pastor Qi is. The sermon was plain and simple, and I appreciated that. After the sermon, Pastor Chao served communion.

I have reached the conclusion that the Chinese have the same curiosity about communion that they have about other things. When they see a line forming in a shop or on the street corner they get in the line so as not to miss anything. When two or three of them stop at a street corner to talk, they attract a crowd of listeners, and in a short time the listeners will be taking part in the conversation. The Chinese people seem naturally curious. Thus it is that they display their curiosity on communion Sunday. When the pastor announces that only those who have been baptized should come forward for communion, those who have been baptized come forward immediately. Then those who have not been baptized come forward. They come slowly, but their curiosity brings them forward. They cannot bear the idea that they are missing out on something. On this particular Sunday, about five hundred people attended church. Consequently, the communion service was long. Most of the five hundred took communion.

Monday, June 29

In order to report grades for my students, I took a taxi to the institute. I also delivered a typewriter and two boxes of miscellaneous materials to be held for Victor Strite, who will arrive in August. I had given money to the school requesting that it be converted to U.S. dollars, and the school auditor informed me that I would have to accompany her and Zhu Zheng to the bank to sign papers. The auditor, Zhu Zheng, and I took a car to the Bank of China, where I was issued traveler's checks drawn on the First National Bank of Chicago. I signed the traveler's checks. I had been a bit apprehensive about signing "papers," but I did not hesitate to sign the traveler's checks. I knew that I was not committing myself to anything.

Throughout the day Wanda and I continued our packing, and in the evening we went to a dinner hosted by the institute. Wanda and I were flattered, for we were given the seats of honor at the head table. We sat on either side of Tang Kai, president of the institute. While we enjoyed a delicious meal, we listened to speeches. President Tang Kai spoke briefly, and we listened to speeches by a number of the departing foreign experts. Some were sincere expressions of gratitude for having had the opportunity to teach at the institute. But some were obviously hypocritical. We enjoyed our farewell dinner, and once it was over Wanda and I were ready to return to the compound and retire for the evening.

Tuesday, June 30

It was the day before the sixtieth anniversary of the founding of the Communist Party in China, but it was also the day before we would begin our journey home to Texas. The night before, programs on television broadcasts had been interrupted to announce that the Central Committee, which had been in session for several days, had elected a new chairman. The most notable news concerning actions taken by the Central Committee was that pertaining to Hua Guofeng and Deng Xiaoping. According to the report, Hua Guofeng settled for being vice chairman, but this means that he will continue to wield tremendous power. Deng Xiaoping became chairman of the military committee, and this likely means that he has made a strategic move to regain support of the military generals, support which he lost to Hua Guofeng last winter. The new chairman is Hu Yaobang, who is a friend of Deng Xiaoping, and being a friend of Deng probably means that he will favor the West, particularly the United States.

Wanda and I had dinner at the Kangle Restaurant with Abner and Mary McCall, Tang Kai, He Jiang, Qi Wenqin, and L. T. Lin. The purpose of the dinner was to discuss the possibilities of an exchange program between Baylor University and Second Foreign Language Institute. As well as being a productive business meeting, the occasion proved enjoyable to everyone present. We enjoyed a delicious meal in an atmosphere of mutual respect and friendship. When the meeting ended, the prospects for an exchange program looked good.

July

Wednesday, July 1

It was the day for which Wanda and I had been waiting, the day on which we would leave Beijing. At 5:30 a.m. we were doing our final packing, and at 7:30 students arrived from the institute to accompany us to the airport. Because Rita Clarke was leaving at the same time, I went to the taxi stand and ordered two cars. By the time I returned to the building in which we lived, enough students had gathered that I ordered a third car.

Finally, we were all in cars and on our way to the airport. The driver of the car in which we were riding took a long time in getting there, driving through country lanes and even through apple orchards. He took his time because he was trying to sell cassette tapes to one of the students while we were en route to the airport.

When we arrived at the airport, we found that other students from the institute had come to bid us farewell. Qi Wenqin and L. T. Lin had also come. We checked our luggage, paying about fifteen *yuan* because our bags exceeded the weight limit, and then checked in to receive our boarding passes. When we started down a long corridor to our gate, we had to leave our Chinese friends behind, and I finally realized what it meant to be leaving. When I turned to wave goodbye, I felt the pain which accompanies only such partings, and I knew there was no way we could turn back.

Wanda and I both knew that our lives would never be the same. We were going home, but the proper emotions had not registered that fact. For some reason, China seemed both far away and far in the past, as though we had never been there. On the other hand, China was very much present. We found not talking about China difficult. Perhaps our compulsion to talk about China indicated something about the depth of our experience there. Or perhaps it indicated nothing more than that we had a major adjustment to make. Whatever the case, I wonder whether we will be able to think and talk about China less when we have returned home and established a routine. I wonder what claim it is that China has on us. Time and circumstances, I tried to convince myself, make us what we are, and our restless thrashing about probably makes little difference in the long run. But I knew better. I had a vested interest in China, and I knew that I would always have that interest.